Power, Knowledge and the Academy

Also by the editors

Val Gillies
MAKING FAMILIES: MORAL TALES OF PARENTING AND STEP-PARENTING
(*with J. Ribbens McCarthy and R. Edwards*)
MARGINALISED MOTHERS: EXPLORING WORKING CLASS PARENTING

Helen Lucey
GROWING UP GIRL: PSYCHOSOCIAL EXPLORATIONS OF GENDER AND CLASS (*with Valerie Walkerdine and June Melody*)
SIBLING IDENTITY AND RELATIONSHIPS: SISTERS AND BROTHERS
(*with Ros Edwards, Lucy Hadfield and Melanie Mauthner*)

Power, Knowledge and the Academy
The Institutional is Political

Edited by
Val Gillies
London South Bank University

and

Helen Lucey
The Open University

Selection and editorial matter © Val Gillies and Helen Lucey 2007
Chapters © their authors 2007

All rights reserved. No reproduction, copy or transmission of this publication may be made without written permission.

No paragraph of this publication may be reproduced, copied or transmitted save with written permission or in accordance with the provisions of the Copyright, Designs and Patents Act 1988, or under the terms of any licence permitting limited copying issued by the Copyright Licensing Agency, 90 Tottenham Court Road, London W1T 4LP.

Any person who does any unauthorized act in relation to this publication may be liable to criminal prosecution and civil claims for damages.

The authors have asserted their rights to be identified as the authors of this work in accordance with the Copyright, Designs and Patents Act 1988.

First published 2007 by
PALGRAVE MACMILLAN
Houndmills, Basingstoke, Hampshire RG21 6XS and
175 Fifth Avenue, New York, N. Y. 10010
Companies and representatives throughout the world

PALGRAVE MACMILLAN is the global academic imprint of the Palgrave Macmillan division of St. Martin's Press, LLC and of Palgrave Macmillan Ltd. Macmillan® is a registered trademark in the United States, United Kingdom and other countries. Palgrave is a registered trademark in the European Union and other countries.

ISBN-13: 978–1–4039–9817–0   hardback
ISBN-10: 1–4039–9817–5   hardback

This book is printed on paper suitable for recycling and made from fully managed and sustained forest sources. Logging, pulping and manufacturing processes are expected to conform to the environmental regulations of the country of origin.

A catalogue record for this book is available from the British Library.

A catalogue record for this book is available from the Library of Congress.

10 9   8   7   6   5   4   3   2   1
16 15 14 13 12 11 10 09 08 07

Printed and bound in Great Britain by
Antony Rowe Ltd, Chippenham and Eastbourne

Contents

Notes on the Contributors   vii

Introduction   1
Val Gillies and Helen Lucey

Chapter 1   Power and the Unconscious in Doctoral Student-Supervisor Relationships   16
Helen Lucey and Chrissie Rogers

Chapter 2   Power and the PhD Journey: 'Getting in' and 'Getting on'   36
Kathryn Almack and Harriet Churchill

Chapter 3   Ambivalent Positions: Ethnicity and Working in our 'Own Communities'   53
Kanwal Mand and Susie Weller

Chapter 4   Interweaving Academic and Professional Power in Higher Education   70
Linda Bell and Maxine Birch

Chapter 5   Power Relationships in Research Teams   88
Melanie Mauthner and Linda Bell

Chapter 6   Making the Right Connections: 'Knowledge' and Power in Academic Networking   105
Val Gillies and Pam Alldred

Chapter 7   Representing Academic Knowledge: The Micro Politics of a Literature Review   122
Jane Ribbens McCarthy

Chapter 8   Measuring What's Valued or Valuing What's Measured? Knowledge Production and the Research Assessment Exercise   147
Pam Alldred and Tina Miller

Chapter 9 Feminism, the Relational Micro-Politics of Power
and Research Management in Higher Education in Britain   168
Natasha Mauthner and Rosalind Edwards

Index   191

Notes on the Contributors

Pam Alldred is Senior Lecturer in the School of Sport & Education at Brunel University, UK, teaching in the Centre for Youth Work Studies. Her current research interests include sex and relationship education, young mothers' values and education policy. Her forthcoming book (co-authored with M.E. David) is *Get Real About Sex: The Politics and Practice of Sex Education*. She was a contributor to the two previous books from the Women's Workshop, and has been involved in other collective book projects; *Challenging Women: Psychology's Exclusions, Feminist Possibilities* (with Burman, E., Alldred, P., Bewley, C., Goldberg, B., Heenan, C., Marks, D., Marshall, J., Taylor, K., Ullah, R. and Warner, S., 1996) and *Psychology, Discourse, Practice: From Regulation to Resistance* (with Burman, E., Aitken, G., Alldred, P., Allwood, R., Billington, T., Goldberg, B., Gordo Lopez, A.J., Heenan, C., Marks, D. and Warner, S., 1996).

Kathryn Almack is a post-doctoral Research Fellow in the School of Nursing Sue Ryder Care Centre for Palliative and End of Life Studies at the University of Nottingham, UK. She has been involved through earlier employment and research activities in working on a range of topics including domestic violence, lesbian motherhood, learning disabilities and more recently palliative and end of life studies. Her doctoral research examines the meanings of motherhood and family life for women who planned and had their first child in a cohabiting same-sex relationship. Her research interests fit broadly within qualitative methodological issues and concerns and in the sociology of parenting and family lives; exploring ways in which people, in a range of circumstances, tell stories about family life and family practices and the mapping out the moral terrains of family lives and intimate relationships.

Linda Bell is currently a principal lecturer in research methods at the School of Health & Social Sciences, Middlesex University, UK. She is an anthropologist who has researched widely in health/social care and family lives, including recent projects on interprofessional education and training, bereavement, gender issues and family support. She is a longstanding member of the Women's Workshop.

Maxine Birch is a Lecturer in Health and Social Care at the Open University, UK. Maxine has worked in higher education for the past 15 years undertaking a variety of teaching, research and managerial roles. Previous research experience has involved the narrative analysis of constructing an improved sense of self in alternative therapies and young people's experiences of smoking. Previous publications reflect her interest in exploring how narrative methods connect intimate and personal stories with understanding social lives. Maxine's recent work as an author for OU learning materials in mental health has encountered many pedagogic issues when developing professional education programmes for health care practitioners. Maxine is a member of the women's workshop and she has contributed to earlier edited collections; *Feminist Dilemmas in Qualitative Research* (with J. Ribbens and R. Edwards, 1997) and *Ethics in Qualitative Research* (with M. Mauthner, M. Birch, J. Jessop and T. Miller, 2002).

Harriet Churchill is a Lecturer in Social and Public Policy at the University of Manchester, UK. Her research interests involve family policy, welfare reform, contemporary family life and social inequalities. She completed her PhD on 'Lone Motherhood: Identity and Agency in Context' in 2004 and is co-author with Teela Sanders of *How I Got My PhD: Experiences, Strategies and Process* (forthcoming 2007).

Rosalind Edwards is Professor in Social Policy and co-director of the Families & Social Capital ESRC Research Group at London South Bank University, UK. Her research interests mainly focus on family policy and family life, especially in relation to gender, class and ethnicity, and she also has an interest in methodology. As well as synthesising work on the inter-dynamics of families and social capital, she is currently undertaking research on parenting mixed heritage children, and a qualitative longitudinal study of children and young people's sibling friend relationships. She is the author of numerous articles and books, the latter most recently including:
Children, Home and School: Resistance, Autonomy or Connection? (2002), *Making Families: Moral Tales of Parenting and Step-Parenting* (with J. Ribbens McCarthy and V. Gillies, 2003), *Sisters and Brothers: Identity and Relationships* (with L. Hadfield, H. Lucey and M. Mauthner, 2006), *Assessing Social Capital: Concept, Policy and Practice*, (ed. with J. Holland and J. Franklin, 2006) and *Key Concepts in Family Studies* (with J. McCarthy, 2007), and with Julia Brannen is founding and co-editor of the *International Journal of Social Research Methodology: Theory and Practice*.

Val Gillies is a Senior Research Fellow in the Families & Social Capital Research Group at London South Bank University, UK. She has researched and published in the area of family and social class, producing various journal articles and book chapters on parenting and social policy, young people's family lives, family and social change, as well as qualitative research methods. Her first sole authored book: *Marginalised Mothers: Exploring Working Class Parenting* was published in 2006. She is currently working on a project exploring the lives and experiences of disaffected pupils.

Helen Lucey is Lecturer in Social Psychology at the Open University, UK. Her main research interest is in the social and psychic processes through which contemporary identities of individuals and groups are formed with particular reference to gender, social class and location. By developing a psychosocial approach in research with children, young people and adults, she has explored these processes in relation to mothering, young girls growing up, educational success and failure, school choice policy and the production of education markets and more recently sibling relationships. Recent and forthcoming books include *Growing Up Girl: Psychosocial Explorations of Gender and Class* (with June Melody and Valerie Walkerdine, 2001), *Sibling Identity and Relationships: Sisters and Brothers* (with Ros Edwards, Lucy Hadfield and Melanie Mauthner, 2006) and *Social Psychology Matters* (with Wendy Holloway and Ann Phoenix, 2007).

Kanwal Mand completed her doctorate in Anthropology at Sussex University and is presently working as a Research Fellow at the Families and Social Capital ESRC Research Group, London UK. Her research interests include transnational South Asian families, the life course and research methods in the study of South Asian transnationalism.

Melanie Mauthner is a social science lecturer at the Open University, UK. She has edited two collections about social research: *Ethics in Qualitative Research* (with Maxine Birch, Julie Jessop and Tina Miller, 2002) and *The Politics of Gender and Education* (with Suki Ali and Shereen Benjamin, 2004). Her research explores siblings and she has written *Sistering* (2005) and *Sibling Identity and Relationships: Sister and Brothers* (with Ros Edwards, Lucy Hadfield and Helen Lucey, 2006).

Natasha Mauthner received her PhD from the University of Cambridge where she conducted research on motherhood and postnatal depression. She took up a postdoctoral fellowship at Harvard University where she continued with this work and subsequently published it in *The*

Darkest Days of My Life: Stories of Postpartum Depression (2002). She is currently Senior Lecturer in the Business School at the University of Aberdeen, UK, where she writes book chapters and journal articles on gender, work and family life, as well as on reflexivity, research practice and the construction of knowledge. These include work on: epistemological issues in archiving and re-using qualitative data; the politics of feminist research management; and epistemological and ontological issues in collaborative research.

Tina Miller is a senior lecturer in Sociology at Oxford Brookes University, UK. Her research and teaching interests include motherhood and identities, fatherhood and masculinities, narrative and qualitative research methods. Her publications include an edited collection, *Ethics in Qualitative Research* (with Melanie Mauthner, Maxine Birch and Julie Jessop, 2002), 'Shifting Perceptions of Expert Knowledge: Transition to Motherhood' (*Human Fertility*, 2003). She has also recently completed a sole authored book, *Making Sense of Motherhood: A Narrative Approach* (2005). Tina has been a member of the Women's Workshop on Qualitative Household/Family Research for 10 years. She lives in rural Oxfordshire and has three very lovely daughters.

Jane Ribbens McCarthy is a Reader in Family Studies in the Department of Social Policy at the Open University, UK. Her interests have centred on qualitative research approaches to everyday family lives, particularly parents and children, and more recently, relationships at the end of life. Her publications include *Mothers and Their Children: A Feminist Sociology of Childrearing* (1994), *Making Families: Moral Tales of Parenting and Step-Parenting* (with Rosalind Edwards and Val Gillies, 2003), *Young People's Experiences of Loss and Bereavement: Towards an Inter-Disciplinary Approach* (2006) and the edited collection *Feminist Dilemmas in Qualitative Research: Public Knowledge and Private Lives* (with Ros Edwards, 1998). Other publications are listed at: http://www.open.ac.uk/socialsciences/staff/jribbens-mccarthy/. She lives in South East England with her daughter and husband.

Chrissie Rogers is a Lecturer in Education Studies at Keele University, UK, a member of the Life Course Studies Research Institute (Keele) and the AHRC Centre for Law, Gender and Sexuality (Kent, Keele and Westminster), and is an associate member of the editorial board *Sociology*. She completed her PhD, 'A sociology of parenting children identified with special educational needs', at the University of Essex (2000–2004) and is in the process of writing this research for publication with

Palgrave Macmillan. After her PhD Chrissie spent a year as an ESRC postdoctoral research fellow in the Centre for Family Research, University of Cambridge (2004–2005). Chrissie has published in *British Journal of Sociology of Education* (2007), 'Experiencing an "inclusive" education: parents and their children with "special educational needs"' and *Auto/Biography* (2003) 'The mother/ researcher in blurred boundaries of a reflexive research process'. She is keenly interested in theories on disability and is also in the very early stages of research on sexual identity/activity and young learning disabled adults.

Susie Weller is a Research Fellow working in the 'Families and Social Capital ESRC Research Group', London South Bank University, UK. In June 2004 she completed her PhD which explored teenagers' spaces of citizenship in rural Britain. She has published a number of articles exploring teenagers' geographies; the use of innovative research methods with children; young people's citizenship; and children's social capital during the transition to secondary school.

Introduction

Val Gillies and Helen Lucey

The institutional is political

Issues of power have long occupied academics. Interpersonal dynamics, institutional workings and the relationships between power, knowledge and control have been the subject of copious study and theorising. However, this scrutiny is less commonly extended to the site of academia itself.

A popular image of the academy as a rarefied haven of detached reasoning and refined culture detracts from a more prosaic truth that universities are structured and sustained through the operation of power on multiple levels. This is graphically illustrated in Pierre Bourdieu's (2001) classic study, *Homo Academicus*, in which he maps the hierarchical workings of academic sociology in terms of status, reputation, distinction and other power practices. In the main though, reflections on power in the academy are restricted to debates about inequality of opportunity, with feminists and others at the margins of academia speaking out about the discrimination faced by women, ethnic minorities and those from working class backgrounds (Malina and Maslin-Prothero 1998; Mahoney and Zmroczek 1997; Morley and Walsh 1996). There is considerably less written about the everyday process of negotiating institutional power relations, despite its central role in building and sustaining an academic career.

Of course, there are exceptions to this. The Women's Workshop is a collective of social science academics of all levels and statuses that have been meeting and publishing since 1995 (see Ribbens and Edwards 1998; Mauthner *et al.* 2002). They have consistently drawn upon and extended the work of those (feminists and others) who have dared to navigate these largely uncharted and potentially perilous waters to reveal some of the 'conflicts, tensions, resentments, competing interests and power imbalances that influence everyday transactions in institutions' (Morley 1999: 4). Nevertheless, the dilemmas and uncertainties that the everyday negotiation of institutional power relations in universities inevitably generates are rarely openly acknowledged or discussed. This institutional denial has produced the sense that such issues lie mainly in the domain of inter- and intra-personal dynamics and are somehow detached from the essential business of teaching and producing research. In the process of maintaining such strong splits between the personal and the institutional, the workings of power in it's multiplicity of sites, forms and effects are rendered crude at best and invisible at worst.

In the established feminist tradition, our edited collection challenges such personal/political, public/private distinctions, to extend our thinking about the ways in which gendered, raced and classed power relations are routinely exercised within a higher education framework. Written from the perspective of a wide range of women researchers positioned at various points in the academic hierarchy, the chapters seek to explore different dimensions and experiences of power as they are lived.

All of the chapters work with a multi-layered conception of power: of what it is, what it can do, where and with whom it lies and how it circulates in the spaces between people, groups and the institutions of higher education. Rather than viewing power as an objective entity either to be wielded, desired or feared, each chapter addresses it as a relational attribute which is fluid, shifting and ever present. The influence of Foucault's work is evident in this book. As he famously pointed out power is everywhere, and 'is not an institution, and not a structure; neither is it a certain strength we are endowed with; it is the name that one attributes to a complex strategical situation in a particular society' (1978: 93). Poststructuralist ideas about power help maintain the dynamism between 'a diverse, contrary social sphere and the many-sided, contradictory subject' (Lucey and Rogers, this volume). Power can operate at many different levels and in contradictory ways. We can think about power as residing in the institution, inscribed in rules, roles and status; as a personal possession of individuals or groups, conferred by virtue of social and cultural position; and as connected to the distribution of resources. We can invoke the forces of rationality when discussing power, knowledge and the academy; but there are less rational though just as powerful *unconscious* forces at play in both the institutional and inter-subjective relations of knowledge production. As the chapters in this book demonstrate, the everyday, mundane practices which form universities and build academic careers are suffused with an emotionality that defies the most rational of interventions. Fantasies, desires, fears and defences of all kinds, some of which we are conscious and some which remain at least partially hidden, play their part in the shape and movement of power from embarking on a PhD to getting published. Importantly, this multidimensional take on power alerts us to the view that power not only has the potential to spoil and destroy, but that it is also constructive, creative and reparative.

A reflexive consideration of the power that researchers engender and exploit in their efforts to study and describe the social world has featured in much of our previous collective work as the Women's Workshop. However, discussions of the relationship between power and knowledge tend to address an imagined, abstract, isolated space inhabited by individuals in their efforts to practice ethically. Less attention has been given to the role of institutional dynamics in setting expectations and parameters which impact significantly on what becomes 'known' and how. As such, the chapters in this book also seek to draw out the crucial relationship between power dynamics within the academy and the production of knowledge. By illuminating the macro and micro processes which underpin and enable the generation of research within universities, their central role in shaping the construction and promotion of knowledge becomes visible.

Spilling the beans

The lack of attention given to the workings of power within higher education institutions reflects the difficulties that we as academics face in discussing topics which threaten or undermine our own (often precarious) place in the hierarchy. Decoding the unspoken and evolving nature of these power dynamics constitutes a major part of our job, yet our experiences and insights tend to be kept to our selves or confined to staff rooms and corridors. We rarely hold back when critiquing higher education policy and practice in the abstract, but drawing attention to the academic power plays we ourselves are engaged in is infinitely more risky. Most of us have witnessed and/or experienced unethical behaviour and misuse of power that is sanctioned and sometimes even compelled by the structures and mechanics of higher education institutions. Some of us also worry that we are complicit in these dubious operations, or at the very least unchallenging of actions that trouble our conscience. Often though we value and enjoy the power we hold, feel we manage it responsibly and seek to augment it.

Our aim in writing this book is to critically reflect on the way power relations within universities are actively navigated. We draw heavily on our own experiences in order to highlight the various ways in which complexities and contradictions of power and research practice are managed and practiced in real life situations. As we outline later on in this chapter, writing this book has not been an easy process. For many of us it has felt dangerous and subversive, akin to whistle blowing or washing our dirty linen in public. On embarking on the project many of us realised we were attempting to say the unsayable, and while the chapters provide a valuable insight they have been self censored, not only to protect individuals and careers, but to protect valuable working relationships. Our intention is not to accuse, moan or expose, but instead to explore the dynamic power struggles that we engage with on a day to day basis, and to examine the real implications these have.

While there is no escaping power as an interpersonal dynamic, the lack of attention given to what Louise Morley (1999) describes as the micropolitics of academic life has profound consequences for the way it operates. Academia is a highly individualised arena in which we are often isolated from and in competition with our colleagues. At the same time our work is often inter-dependent on that of peers, senior staff such as grant holders and professors, and more junior staff such as secretarial staff, research assistants and research students. As we develop our 'feel for the academic game' (Bourdieu 2001) our un-reflexive practices may become ever more ruthless as we grapple with the constraints and affordances that flow from the circulation of power in universities. Most academics can recount experiences of being on the wrong end of power. Marginalisation within departments or research teams, unfair allocation of teaching hours and administrative duties, undue pressure to raise external funds and publish in the 'right' journals and pilfering of ideas or work are staple academic gripes. But these and many other perceived injustices operate at a complex interpersonal level, making them extremely tricky to discuss. Few academics would position themselves as misusing power. Far more would identify as victims rather than perpetrators of such abuses. Yet whether or not we are prepared to admit it, exclusion, bullying, exploitation and racial and sexual discrimination are widespread in university departments (Abbott, Sapsford and Molloy 2005; Lipsett 2005; Westhues 2005). More often than not such practices go unchallenged, chiefly because there is no safe method to recognise and confront them. By bringing these issues out into the open and highlighting their complexity we hope to initiate a more honest and inclusive debate.

The prevailing silence on the management of power dynamics in the day to day running of university departments and faculties has much broader political as well as personal consequences. The power relations that characterise higher education in the UK profoundly impact upon what becomes 'known', how and by whom. As Bourdieu (2001) argued universities were fundamentally designed to reinforce and reproduce existing structures by legitimising and promoting elite understandings, practices and values. From this perspective, institutional power structures are regulatory in that they work to preserve the *status quo* in society. At a visible structural level policies and procedures inform and justify the university hierarchy, but despite equal opportunities checks and balances, white, middle class men continue to occupy the most powerful positions in academia. This inevitably impacts on the kind of knowledge that is produced and valued. The chapters in this book extend current perspectives on power, knowledge and the academy by integrating understandings of institutional and interpersonal dynamics, thereby highlighting the politics of knowledge production.

The micropolitics of an edited collection

Perhaps inevitably, the production of this book has been characterised by our own hyper-awareness of issues of power in shaping the process and construction of this final version. Reflections on how we formulated the idea, secured a publishing contract and produced this edited collection effectively illustrate the kinds of macro and micro dynamics discussed further in the chapters. In order to demonstrate what we mean by micropolitics we will attempt to give a candid account of how power was exercised, resisted and managed during the course of writing this book. We begin by contextualising the project and our research group, outlining the structural and interpersonal framework we are located within. We then reveal the particular concerns and issues that were encountered and how they were (not always satisfactorily) dealt with, before we introduce the specific chapters that make up the book.

The Women's Workshop

Following on from previous collective work, this book has been authored by members of the Women's Workshop, an established research group with a history of exploring critical issues around feminist ethics and research dilemmas.

Previous publications have included *Ethics in Qualitative Research* (eds Melanie Mauthner, Maxine Birch, Julie Jessop and Tina Miller, 2002) and *Feminist Dilemmas in Qualitative Research: Public Knowledge and Private Lives* (eds Jane Ribbens and Rosalind Edwards 1998). The group also produced a Special Issue on researching private life as part of the Women's Studies International Forum in 1995. Originally founded as a PhD support group for women studying family and household issues, the workshop has evolved over the years as original members moved up the hierarchy and new members at various stages of their careers joined. We currently have 23 research active, female academics from England and Scotland on our mailing list, with our disciplinary backgrounds spanning sociology, psychology, education, geography, social policy, health studies, social work, anthropology, childhood studies and criminology. Not all of us are able to attend monthly meetings regularly but we share a broad interest in qualitative research on family and intimacy. Ostensibly the aim of the group is to provide a space for members to present and discuss their work. However the last few years have seen workshop meetings focus more explicitly on particular publishing projects, a move that to some extent excludes those members not able to contribute.

The last edited collection by Women's Workshop (*Ethics in Qualitative Research*) appeared to have been well received. Positive book reviews and comments drew attention, not only to the content of the book, but also the fact that it was written by a feminist collective. We were congratulated and envied by our colleagues for being part of such a stable, committed, supportive and productive group. While this praise was welcome and not entirely undeserved it provoked slight pangs of guilt in many of the contributors. Production of the book had been characterised by discord, dissatisfaction and hurt feelings among the group as well as pleasure, accomplishment and pride. These more negative experiences were private and known only to the group members, while our public image was of a harmonious feminist collective. Those who were group members when the previous book (*Feminist Dilemmas in Qualitative Research*) was produced remember similar upsets and difficulties alongside a more general sense of achievement.

On reading these two books there is little trace left of the arguments, pressures, negotiations and compromises constituting their construction. As with most academic work the messy, slippery, convoluted nature of its construction is polished out of existence. Yet these underlying dynamics are fundamental to the finished product. They act as unseen parameters within which research projects, articles, books and ultimately academic careers are developed. Reflections on this theme, combined with informal discussions in the workshop about the intricacies and perversities of climbing the greasy academic pole, sparked the idea for this edited collection on power relations in universities. It was proposed that we explore how the everyday process of negotiating institutional power relations generates ethical and political dilemmas for academic researchers. How should hierarchical working relationships be managed and what impact does this have on the research process? To what extent do institutionally ingrained conventions and practices shape what becomes known, and what are the personal consequences of challenging them? Can the mechanisms of academic career progression be reconciled with broader ethical and feminist principles?

While many of us were enthusiastic about this new venture, concerns were raised about initiating another project that would set book contributors apart from the wider group. At the time, however, meetings were sparsely attended and dominated by those of us keen to develop another edited collection. A decision was taken to pursue a publishing contract whilst also retaining space for members to bring unrelated pieces of work for discussion. In practice this has meant that for the past year or so Workshop meetings have been almost exclusively devoted to this editorial book. As with all aspects of academic life, proposing and initiating a book about power relations in universities is itself characterised by the exercise of power.

Negotiations and issues

As the then convenor of the group, Val was keen to see the project get off the ground and wrote a book proposal which was circulated to the group for comments. At this stage ideas for chapters were discussed at Workshop meetings and a more general call for chapter abstracts was sent round. But before we could progress further important decisions had to be made about how we would organise the process of writing and editing. Some group members felt we should explore a more collective approach and co-write the book together as the Women's Workshop. Others expressed concern about how this would work in practice. This debate took place at a time when many members were over worked, stressed and unable to make regular meetings. Few felt able to make the commitment that would be required to work in such a close and intensive way.

Also, many of us could not imagine how the delicate and often precarious process of co-writing would work extended across such a large group, particularly in the context of ever increasing pressures on academic staff. It was anticipated that work loads would end up falling unevenly, causing resentment and denying credit to those who took on most responsibility. Being able to point to named publications has particular significance in the UK since the introduction of the Research Assessment Exercise (RAE) (see Chapter 8) which rates academic performance on this basis. Worries were also expressed about how we would negotiate existing power differences within the group. Would a PhD student feel confident in asserting their views to an established professor? Would newer members feel less able to contribute? These issues were complicated by interlinked working relationships across the group. Some members had been, or still were supervised by/supervisors of others, while many of the group have worked and written together in the past. It was eventually decided that these dynamics were best suited to a more traditional approach involving an editor and named chapters.

Having written the initial book proposal it was decided that Val should take on the role of editor. Not wanting to shoulder this alone she approached Helen to act as a co-editor, mainly because she felt confident of their ability to work well together. By this point nine abstracts for chapters had been written by individuals and pairs and all were included in the proposal that was sent to publishers. Initially we returned to the company that published our last two edited collections, but we were told there was no market for this kind of work and advised instead to write text book on 'how to get a PhD'. An approach to a smaller publisher was similarly disappointing. Our response was to adopt a more strategic method drawing on contacts we had made in the publishing industry. At the time Helen had recently published a book through Palgrave, and was able to pitch the book to the then commissioning editor. Having received broadly positive and helpful comments on the proposal from reviewers we were offered a contract.

Although we were very pleased to be able to move ahead, one of the reviewers drew our attention to the fact that none of our original chapters focused on the issue of ethnicity in academia. All of the active members of the group at the time were white and we had failed to critically reflect on our own whiteness. Our ideas for chapters inevitably explored issues that impacted upon our day to day lives, and as white academics, for whom our whiteness was invisible, we did not view ourselves as 'raced' or belonging to ethnic groups. Nevertheless, to leave out an issue that is so central to power dynamics in universities felt unforgivable and we decided that an additional chapter on the subject must be included. During this time Kanwal Mand and Susie Weller joined the group and were more immediately attuned to the way ethnicity impacts on their roles as researchers. Just as their chapter was included, another chapter was withdrawn when a member started a new job and felt unable to continue her commitment to the group.

Having secured our publishing contract our thoughts turned in earnest to producing the book. More serious negotiations began around who would be involved in writing individual chapters and exactly how they would be written. Everyone wanting to take part in the book was able to find a role, although this had not always been the case in past projects. Minor upsets occurred in the process of adopting writing partners. Most members actively sought to co-write, while some more reluctantly included others in an attempt to embrace a more collective approach. It was established that named authors would take responsibility for chapters, with drafts read and commented on by all group members. But on facing the actual prospect of writing about highly sensitive subjects, practical and ethical constraints loomed large. While important, much of what we wanted to say was personal, challenging and potentially hurtful. We soon realised that we would be restricted to describing the tip of a micropolitical iceberg.

Given that our aim was to illuminate interpersonal and structural machinations rather than point the finger at individuals (or each other), we each developed different strategies to avoid implicating or exposing others and ourselves. For obvious reasons we are unable to go into details about this, beyond our acknowledged use of pseudonyms, generalisations, and drawing on anonymous experiences of group members. In spite of our efforts, and the significance we attach to this project, we have left much unsaid simply because we do not feel safe enough or ruthless enough to articulate it. Inevitably though, 'is that supposed to mean me?' conversations were a feature of some of our meetings, alongside much unspoken speculation. Several of us were forced to drastically alter plans for our chapters because we were unable to describe incidents or issues in a format that avoided identification of those involved. Many of us still feel we are taking a risk in writing our chapters, making this a difficult but enormously satisfying book to produce.

Editorial dynamics

As the book progressed our role as editors came more to the fore. Neither of us has acted in this capacity before and we were unsure about how, when and to what extent to exercise our editorial power. The fact that we were members of a feminist workshop writing about power dynamics made this uncertainty particularly acute. Deadlines for first drafts were set in agreement with the group, but hardly any members were able to meet them. At this point our lack of power became only too evident. The rigors of the academic year were impacting heavily on group members and the RAE was looming. More senior members were being pressured to prioritise work that would generate high status publications, and were told participation in this edited collection would count for little. As they speculated about whether they could sustain their commitment, we wondered whether we could sustain the book as a whole.

As first drafts began arriving Workshop meetings were scheduled to discuss and give feedback to contributors. Not all members could attend these meetings and so we felt a responsibility as editors to provide detailed written comments. Some drafts came in a relatively polished format while others were in note form and clearly required considerable work. By issuing our comments we were to some extent imposing our own vision of the book onto contributors. This was further complicated by our dual status as editors and chapter co-writers, giving us extensive control over our own chapters. Again though, our power to shape the content of the book was limited. Our comments were not always accepted or appreciated, while some co-writers were themselves engaged in a power struggle over the direction of their chapters. As the deadline for the manuscript to be delivered to the publishers lunged into view, we found ourselves waiting on second drafts and as well as a significant number of first drafts. We ourselves were subjected to significant work pressures and as a result we contacted the publishers and extended our deadline by 6 months.

As our new delivery date approached we spent considerable time negotiating with individual authors over chapter content, deadlines and in some cases over whether it would be possible for the chapter to be written in time. We had been informed by the publisher that the book would not be out in time for the RAE cut-off point if we pushed the delivery date back any further. While this did not affect more senior members, some in the group were depending on their chapters as RAE submissions. Eventually we reached a point where all but two second drafts had been written, and we began to feel more confident that the book would actually be completed. At this stage we took an editorial decision not to ask for any more amendments. Time pressures, our personal workloads and respect for the contributors own choices underpinned this move.

In short, our editorial style has been tentative and light handed for a number of reasons. These include uncertainty, the nature of the topic in hand, a commitment to working as collectively as possible and our own job related pressures. We have been criticised by some in the group for not providing enough guidance and failing to enforce universal deadlines. We are just grateful that we have managed to support the book through to publication. We also wonder if, realistically, it would have been possible to edit the book without causing some offence or eliciting criticism. We have tried to reflect honestly about the micropolitics of producing this book, but as with all aspects of this topic there is much that has to remain secret. Keeping things to a broad level, we can admit that the process has been characterised by spats between co-authors, misunderstandings, indignation and frustration as well as acute anxiety about revealing too much. Nevertheless, we have managed to work through this to produce what we feel is important and original book.[1]

Outline of the book

In the chapters that follow authors explore aspects of power that characterise academic relationships and career structures, impacting on the essential business of knowledge production in universities. While all of the chapters are united by a feminist perspective and an understanding of power as an inevitable feature of everyday life, they span a variety of topics and draw on a range of insights and theories. In terms of the chapter order, our initial intention was for the book to move from a focus on micro relations to an exploration of more macro structural issues. However, during the writing of the book it became clear that this would be imposing a false distinction. Each chapter has micro and macro implications, regardless of the extent to which these are explicitly addressed by the authors.

Nevertheless we begin the book with a sustained focus on interpersonal dynamics. In Chapter 1, Helen Lucey and Chrissie Rogers take a psychosocial perspective on experience to explore some of the unconscious and less rational dimensions of relationships between research students and their supervisors. They draw on three case-studies to examine the power of unconscious processes in the shaping of this particular institutional dynamic. Through a psychoanalytically inflected analysis they illuminate some of the ways in which internal, personal worlds merge with and mutually form external, institutional worlds and in this way address some of the gaps in current accounts that advise students and supervisors and that assume an entirely rational subject.

In Chapter 2 Kathyn Almack and Harrie Churchill also explore the dynamics of carrying out PhD research, reflecting upon and analysing the shifting power positions they experienced during this time. They note how research students may find themselves in a complex position involving simultaneous experiences of being powerful and powerless. Based on personal narratives this chapter draws out some of the contradictions that shaped their successful journeys through doctoral research in the UK. In particular the chapter focuses on the role of subjectivity, status and resources in the working out and maintenance of power relations. They conclude by discussing how these dynamics have considerable implications for the control over and direction of the research produced.

Kanwal Mand and Susie Weller speak from the perspective of contract researchers in Chapter 3. They explore the way many female academics carve out a 'niche' which involves working with and sometimes in their own ethnic and cultural communities. Drawing on their own and others' experiences they demonstrate how such 'niches' can be both enabling and disabling. Their nuanced account examines the workings of broader power dynamics around gender and ethnicity, and highlights the way in which inequalities in academia are often sustained through subtle micropolitical processes. Their experiences as Asian and white British researchers are contrasted to show how ethnic minority academics are more likely to become trapped in such niches, while white researchers might be seen as more flexible. Since writing this chapter the real material consequences of this have been explicitly demonstrated. While Susie's contract to research children-centred issues has been extended, Kanwal was made redundant in light of their being no further funding available for research on South Asian families.

In Chapter 4 Linda Bell and Maxine Birch examine the way processes of power within academia shift between acquired academic knowledge, and 'practitioner' knowledge. In particular they highlight the way practitioner qualifications have become more 'powerful' in commanding high status, with Government policy demanding higher qualification standards of many public sector careers. Via a discussion of the centrality of 'writing', they explore the many tensions associated with educational standards in the public sector. In the context of widening access to higher education they consider their own work trajectories to explore the impact these changes have had on their academic careers.

Melanie Mauthner and Linda Bell consider how power relationships in research teams influence project methodology and findings in Chapter 5. Drawing on knowledge of sociological, health, social care and education research they highlight issues of working collaboratively during all stages of research. They also focus on intersections of career status, teamwork experiences and reflexivity, examining how team members share out tasks stemming from their investment in teamwork and awareness of rights and responsibilities. They conclude by offering a framework for researchers to consider the effects of power dynamics in teams during the life of a project.

Val Gillies and Pam Alldred focus on the dynamics of social networking as an integral part of being an academic in Chapter 6. Exploring their own and others' experiences they show how implicit rules of academic socialising are central to career development. While they acknowledge the positive value of sharing ideas, collaborating and generating support, they also explore the less benign aspects of academic networking to show how the currency of 'social capital' can sustain a distinct, exclusionary culture. They argue that confined circles of power and influence socially produced within academia ultimately ensure a shared interest in preserving the *status quo*.

In Chapter 7 Jane Ribbens McCarthy critically examines the process of conducting a literature review to explore the power issues involved in the interpretation and representation of academic knowledge. Based on her recent experience of undertaking a commissioned review on the topic of 'loss, bereavement and young people' she describes a personal journey, during which she uncovered the various ways in which 'facts' can be used to support specific arguments, regardless of original context. In this highly reflexive and autobiographical account Jane reveals the complex issues she faced and their implications in terms of individual and academic power to select and shape what is counted as 'knowledge' in any given field.

In Chapter 8, Pam Alldred and Tina Miller give an analysis of the more formal and abstract relations of power embedded in the UK Research Assessment Exercise. They look at the ways in which practices which were intended only to measure research productivity themselves produce and sustain hierarchies regarding types of research and models of knowledge production. They demonstrate that what appears to be a rational, bureaucratic, measuring exercise is, in practice, a variable and shifting endeavour that rests on highly subjective 'measures'. They draw upon their own and colleagues' experiences of trying to make sense of and navigate the RAE and the enforced requirement to produce certain types of 'output' in certain types of publication for RAE purposes. They argue that as academics become increasingly self-conscious of performance indicators and individually more visible through them, we are more tightly disciplined by them.

We end the book with an exploration of inter-subjective and institutional dynamics at the other end of the academic hierarchy. In Chapter 9, Natasha Mauthner and Rosalind Edwards explore the tensions in attempting to be a feminist research group manager, where the very idea of a feminist manager has been termed an oxymoron. They address the nature of contemporary higher education and how it forms the contextual underpinnings of institutional power dynamics in which attempts at feminist research management take place. In particular they consider the dilemmas that arise when trying to practice research management in a 'feminist' spirit within an individualistic system that fosters competition rather than cooperation and celebrates individual rather than collective successes.

While each of the chapters explore very different themes from very different perspectives, all articulate similar experiences of exercising, resisting or subverting power in an academic contexts. We are not pretending that the power struggles described in this book can ever be overcome or transcended. But by discussing them openly we aim to create space for a more reflexive and ethical management of the issues involved. In particular we hope our own experiences will provide a resource for those currently navigating academic careers and wrestling with similar problems. Writing this book has certainly proved useful and enlightening for us.

Note
1   We would like to acknowledge all the help and support we received from workshop members who were not able to author chapters. Particularly Jean Duncombe whose contribution in the early stages of the book was much appreciated, and Jane Franklin who joined the group towards the end of the book's production and provided valuable feedback on chapters.

References
Abbott, P., Sapsford, R. and Molloy, L. (2005) *Statistics for Equal Opportunities in Higher Education: Report To HEFCE, SHEFC, HEFCW*, Glasgow, Caledonian Centre for Equality and Diversity.
Bourdieu, P. (2001) *Homo Academicus*, Oxford: Polity.

Foucault, M. (1978) *History of Sexuality Vol 1*, New York: Random House.
Lipsett, A. (2005) Bullying rife across campus, *Times Higher Education Supplement*, 16th September.
Mahoney, P. and Zmroczek, C. (eds) (1997) Class matters: 'Working-class' women's perspectives – on social class, London: Taylor and Francis.
Malina, D. and Maslin-Prothero, S. (eds) (1998) *Surviving the Academy: Feminist Perspective*, London: Falmer Press.
Mauthner, M., Birch, M., Jessop, J. and Miller, T. (eds) (2002) *Ethics in Qualitative Research*, London: Sage.
Morley, L. and Walsh, V. (eds) (1996) *Breaking Boundaries: Women in Higher Education*, London: Taylor and Francis.
Morley, L. (1999) *Organising Feminisms. The Micropolitics of the Academy*, New York: St Martins Press.
Ribbens, J. and Edwards, R. (eds) (1998) *Feminist Dilemmas in Qualitative Research, Public Knowledge and Private Lives*, London: Sage.
Westhues, K. (2005) *Workplace Mobbing in Academe*, New York: Edwin Mellen Press.

1
Power and the Unconscious in Doctoral Student-Supervisor Relationships

Helen Lucey and Chrissie Rogers

Introduction

In this chapter we explore some of the ways in which power is experienced within the intersubjective relations between the doctoral research student and her supervisor(s). Taking a case-study approach, we will address some of the gaps in current accounts of those relationships and their place in the construction of academic subjectivities. Rather than keeping the individual separate from the social, as is customary in the social sciences, we assume that while it is impossible to conceive of entirely autonomous individuals who are beyond or outside the social, it is simultaneously the case that there is a sphere of personal subjectivity that is immensely powerful in the unfolding of institutional and interpersonal relations (Frosh, Phoenix and Pattman 2003). Our aim is to explore how the relationship(s) between research students and supervisors are constituted both psychically and socially, between personal lives, social structures and public institutions. Through a psychoanalytically inflected analysis, we will explore the less rational, more unconscious aspects of the researcher-supervisor dynamic to illuminate the pleasures and difficulties, satisfactions and frustrations, obstacles and resolutions that women have experienced in their student-supervisor relationships.

There are many worthwhile books which aim to provide help, support and practical advice for PhD students and their supervisors in British institutions of higher education (see for example, Finn 2005; Phillips and Pugh 2000; Delamont, Atkinson and Parry 2004), and these publications contribute towards improving the experience of those involved. The emphasis in these texts is how to build a positive student-supervisor dynamic that will support as smooth a progress as possible of the student's work through all the various stages of their research and end in the desired outcome for both student and supervisor – the successful completion of a doctorate and award of PhD. Such texts often construct the relationship as a pragmatic and prescriptive one where imbalances in power, although a taken-for-granted aspect of the interpersonal relationship, and thoroughly inscribed in institutional conventions and practices, is rarely made explicit in either personal or institutional discourses. There are strengths to this approach that should not be undermined: students and supervisors need to gather a set of practical and intellectual skills. Supervisors must be able to properly direct the student and help her towards a gradual accumulation of successes in the various tasks that need to be undertaken. Meanwhile, students need to take the supervisor's direction as well as take responsibility for delivering on these tasks.

Power: sites and circulation

How can we understand power and its effects in this situation? Power can operate at many different levels and in contradictory ways in student-supervisor relationships. Its' domains include those of the institution (rules, roles, status) but also of the person (emotions, memories). We can think about power as a possession or attribute, bestowed on individuals or groups by virtue of their social and cultural position and giving them the capacity to exert influence on others, to have one's wishes respected and acted upon and to have relatively unrestricted access to resources. Interpersonal power, according to Scott can combine both mainstream and second stream power where mainstream power is 'principally concerned with the episodically exercised power that one agent has over another' (p. 7) and the second stream 'of power research focuses on the dispositional capacity to do something' (2001). The former may be explicit in an abusive marriage, for example, the latter more likely to be apparent in a student-supervisor relationship. However, interpersonal power is rooted in face-to-face contexts of interaction. It involves an interaction whereby individuals bring to the event (a meeting, for example) physical and personal selves. It is not simply about the occupation of a powerful social position delegated to that person. It operates at a personal level too, whereby particular individuals are authorised to issue orders and decisions over others (2001: 28).

Here, power can be linked to the notion of agency which in modern conceptions of individualised selfhood is in turn connected to autonomy: self sufficiency and freedom from dependence on others is currently lauded as an ideal state of the citizen. This raises some interesting questions about empowerment. Contemporary discourses of the 'consumer-citizen' construct students as rational and powerful choosers in an un-restricted Higher Education market (Reay, David and Ball 2004). Although this may be a chimera, different, sometimes competing discourses order and evaluate knowledge and experience and position people in different ways, with varying degrees of power. Students may feel more (or less) powerful as 'clients' in a competitive educational market rather than as recipients of welfare. In any case, within a discourse of 'choice', it is up to the subject to realise their agency and use their power to make the right decisions and then act upon them.

Power can circulate and become visible through the distribution of resources. It depends upon access to, as well as equity and inequity in, the distribution of those resources. But not all of the resources available to people are on the material, economic or cultural planes; inner emotional resources such as trust and hope can be just as important in the building and sustainment of good experience and the fulfilment of goals. Nor are such possessions easily distributed more fairly: one cannot straightforwardly 'give' confidence or a willingness to learn to another who has less of these vital assets. This is not to say that one person cannot help another; empathy and generosity towards as well as recognition of the other can be immensely powerful in helping one to grow and even in repairing emotional damage (Benjamin 1998).

Much has been written about the destructive potential of power and there is certainly no shortage of evidence to attest to its misuse and malignity. Some writings from feminist researchers emphasise the corrosive effects of gendered and classed institutional hierarchies and personal power differentials between women in higher education (Morley 1999). However, the creative potential of power, to resist oppressive structures and relationships and to use one's own power to help another, must also be kept in mind (Rustin 1991). As Hoggett notes, 'power may be exercised to build trust and assemble the preconditions for dialogue. If power has the capacity to systematically distort communication then it may also have the capacity to systematically facilitate communication' (2000: 51).

A poststructuralist model casts power as not necessarily oppressive nor imposed from above by a privileged group on a subordinate and disadvantaged group. Foucault's work enables us to make links between a diverse, contrary social sphere and the many-sided, contradictory subject. In his conceptualisation, power is not simply a commodity that can be acquired or seized, rather it has the character of a network – its threads extend everywhere. Nor is power only a limiting force: it is productive, producing forms of knowledge and discourse, categories of normality, through the production of domains of objects and rituals of truth. Within a structuralist framework, power is seen to conceal or 'distort' truth, but for Foucault it is through the operation of power that what is held to be the truth of a situation is produced. Knowledge cannot be seen as an unalloyed or see-through representation of objective truth, but is itself fundamentally tied up with the workings of power in specific social and political contexts and histories. More than this, power also induces pleasure. Foucault asks 'if power were never anything but repressive, if it never did anything but to say no, do you really think one would be brought to obey it?' (Foucault 1980: 119, quoted in Lawler 2000: 21).

Existing discussions of student-supervisor relationships are often premised on the assumption that all aspects of the dynamic, including dimensions of power, can be known about, talked about and institutionally governed. This presupposes a hyper-rational model of the subject and indeed, of institutional life, in which people relate to one another in clarity and 'truth', seeing and hearing only that which is 'really there' and entering into the relationship entirely free from the traces of previous experience. Whilst literature on how to get a PhD and/or how to supervise one does not steer clear of the kinds of difficulties that can arise in student-supervisor relationships, there is an underlying assumption that the source of the problem is open to identification; that it can be known and named and then solved within the framework of a professional, institutionally bound relationship. Rose (1992) notes that a commonplace view of power is of an oppressive, limiting force that works from outside the person. It is against this model that 'true' knowledge becomes the key to defeating the hold that power can have upon us, because by gaining truth, we also gain the capacity to see through power. Here, knowledge has the capacity to liberate us from the workings of power. This calls to mind the Enlightenment notion of a 'true self' that is knowable through reason and self-reflection. Once known, this 'autonomous' self can stand beyond the workings of power, in order to realise its full potential, and, to be 'free'. Autonomy, in this formulation, is presented as lying at the opposite pole to regulation and government, and indeed, to the workings of power (Lawler 2000: 20).

In this chapter, we take a different view of human experience and the dynamics of intersubjectivity and foreground the possibility that there are unconscious aspects of our own and others experience that cannot easily be known or made available to rational, conscious intervention. In this view of experience, unconscious processes, although heavily cloaked or hidden, are nevertheless extremely influential. They are interwoven with more conscious processes, not only at the level of the individual but in the very structures of collective human life, including in institutions such as schools and universities.

We would take the view that there is no straightforward correspondence between external and internal 'realities', for instance, between what is actually said between supervisor and student, and what each understands to have been said. How each may feel about what is said and/or meant cannot be easily taken for granted, but is subject to the distorting effects of anxiety, desire and fantasy that circulate continuously within and between individuals and groups. Because of this, even the best of rational intentions and conscious goals can lose their way, become obscured or even thwarted in student-supervisor relationships. Furthermore, interpersonal relationships are never as free from the past as we might like. The echoes and vibrations of past experiences, particularly those with our childhood carers, have a tendency to resonate in the present and thereby help give shape to our understanding of the here and now, of ourselves and others.

Student-supervisor relationships are constituted in and through multiple locations and sites. As institutional relationships, they are inscribed with the dynamics of hierarchy and subject to formalised codes of practice and conduct. As well as institutionally and professionally defined, these relationships are personal: they may be conducted in relative privacy; they may be intimate and at times intense. Of course there are always exceptions to this rule; Silverman (2005) describes in his discussion on supervisors a student that went from the beginning to the end of his doctoral journey without supervision through his own choice and yet came through with 'flying colours'. But this is not the norm. Most first time research students need, want and indeed expect support and guidance throughout this journey. Regardless of this, the PhD process carries a multitude of investments for the student and the supervisors. All sides often share an investment in the process as part of the way in which they can enhance their career prospects and potential.[1] For these reasons there is no one model of power that is adequate to describe or analyse its character, circulation, medium and effects in PhD students' relationships with their supervisors.

We will draw on concepts from social theory and psychoanalysis to try and shed light on the interplay of private, emotional and structural, institutional features of such relationships. However, moving between inner experiences of the self, to those of the interpersonal and group relations and out into the wider culture and institutions, involves crossing disciplinary boundaries; movements that can sometimes be seen as transgressions rather than explorations or bridge-building projects (Froggett 2002). A basic tenet of psychoanalytic perspectives is that our early experiences of intimacy and attachment have a profound influence on the shaping of our internal world and are heavily, though often unconsciously brought to bear on the dynamics of subsequent relationships in adulthood. This is not so different from a diverse array of sociological work which draws strongly on the idea that family and friendship relationships of childhood are critical in the production of socially competent adults, for structuring the gender and sexual identities of individuals and for helping sustain societal patterns of difference and therefore is crucial in maintaining social divisions.

Of course it is not early family experiences alone that shape our feelings about higher education. Bowler (1999) reminds us that most of us will have undergone about ten years of compulsory schooling, which will have contained many different kinds of experience and shades of emotion. As numerous female academics from working class backgrounds have attested to, these emotions are likely to include failure, humiliation and shame as well as, for some, success and pleasure (Walkerdine, Lucey and Melody 2001; Plummer 2000; Reay 1997).

Our discussion focuses on processes rather than structures. As Morley says 'both feminism and micropolitics privilege processes rather than structures' (1999: 6). These processes, conscious and unconscious are bound up in official structures enshrined in hierarchical patriarchal structures between male and female academics, and now the 'new managerial' philosophy of economy, efficiency and effectiveness (*ibid.*: 28). However, the experiential nature, the different expectations and the constant negotiation and renegotiation of the self in relation to another as a supervisor or a research student is of importance here in unpacking personal powerful and empowering relationships within the micro-academy.

Over the course of doctoral study the supervisor-research student relationship may involve two or even three supervisors, all of whom are likely to be at different stages in their academic careers and emotional development. For the supervisor this relationship is one of many working relationships. For the research student however, it may be an extremely important, even the *most* important one, for three or four years. Much of the interaction between research student and supervisor(s) happens in private. In the space of the supervisor's office, interpersonal dynamics shape the experience that each has of the other. There are rules, but these may be subject to the personalities and preferred working styles of the two parties. Here, the dry rationality of university board and funding-body rules and regulations gives way to the ebb and flow of emotions, investment, wishes and needs, where the messiness of everyday human states such as vulnerability, anxiety, expectation and the need to trust are part of the matrix that makes this relationship work, or falter.

Three women's accounts

Three women who were accessed by us through personal networks and had completed a doctorate were asked to write something about their relationships with their PhD supervisors. All of the respondents had two supervisors at some point in their studies (as is the case in most British universities) and we asked them to comment on each supervisor. All were currently working as academics. Importantly for our analysis, all of them were sympathetic to the idea of unconscious dynamics and two had undertaken personal psychodynamic therapies. We began by asking them to write a few pages describing and reflecting on various aspects of their relationships with supervisors. We subsequently interviewed them in order to explore the themes they had raised in their written pieces and add explanatory detail to their narratives. The three women all had strong, highly reflexive analyses of their experiences of supervision, which we have taken as the basis for the rest of the chapter. We did not alter the women's analyses, but we did theorise them in the light of a psychosocial framework. We then showed our final draft to the women for their approval, which they gave.

At this point we must stress that these are necessarily one-sided accounts, from the students' rather than supervisors' perspectives. However, we hope that the reader will appreciate that the women have presented a psychologically realistic analyses, by endeavouring to take responsibility for their part in what went right and what went wrong in their relationships with their supervisors.

Laurel

In Delamont *et al.* 'Supervising the doctorate: a guide to success', the authors state that at the core of successful supervision lies 'self-consciousness, not intuition or flying by the seat of your pants' and that the processes and issues involved in doing research must be made explicit by the supervisor both to themselves and to the students (2004: 1). Later on the same page however, the authors point to the professional and personal hopes and desires that the supervisor brings to the relationship.

> Supervising doctoral students is one of the most satisfying things anyone in higher education can do. Watching a new scholar become an independent researcher, conduct a project, write up the results, present them at a conference and see the first publications is a wonderful experience. Guiding a new scholar into your specialism is intrinsically rewarding and the best way to ensure that your own work echoes down to the next generation and beyond (Delamont et al. 2004: 1).

This comment clearly reveals that the relationship between students and supervisors is saturated with emotion. Not least, it illuminates the possibility that the relationship can be 'satisfying' for the supervisor and thereby goes some way to balance the idea that because of the imposition of a 'quality culture' in British universities, students are a terrible burden on the teacher (Morley 1999). Most strikingly it brings to our attention that this is a relationship that is deeply parental. O'Leary and Mitchell describe a mentoring relationship within the academic environment as that of a more experienced adult guiding and supporting a younger, less experienced adult through the world of work (1990: 66). For the supervisor it carries the desire to nurture another through a demanding process, from dependence to independence, to become just like oneself. It also reveals the narcissism of parenting and of the academic world; the desire for our work to survive beyond ourselves, for it to influence subsequent generations, for it to matter, for us to matter. It is clear that there are dimensions to this relationship that cannot easily be made explicit and are neither entirely rational nor consciously felt but that are nevertheless 'active' in the relationship between student and supervisor.

Laurel is a white, British woman from a middle class family background, who was awarded her PhD five years ago. Her doctoral research spanned two distinct disciplines; the natural sciences and the social sciences. Because of this, she felt that it would be helpful for her to have two supervisors, even though joint supervision was fairly unusual at the time when she began her studies, and for them to have expertise in one or other of these disciplines. Laurel chose her supervisors herself and supervision sessions were always with both of them. Dr Aston, a physicist, was extremely well-known in her field and had high status in the department. Dr Brant, a social scientist in the same department, had an excellent reputation in her specialist area, but did not enjoy the same kind of standing as Dr Aston. Laurel describes Dr Brant as being 'in awe' of Dr Aston.

That a one-to-one student-teacher relationship necessarily holds something of the dynamic between parent and child is fairly obvious and well documented (Wisker 2005). However, having *two* supervisors and thereby making it a triangular relationship adds a distinctly Oedipal family dimension. Laurel connects her early family experiences and her perception of her mother and father's relationship to her understanding of supervision and its' three-way dynamics. She describes her father as 'overwhelming, bullying, egotistical'; an emotionally immature and withholding man who 'dribbled out just enough love to keep [Laurel and her mother] trying for more'. In the face of her father's power to hold back affection, encouragement and praise, her mother 'became more like a sibling', never able to stand up for the young Laurel and ridiculed for her attempts to do so. The emotional inequality in her parents' relationship and the ways in which this was communicated, were to provide a strong unconscious framework for Laurel's experience of her supervisors and herself with and in relation to them.

In psychoanalytic thought, there is an assumption that early life and experience is highly influential in the formation of emotionally charged and lasting internal worlds. Internal psychic reality is not a straightforward mapping of the external world or experience, but is profoundly subject to the effects of anxiety and fantasy. In the Kleinian and object relations school of psychoanalysis, versions of people (and other 'objects') are internalised from an early age and are central to the shaping of internal worlds. The Freudian concept of transference also helps us to think about the unconscious aspects of the significance of the past. It describes how feelings, impulses or fantasies about someone may originate in an earlier relationship, but are nevertheless experienced as belonging to the person with whom one is relating to in the *present*. This concept was originally formulated in the clinical context, where the patient transferred feelings (which could be negative or positive) from an earlier, often parental relationship, onto the analyst and experienced the analyst accordingly. But other professional relationships that are structured in terms of power also elicit transferences. 'There is expertise and professional status on the one hand, and lack of knowledge and perhaps dependence on the part of the patient/client; and it is probably this that promotes transference *via* a re-creation of the power differential of the parent-child relationship' (Thomas 1996: 169). This power dimension is foregrounded in student-teacher relationships where the whole enterprise rests on the student needing help and being able to receive it from a more knowledgeable supervisor.

Laurel articulates clearly how her positive and negative feelings in supervision were connected with early parental experiences. She understood Dr Aston (the physicist) as embodying the certainty and authority of her father. She brought feelings originally experienced in relation to her father into this relationship and looked to Dr Aston, as she had to her emotionally withholding father, for 'love, acceptance, a modified authority'. The transference was quite different with Dr Brant who seemed unconfident about her own knowledge and deferential to Dr Aston. Her insecurity about the scientific side of Laurel's work meant that Laurel had to keep the physics from her – 'she [Dr Brant] found sessions where the physics was pivotal really hard I think and I'd feel the need to find ways of talking and being that enabled her to participate'.

Laurel wanted to bridge the distinctions and divisions between the two disciplines that were embodied in the two supervisors; a compelling feeling that resonated strongly with the young Laurel wishing that her parents could bridge their differences and fantasising that she might be able to facilitate this.

> There were times when nearly half a supervision would be taken up with them negotiating their relationship. This generally took place through discussions of local politics. [...] Part of me loved these conversations – they both seemed to enjoy them – the finding of connections.

That difficult feelings from her childhood were being transferred to these contemporary relationships is best illustrated by one incident in supervision when Laurel wanted to bring the two disciplines together in her work and began moving away from the scientific research on her topic towards a wider reading of sociological research. Laurel wrote:

> Dr Brant was encouraging me, but as soon as it became clear what direction this was taking, Dr Aston said 'No' (quite literally). I think

she said it didn't have a place in my PhD... That was a real shock – a blow. I didn't argue about it, I just accepted it. And Dr Brant buckled under this one too. [...] The silencing shock of Dr Aston's 'no' was repeated later when she thought my ideas for a research project were 'boring'. [Laurel was subsequently funded by the ESRC for the same project].

The power of a more senior and well known academic to decide what does and does not count as appropriate academic endeavour or knowledge to a relatively junior colleague and student is made abundantly clear in this example. Hierarchical subject positions which may have been muted at other times are made visible and taken up by these three people who are at different places in that institutional hierarchy. Feminists and others have written of the difficulty of finding a voice in the 'expert system' of academia where so often power is established and exercised in the silencing of counter-arguments. Furthermore, the problem of speaking cannot be separated from the audience that one is speaking to and as Laurel's account illustrates, 'Many students experience the presence of this academic Other in terms of the theft of their capacity to speak and make sense of their own experience' (Hoggett 2000: 116).

In the following example of Sarah, we see how the problem of finding and keeping an academic voice is not only linked to hierarchical structures in this expert system, but can also be intertwined with strong tendencies towards disowning one's own creative capacities.

Sarah

Sarah is a white, British woman, from a working class background who was awarded a doctorate four years ago. During her doctoral studies she had four different supervisors. Her account of these relationships brings to our attention the power of a different kind of transference, not so much to do with early parental relationships but with strong childhood bonds with older sisters (Coles 2003; Mitchell 2003). This example also highlights that, while positive transferences and projections may be hugely beneficial for student and supervisor, they can also eventually come to be a bar to a realistic understanding and appreciation of our own creative resources.

Sarah first registered for a PhD in the social sciences in 1995 and got along so well with her supervisor, Dr Fraser, that when she offered Sarah some part-time research work she didn't hesitate in saying yes. Sarah felt hugely supported by Dr Fraser. Importantly, she felt that

Dr Fraser was able to recognise her potential as an academic and wanted to nurture that.

> She would ask for my opinion about the research and really encourage me to take risks, to say what I thought. Then I couldn't believe it when she thought that my ideas were really good. She seemed to be able to do something with my words and ideas. I don't know, turn them into another language, an academic language that I was dazzled by. I was dazzled by her to be honest.

In Sarah's written account of her relationship with her supervisors she linked her tendency to form 'strong, positive bonds with women who are about 10 years older than me' (as was Dr Fraser) with her relationship with her sister, also 10 years her senior. This much loved and admired older sibling provided protection and safety (from older brothers) for Sarah when she was a child as well as acting as a patient and kind intermediary between home and the outside world. This mediating aspect of the sisters' relationship was mobilised again in Sarah's growing bond with Dr Fraser, who Sarah felt offered her recognition for her cleverness, understanding of her lack of confidence and a bridge between Sarah and a terrifying academic world. Additionally, when Sarah was a child she watched her teenage sister grow into, in her eyes, 'a beautiful young woman, who was incredibly confident and glamorous and had impossible amounts of freedom'. In Sarah's mind, her 'dazzlement' by her supervisor was somehow connected to her childhood fantasies about her glamorous older sister.

Although this was a mainly positive sibling relationship in which Sarah received care and protection, what she perceived to be her elder sister's confidence, beauty and autonomy also provoked some difficult feelings for Sarah. At the level of the unconscious Sarah's admiration of her sister had led to envy and a psychic diminution of her own talents and qualities. As Sarah grew older tensions began to emerge in their relationship with Sarah feeling 'completely inadequate' around her sister. In her mid-twenties, a row that 'came out of nowhere' caused the sisters to break all contact for two years.

Joanne Lacey's (2000) frank description of her emotional and academic relationship to both a body of work by working-class feminist writers and her PhD supervisor in terms of 'academic fandom' is important here. Although she 'worshipped' the supervisors' work and constructed her as a 'powerful mentor', Lacey also raises the spectre of envy of the supervisor. She fantasised that these idealised figures had everything that she wanted but was struggling hard to get.

The concept of projective identification helps us to understand how subjectivities are developed in dynamic relation with others at the level of both the psychic and social. It has lately been employed in the social sciences to explore the ways in which the destructive parts of the self, such as greed, self-centredness, envy, hate, pomposity (these are just a few of the things most people would rather not know about themselves) are psychically expelled out of the self onto another. Individuals and groups such as ethnic, religious, cultural and class groups can become strongly invested with negative qualities and characteristics, which they are then seen to possess (Lucey and Reay 2002; Clarke 1999). Through projective tendencies the self is then cleansed of the possession of these difficult elements as they are now experienced by us as belonging to the other.

But it is vitally important for our discussion here to remember that good parts of the self may also be defensively projected. It can be equally difficult for a person to own their positive qualities, their assets and talents, because of guilt, fear of envy, retaliation, abandonment or loneliness. These good parts of the self may also need to be protected from the more destructive capacities of the self and so may be attributed to or deposited into someone else so as to be kept safe. Because this object (person, group, place) must now contain the good things about the self – kindness, generosity, creativity, cleverness – it quickly becomes idealised.

Of course, the capacity to idealise is important; it helps us to fall in love and to maintain hope for a brighter future in conditions of adversity. Sarah's positive identification with Dr Fraser worked well for them both at first; they wrote and published well-received work together. Sarah however, had so thoroughly disowned her own capacity for intellectual work and her creativity into the figure of Dr Fraser that she was convinced that

> all the ideas, all the good bits about the articles, all the cleverness belonged to Dr Fraser and not me. I knew that I couldn't do anything without her.

This meant that all the capacities that Sarah needed to function and grow as an academic were no longer available as internal resources for her to draw on. By locating them in another, she ended up feeling utterly depleted of her own talents, disabled in her work and entirely dependent on Dr Fraser.

This is rarely a dynamic that can be sustained in perpetuity: it is a common experience for idealised objects to fall off the pedestal on which they have been installed. The idealised object inevitably fails to live up to the ideal expectations and quickly turns into its opposite. Just as Sarah's relationship with her sister could not continue under the weight of her distorting idealisations, neither could her relationship with Dr Fraser survive Sarah's persistent rejection of her own capacities, nor her subsequent disappointment in this 'dazzling' object.

We have concentrated on Sarah's story here because that is what we know most about. Although we can safely surmise that Dr Fraser brought her own unconscious defences, anxieties and fantasies to this relationship, we cannot know about the precise nature and effects of these in this particular relationship. What we can suggest is that Sarah's idealising and highly flattering projections appealed so strongly to the narcissism of the supervisor (and were perhaps just as dazzling to her), that she was unable (or unwilling) to adequately repel them.

Although they may originate in internal, psychic conflicts, these disjunctions and distortions of experience are well supported in the competitive, highly critical world of academia (see this volume Chapters 4 and 6). Here, systems such as peer review, although sounding innocuous enough, merge powerfully and painfully with the critical dimension of the superego – the internal, nagging, often highly judgemental and surveying authority figure.

Sarah's relationship with Dr Fraser gradually broke down to the extent that when Dr Fraser moved institution, Sarah was so 'furious' with her that she took the opportunity to continue her studies with two new supervisors. Sarah could easily have repeated this pattern, of idealisation followed by furious disappointment, within the new supervisory relationship, but managed not to. While the pain of disillusionment is hard to bear, if it can be tolerated, it can provide the basis for relationships in which the failings of the self and the other can be recognised and (at least some of the time) accepted. Sarah's new supervisor relationships worked well for her and she was able to construct and hold a much more realistic and 'bounded' view of her own and their roles and capacities. She and her sister also gradually repaired and rebuilt their relationship on less projective grounds.

In the following example of Elaine we focus again on the parental dimensions of the research student-supervisor relationship and extend our discussion of disillusionment with reference to Ian Craib's (1994) discussion of 'the importance of disappointment' in emotional development. In this case we see how resistance and a struggle for power with the supervision relationship resonates with experiences of powerful mothers and 'absent' fathers.

Elaine

Disappointment in the development of the self is important, not least of all because as offspring we often have to deal with the fact that our parents are not always what we expect them to be. It is a constant negotiation and renegotiation of disappointment that fundamentally is part and parcel of this development of the self. As Ian Craib suggests,

> Disappointment comes not only from having to restrict ourselves, from having to share with other people and from having to make choices in our lives; it also comes from the recognition of what we are, and it is not a world-shattering announcement that we are not always what we might like to think we are (1994: 44).

Elaine, a white, British, single mother, from a working class background, was awarded her PhD in the social sciences, in 2005. In 1999 she began her journey as a part time postgraduate whilst working full time. Four years earlier she had completed a Masters degree at the same institution. When thinking about a doctoral supervisor she decided on the same 'aging' male, Professor Baker, who had supervised her Masters dissertation. She liked and respected him and was drawn to her experience of him as a 'hands off' of supervisor, who gave her space to think independently. She felt that there was a good 'fit' between his model of supervision and her style of learning. Crucially, he seemed familiar, and not only because he had supervised her Masters work but because he reminded her of her dad: 'a bit fluffy, preoccupied and distant, but a deep thinker'.

Elaine's father had left her mother when she was seven years old. In his absence she had constructed an idealised internal picture of her father, one that stood in stark contrast to her mother who, as 'supportive, but very controlling and rule driven', was experienced as rather all too present. Elaine viewed Professor Baker (not much younger than her father) in the light of this internal construction of her father. He listened, interjected at times and guided her. Importantly, practical circumstances (Elaine was a part time research student with a child and a full time job) meant that she rarely saw Professor baker. This was similar in some aspects to the relationship she had with her father who lived some distance away. Furthermore, Elaine's mother had consistently made access to Elaine difficult for him.

Elaine does not know quite why she chose the path that she did, but after a postgraduate conference early on in her PhD she decided to change supervisors. It is not that she consciously found Professor Baker problematic, but once she had heard the junior female academic, Dr Alice, speak so passionately about her own research, she approached her. It could be argued that Elaine was disappointed with her dad; after all, her experience of the situation was that he left *her* (not her mother). Similarly, as much as Elaine liked Professor Baker he did not really match up to the unconscious expectations she had of him. She wanted someone more dynamic as a supervisor, just as she wanted a more dynamic father. Here we say 'unconscious expectations' because she had strong feelings for Professor Baker and she liked his 'relaxed' way of working, but felt she needed more. However, she also needed and wanted an active and productive engagement with her research: a promise that the younger, enthusiastic female academic seemed to hold:

> She was so enthusiastic about her research that I wanted to chat to her about it. We did so and she suggested that maybe I should go to her to rework my ESRC proposal. We then spent some time doing this and we both worked hard. During this process she was seductive, engaging and remained enthusiastic. I was converted. I knew that she would work me harder than Professor Baker, but this seemed a small price to pay for her engagement with my work.

This is where Dr Alice (as the figure of her mother) became the more dominant force and indeed Elaine's feelings of disappointment in her self and with her new supervisor developed early on. Another interesting point here is Elaine's use of the word 'seductive': as if this was a conscious manipulation of Elaine on the part of the supervisor. But rather than something that was being done to her, we can see her feelings of being seduced as referring to the pleasure she experienced in receiving that which she longed for – attention and enthusiasm for her ideas and work. We could also say that enthusiasm and attention should be a rule of good supervision.

During the period where Elaine and Dr Alice worked on her proposal the workload was hard, but what was harder for Elaine was the development of a cantankerous and argumentative relationship between them. Elaine thought that maybe it was the process of writing and rewriting the proposal that provoked this, but once the full-time funding had been secured she still felt 'stifled and hemmed in' – the opposite of how she felt with Professor Baker, and explained, and to a certain extent analysed this aspect of her relationship better than we could:

> Since she was my supervisor I was no longer able to take time to pontificate over my work. No, I had to plan, plan and plan! We had to meet regularly and every single thing I wrote she commented on with great criticism. 'Maybe this is what 'real' supervision was like', I thought at the time. I didn't like this way of working. We constantly argued and I even suggested that I didn't like the conflict, but she assured me this was normal. She had it during her PhD and that's what doing a PhD required. I was not convinced. It reminded me of my relationship with my mother and she actually had the gall to remind me that my relationship with my mother was like that! (as we had spoken about my mother). But for all the warts, I can accept that with her – she's my mother! My supervisor on the other hand was only a few years older than me and made me feel like I was inferior.

In this highly emotional relationship Elaine became not only disappointed with herself because she was unable to control her hateful thoughts for her supervisor, she was also disappointed with her supervisor (as she had been with her mother). As a teenager without her father around she was unable to accept the rule driven boundaries her mother imposed upon her, and as with Dr Alice, her rules brought out her reminiscent teenage struggle with authority as she clearly describes here.

> She *told* me what to do and said that I should use her experience. I'm afraid this way of working brought out the rebellious and maybe even childlike aspect of my self. If she was going to treat me like a child then I guess I would behave like one. Supervisions, in the main, took place in her office, and were for all intents and purpose a battleground. I went in expecting what I considered petty criticism and that's what I got. What I desired was intellectual conversations about my ideas! As I remember it got so bad that I decided I could no longer work with her. I went to my graduate head (in confidence) and told her my dilemma. She advised that I talk with her and that maybe she would be happy to 'let me go'. I did this and she was not. [...] we came up with an alternative. I gained another supervisor, another young female lecturer.

At the same time, her contradictory feelings for 'the father' that had left her were played out with her actual father *and* with Professor Baker. While she yearned for this absent, idealised father, when she did see him the visits did not always go well: 'he simply did not have the personality to rein me in, as I got older, during my visits'. In hindsight, Elaine noticed that Professor Baker also never quite got her full attention and towards the end of her PhD he too 'left' by passing away. Elaine wrote that she was unable to 'grieve properly as he was no longer my supervisor'.

It could be argued here that disappointment is a negative experience and that as with the experience of power/subordination cannot be used positively. However as Foucault (1980) and Scott (2001) unpack the positive aspects to power, so too does Craib (1994) highlight the positive, if not necessary attributes of experiencing disappointment. In fact he goes as far as to say in late modern society what we once called 'life' now includes disappointment whereby psychotherapy has had a big part to play, and suggests:

> If I put my hand in the fire and it is burnt, I will not do it again in a hurry; psychotherapy says, in one sense, put your hand in the fire and keep it there. Psychological development depends on 'staying' in the fire, to the point where we begin to understand the pain and find that it is bearable, and that it might even be used in some way (1994: 193).

Elaine described her supervision as 'difficult' and wished she had experienced a more collegial relationship with Dr Alice. However, by repeatedly experiencing a struggle with authority (as she did with her mother), she suggests now she can look back with respect for the struggle too that her supervisor had with her in experiencing that 'childlike' and negative reaction to being 'guided'.

Conclusion

In this chapter, we have posited a psychosocial view of subjectivity and experience in order to explore some of the ways that student-supervisor relationships are shaped intersubjectively. Through the case-studies we have discussed how subjects are both constructed and constructing, the subject *of* forces as well as subjected *to* 'forces operating from elsewhere – whether that be the "crown", the state, gender, "race" and class, or the unconscious' (Frosh 2003: 1549). Although we have applied different psychoanalytic concepts and ideas to Laurel,

Sarah and Elaine's narratives, some common themes have emerged. For instance, the transference of feelings connected with early caring relationships with parents and sisters to supervisor relationships surfaced for all three women, albeit in different ways, as did the power of positive and negative projections of difficult emotional material into their supervisors. The anxieties involved in the construction of academic subjectivities were also illuminated, as were the ways in which these were defended against institutionally; in viewing projects which bring different theoretical perspectives together as transgressive rather than bridging and in the policing of the production of 'correct' academic knowledge by supervisors.

Where does this kind of analysis leave us? We are not saying that by taking up a psychosocial perspective we can guard against the difficulties, failure even, of student-supervisor relationships. But we would claim that there is immense value in casting this theoretical light on questions of power, intersubjectivity and the production of 'reality' in higher education. Reflecting within this model will not 'liberate' PhD students and their supervisors from ever experiencing anxiety, disappointment, fury or feelings of worthlessness in their academic lives. But it can allow for an examination of the psychological investments in maintaining the psychic and social *status quo* and in striving for change. These are core questions for any personal or political project.

Notes

1 Students who want to study for a PhD out of a desire to learn about and develop their own interests may not be as concerned about enhancing their careers and therefore may be less concerned with producing a thesis within a given time. However, these students are antithetical to the advent of a performance and auditing culture in HE. This kind of laissez faire attitude towards completion is not only discouraged but also actively legislated against in most universities, leading to far fewer who are motivated in these ways.

References

Benjamin, J. (1998) *The Shadow of the Other: Intersubjectivity and Gender in Psychoanalysis*, London: Routledge.
Bowler, M. (1999) *Feeling Power: Emotions and Education*, London: Routledge.
Clarke, S. (1999) Splitting difference: psychoanalysis, hatred and exclusion, *Journal for the Theory of Social Behaviour*, 29 (1) 21–35.
Coles, P. (2003) *The Importance of Sibling Relationships in Psychoanalysis*, London: Karnac Books.
Craib, I. (1994) *The Importance of Disappointment*, London: Routledge.
Delamont, S., Atkinson, P. and Parry, O. (2004) *Supervising the Doctorate: A Guide to Success*, Bucks: SRHE and Open University Press.

Finn, J. (2005) *Getting a PhD: An Action Plan to Help Manage Your Research, Your Supervisor and Your Project*, London: Routledge.
Foucault, M. (1980) *Power/Knowledge: Selected Interviews and Other Writings, 1972–1977*, Brighton: Harvester Press.
Froggett, L. (2002) *Love, Hate and Welfare: Psychosocial Approaches to Policy and Practice*, Bristol: Policy Press.
Frosh, S. (2003) Psychosocial studies and psychology: is a critical approach emerging?, *Human Relations*, 56 (2) 1545–1567.
Frosh, S., Phoenix, A. and Pattman, R. (2003) Taking a stand: using psychoanalysis to explore the positioning of subjects in discourse, *British Journal of Social Psychology*, 42, 39–53.
Hoggett, P. (2000) *Emotional Life and the Politics of Welfare*, Basingstoke: Macmillan.
Lacey, J. (2000) Discursive mothers and academic fandom: class, generation and the production of theory, in S. Munt (ed.), *Cultural Studies and the Working Class*, London: Cassell.
Lawler, S. (2000) *Mothering the Self; Mothers, Daughters, Subjects*, London: Routledge.
Lucey, H. and Reay, D. (2002) A market in waste: psychic and structural dimensions of school-choice policy in the UK and children's narratives on 'demonized' schools, *Discourse: Studies in the Cultural Politics of Education*, 23 (3) 23–40.
Mitchell, J. (2003) *Siblings, Sex and Violence*, Cambridge: Polity Press.
Morley, L. (1999) *Organising Feminisms: The Micropolitics of the Academy*, New York: St Martin's Press.
O'Leary, V. and Mitchell, J. (1990) Women connecting with women: networks and mentors, in S. Stiver Lie and V. O'Leary (eds) *Storming The Tower: Women in the Academic World*, London: Kogan Page.
Phillips, E. and Pugh, D. (2000) *How to Get a PhD: A Handbook for Students and Their Supervisors*, Maidenhead: Open University Press.
Plummer, G. (2000) *Failing Working-Class Girls*, Stoke-on-Trent: Trentham Books.
Reay, D. (1997) The double bind of the working class feminist academic: the success of failure or the failure of success?, in P. Mahoney and C. Zmroczek (eds), *Class Matters: Working Class Women's Perspectives on Social Class*, London: Taylor and Francis.
Reay, D., David, M. and Ball, S.J. (eds) (2004) *Degrees of Choice: Social Class, Race and Gender in Higher Education*, London: Trentham Books.
Rose, N. (1992) Governing the enterprising self, in P. Heelas and P. Morris (eds), *The Values of the Enterprise Culture: The Moral Debate*, London: Routledge.
Rustin, M. (1991) *The Good Society and the Inner World: Psychoanalysis, Politics and Culture*, New York: Verso.
Scott, J. (2001) *Power*, Cambridge: Polity.
Silverman, D. (2005) *Doing Qualitative Research*, London: Sage.
Thomas, K. (1996) The psychodynamics of relating, in Wetherell, M. and Dallos, R. (eds) *Social Interaction and Personal Relationships*, Milton Keynes: Open University Press.
Walkerdine, V., Lucey, H. and Melody, J. (2001) *Growing Up Girl*, Basingstoke: Palgrave Macmillan.
Wisker, G. (2005) *The Good Supervisor: Supervising Postgraduate and Undergraduate Research for Doctoral Thesis and Dissertations*, Hampshire: Palgrave Macmillan.

2
Power and the PhD Journey: 'Getting in' and 'Getting on'

Kathryn Almack and Harriet Churchill

Introduction: reflecting on doctoral experiences in higher education

In this chapter we examine power processes within academia through an analysis of our personal narratives of undertaking doctoral research (in social sciences) against multi-dimensional frameworks of power (McNay 2000; Morley 1999). The PhD process can encompass a wide range of issues including those related to research methodology, practice and theory as well as the contextual significance of personal and institutional settings to knowledge production, but we focus on issues of power emerging from our transitions and experiences in *commencing* doctoral research, on what we have called the achievement of 'getting in' (accessing doctoral research opportunities) and 'getting started' (the first months of study). We write this as two White British able bodied women from differing class backgrounds (as we discuss later). However, commencing PhD research for both authors involved ambivalence and struggle in the transition towards an academic career negotiated within particular personal, biographical and institutional sets of circumstances. The relationship between achieving a PhD, taking our academic careers forward and the wider context of social positioning, institutional settings, power and knowledge constitute our central concerns. The narratives we present in this chapter are based on reflections guided by personal memory, journal entries, and discussions within the Women's Workshop and elsewhere and situated alongside the analysis of power relations, processes and outcomes in higher education (Morley 1999; David 2000; Wisker 1996).

It is worth noting the sensitivity and ethics of such an endeavour, as we seek to move beyond the micro-picture offered by our personal narratives towards broader theoretical frameworks that conceptualise the socially constructed nature of advantage and disadvantage (such as those constituting class, gender, age and disability based inequalities) which also pervade academic hierarchies. Making use of and writing about one's own biographies in a public arena, where we do not have the benefits of anonymity provided to research respondents, raises salient questions about what we might want to reveal or conceal. The biographical texts within this chapter are inevitably selected (and re-worked) aspects of our PhD trajectories developed from materials we wrote at the time but written primarily as retrospective accounts. To some extent we have 'sanitised' aspects of our lives for public consumption; we have imposed an orderliness, a shape on lives that are essentially irrecoverable (Hollway and Jefferson 2000: 167).

Our individual biographies are not seen as the basis for making large scale generalisations. Our aim is to examine some of the challenges, problems and pressures that we felt, located in the wider social and cultural context, as well as 'imagining an alternative' – what might facilitate an empowering set of conditions (Hoggett 2000). This paper thus begins to examine relatively neglected aspects of the biographical, institutional, material and relational contexts to the PhD process.

Our focus: 'getting in' and 'getting started' as a doctoral student in the social sciences

Despite a considerable expansion in university education and the transition from elite to mass system of higher education (Egerton and Halsey 1993; Black 2005), differentials in access remain strong (Reay *et al.* 2001). Subsequently there has been considerable interest in capturing the experiences of marginal groups such as working class, mature or ethnic minority undergraduate experiences of higher education (Edwards 1993; Reay *et al.* 2002; Wisker 1996) and the experiences of working class and women academics within the academy (Mahoney and Zmroczek 1997; Morley 1997).

Within the literature on postgraduate teaching and learning, the power dynamics of the supervisor/student relationship are often acknowledged. Indeed the subject of supervisor-student relationships is a major area of study itself (see Lucey and Rogers, Chapter 1 in this volume) and many texts now offer advice on establishing less hierarchical PhD supervisory relations (see Pugh and Phillips 2000). However, power dynamics within the PhD process beyond supervisory and research relationships have rarely been the focus of analysis and reflection. In the following section we outline the theoretical framework that we draw upon and then consider how this framework, applied to our personal narratives, can illuminate wider issues of the connections and power dynamics between personal experience and the broader social and institutional setting of higher education.

Power 'operating on us and through us': theoretical influences in linking the relational, cultural and material aspects of power

In our collaboration for this chapter, we noted differences in our personal accounts but we were also struck by the similarities. Centrally, our research interests emerged from our gendered, classed and biographical life experiences; in Bourdieu's terms, shaped by our individual *habitus* (Bourdieu 1990b).[1] Other central aspects of a shared location were firstly, being mothers with young children and secondly, embarking on a biographical transition in commencing PhD research and aspiring towards an academic career. We felt we had come to PhD research through non-traditional paths (although suggesting a uniform traditional path is dubious).

Underpinning these themes, we examine the complexities of classed and gendered experiences of power. We draw upon Bourdieu's interconnected concepts of habitus, fields and forms of capital. Habitus can be understood as an internalised core derived from biographical experiences and social location, that although amenable to change and generative, forms the conscious source of everyday practices. This core constitutes a 'socialised subjectivity' (Bourdieu and Wacquant 1992: 126), a set of predispositions to thinking and behaving that have been acquired 'through experience and explicit socialisation in early life' (Jenkins 2002: 79). For Bourdieu, class relations are deeply embedded in what 'one is' and are deeply internalised, and hence reproduced through habitus. Bourdieu's writings have been criticised for overemphasising the role of class and, particularly in relation to habitus, for being overly deterministic. We would not want to deny the importance of other categories such as gender, ethnicity and sexuality and issues of both gender and class form our main focus in this paper. From a feminist materialist perspective, theorists such as Skeggs (2005), Lawler (2005) and McNay (2000) have attempted to make space for the dynamic and generative possibilities of habitus, which can be subject to change in relation to context. We aim to understand the multi-dimensional aspects of class and the interconnections with other structural inequalities and in doing so, we find Bourdieu's notion of habitus most useful when considered alongside the related concepts of social fields, different forms of capital and the potential for transformation. As Lawler (2005: 112) argues, 'habitus only makes sense in the context of specific local contexts or 'fields' – the 'games' for which 'the rules of the game equip us'. The related concept of field gives the habitus a dynamic feel. As social actors in social worlds encounter new and different experiences in the 'field', the habitus continually restructures. Thus, while the individual's early habitus reflects the social position in which it developed, it also carries within it the genesis of new creative responses that are capable of transcending the social conditions in which it was produced (Reay 2004: 434–435). The location of a social class position further relies on amounts and composition of capitals available. Capital takes different forms, usefully outlined by Black (2005: 129): economic, which relates to income and wealth; cultural, which is possessed in different forms – in an objectified state in the form of cultural goods, in the form of dispositions of the mind, and in an institutionalised state, most often recognised as educational qualifications; social which consists of resources based on networks and relationships that an individual is embedded in and can draw upon; and symbolic, which is the form other capitals take once they are perceived and recognised as legitimate. As Skeggs (1997: 128) notes 'legitimation is the key mechanism in the conversion to power'.

The dynamic interconnections between habitus, field and forms of capital allows for a 'microtheory of power' (see Moi 1999) that allows us to incorporate mundane details of everyday life into a social analysis of power. Morley (1999: 5) discusses how a series of seemingly small incidents/transactions and individual endeavours can acquire a new significance when located within a wider analysis of power relations. As Reay (2002) and others have noted (Edwards 1993; Wisker 1996) issues around belonging, fitting in and feelings of authenticity/ inferiority are key to understanding working class, ethnic minority and women's experiences of the move into higher education.

We now turn to setting out aspects of our experiences in 'getting in' and 'getting started', with an analysis of the theoretical implications of these experiences.

Getting In: 'non-traditional routes' into doctoral research:
Our routes into higher education differed but neither of us followed a 'traditional' middle class route of 'A' levels followed by degree, MA then PhD and both came to post graduate studies as 'mature' students

after a break from full-time education and with responsibilities as parents of young children.

We both noted how our biographical pathways towards a doctorate were far from linear or expected:

Kathryn
I come from a rural working class background, occupying what Reay (1997a: 21) describes as the 'borderlands of social class'. Passing the 11+ I went to the local girls' grammar school, which had a reputation of high academic achievement. Differences in background were present but only began to really show at 16+ when most of my (working class) friends left school. There was little expectation that working class girls stayed on to do A levels. Questioning now why I and not others stayed on to do A levels, I identify a possible connection to my 'borderlands of working class', which include a rural background as well as a familial pursuit of signifiers of middle class identity – associated with home ownership, grammar schools, elocution and piano lessons. At the time, I could not then articulate the differences; it was only much later, when I read feminist accounts of working class school experiences (Steedman 1986; Walkerdine 1990; Mahoney and Zmroczek 1997) that I felt able at last to make sense of my feelings of alienation and struggles within this middle class environment – and my downward spiral from good O level grades to low A level grades. Rather than teachers being concerned about a bright girl achieving such poor results, I, like many (see, for example, Holloway 1997), experienced the kind of low teacher expectations that contributed to a longer-term sense of not belonging in an academic world. However – a chance comment (that I ascribed to luck rather than a sense of worth) by one teacher about applying to universities and widening participation in higher education did open up possibilities. In common with many working class girls of my generation, I was the first in my family to do a degree. I did so at a polytechnic in my 20s, – and here I don't recall questioning my sense of belonging as I had at school. Polytechnics were more likely to attract students from a range of backgrounds, but also being perceived as a mature student may have made some difference in obscuring class differences. Post-degree, I entered employment in the field of social care/community work, which again opened up further training opportunities and ultimately led me to doing an applied MA course in my 30s. I subsequently harboured ambitions to go further and do a PhD although this seemed even then so unrealistic/unattainable that I did not actively pursue it. This was 'not for the likes of me'.

Harriet
My educational trajectory towards a PhD was quite complex. Firstly, my educational background through primary, secondary and A level education was

one of perceiving myself as having fairly low academic abilities, something confirmed by lower academic grades and the low expectations of others (in relation to academic achievement). Secondly, educational aspirations were not central in our family (my parents were heavily involved in the horse racing industry and as a family we had a daily routine orientated around training and keeping horses). Thirdly, at the time of completing A Levels there was a general expectation that earning your own money was a priority and university was too costly and financially risky. Post A levels I attended a vocational course at the local college and took up retail paid work for a couple of years. During this time I also got interested in local politics and equality campaigning. This interest turned into an aspiration to study politics and as a mature student I began an undergraduate degree. I felt some differences from my undergraduate peers in being a few years older, having taken some time out from the education system and needing to work part-time to fund my studies. Ultimately though learning about political and sociological theories of inequalities as well as getting involved in student political campaigning I felt my life was 'turned around'. Undertaking a politics degree was a transforming experience for me opening up a new world of political ideas and theoretical approaches, leading to a new awareness and alternative aspirations towards an academic career.

Our motivations for undertaking doctoral research were related to how inspiring we had found the subject area at the undergraduate level:

Harriet
Following my degree I was employed as a researcher at the same university within a research unit conducting critical social science research for social welfare and equality. Research at this point had become a means of generating critical knowledge and action towards social justice. After three years as a research assistant I began an MA in research methods although later gave up this course and ultimately my job when I became pregnant and experienced difficulty in moving to part-time hours and securing childcare. I then looked after my daughter full-time and was reliant on welfare benefits for three years. After three years out of the labour market I felt extremely fortunate to gain a PhD studentship, which had been advertised within a family research centre at a university. As a fully funded PhD studentship, this vacancy fitted my search for research employment (so beginning a PhD for me was not dependent on applying to a research council for PhD funding). This appeared to be a very good way of getting back into research work as well as developing my own research interests. I had been very surprised to gain the studentship and felt uncertain about ultimately achieving completion. I was aware that I

had not completed an MA and had been out of research for a few years. I was also uncertain about coping with doing a PhD and raising a young child. However, these same circumstances led me to pursue a research topic that had emerged from my previous interests in feminist research and my own experiences – to explore how lone mothers' negotiate paid work opportunities. My motivations for doing PhD research therefore were political, theoretical and personal as doing a PhD was a means of earning an income (that was still considerably more than Income Support), gaining a qualification, critically reviewing policies towards mothers and families, recognising mothers' lay knowledges and developing my engagement with social science theories. These diverse motivations were also not necessarily complimentary.

Kathryn
My MA studies were self funded on a part-time basis while working as a Community Worker – an applied course so perceived to be 'not too academic' and therefore not too daunting. Doing an MA led to an interest in academic studies that I wanted to take further, but as noted above I felt this was an unrealistic aspiration. The barriers were both real and self-imposed. I felt uncertain about achieving this in terms of competence, funding, and leaving employment to become a full-time student. However, circumstances conspired to give me the push I needed. My Community Work post was cut while I was on maternity leave and, while offered alternatives, I took voluntary redundancy. I found part-time work but redundancy and motherhood had made me think again about future work (career?) prospects. I was also influenced by two close friends working in academia who encouraged me to apply for a PhD studentship that was advertised at my local university, exploring the fields of homelessness and domestic violence – areas I had worked in as a practitioner and therefore knew about. I still might not have applied for this had it not been for the support of these friends who took it for granted that I was more than capable of applying. Like Harriet, being successful in my application felt more like a stroke of luck than anything to do with my capabilities! At the same time however, doing a PhD might well have involved an element of empowerment; resistance to the deeply ingrained notion that I was moving into spaces where I perceived I did not belong.

Access, entitlement, luck

In diverse ways undertaking PhD research was not an expected part of our personal aspirations or those communicated to us by others who formed early influences in our lives – family and school. We therefore began our PhD journeys with perceptions of difference that raised concerns about entitlement, competence and belonging as well as pursuing research areas that connected in some way to our own personal trajectories and political values. While our perceptions of 'inferiority' differed, with some around cognitive ability, some around family commitments and others stemming from our gendered class backgrounds, they signal an internalisation of perceived disadvantage so often remarked on in studies of disadvantage and non-middle class student experiences (Edwards 1993; Hoggett 2000). The delayed entry among working class or low income women into higher education operates not only at the level of undergraduate degrees (Reay 2002) but also disrupts the normative trajectory (full-time education in one's twenties) of moving from a degree to post-graduate studies – as we have experienced. As Morley (1997) has argued, this temporal dimension is a by-product of the class system but one that can reinforce a negative image of working class women being less scholarly than their middle class counterparts. In sharing accounts of our experiences we recognised feelings of doubts about our educational competence and lack of confidence in pursuing a PhD as a viable possibility. We attributed our educational attainments thus far as down to 'luck'; getting in through luck rather than through entitlement. Aspirations or access to higher education did not form part of our familial habitus but we both noted that in more recent years we knew of friends who were doing MAs/PhDs. However, while transcending the conditions of one's early habitus is possible, the influence this holds over our life choices is never fully left behind. The habitus can be understood as a 'durable set of cognitive and affective dispositions, rooted in early socialisation in the family and at school' (Aldridge 1998) and as such can continue to work long after the early conditions of its emergence have been dislodged. Despite having gained degrees and seeing the opportunities taken up by others, there was still a strong theme running through our accounts that PhDs were something that other people did – which was 'not for the likes of us' (Bourdieu 1990a). Bourdieu's conceptualisation of the interactions between habitus and field, with access to varying amounts of capitals allows us to develop an understanding of being located in this space of unease. Education is one particular field where possessing the types and volume of capital available for example to the middle classes can assist the (middle class) individual moving into this field in ways which can be taken for granted. In other words, for the middle classes there may be a greater and taken for granted disposition to enter into higher education and to perhaps progress further in an academic career via a PhD:

> Middle class people are able to operate with a sense of entitlement to social space and economic rewards that would be beyond

comprehension to those of the working class for whom limitation and constraint frame their social movement. (Skeggs 1997: 132–133)

This is not to say that middle class students 'have it easy', but that they may be better equipped to move into the academic habitus. The predispositions, habits, tastes of a middle class habitus provide a sense of knowing the 'rules of the game' or having a 'feel for the game' in the predominantly middle class field of higher education. Coupled with the right kinds and volume of capital this can, as identified by Black (2005: 129–130) 'facilitate a smooth and privileged movement into a field', allowing 'the person to exist like a "fish in water", never needing to be conscious of the water that surrounds her'. As noted, our experiences of 'getting in' included feelings of vulnerability and insecurity, of not belonging. These experiences are not exclusive to those outside the middle class habitus. However we recognise the particular sense of not feeling at home in the academic environment, of feeling fraudulent and anxious that the fraud may be exposed – feelings eloquently written about by others (Mahoney and Zmroczek 1997) and indicative of class location. As Black goes on to observe: 'In contrast, the water can become very murky indeed where the knowledge, skills and tastes possessed are "wrong".'

Having recognised some of the constraints, it was the institutional opportunity towards widening participation in higher education that facilitated entry as well as the personal transformation of understanding and awareness generated from feminist theory. It is important to recognise that these experiences may also be the impetus for agency and resistance. Another narrative can be told where we need to recognise that although in some sense marginal, our social positions and PhD trajectories included aspects of privilege and social support. For example, meeting students from similar backgrounds and with family commitments provided some sense of belonging and support. Furthermore, occupying a social positioning which amalgamates current privilege and historical disadvantage and having the cultural capital of the working class educated can also be an asset in allowing different insider/outsider perspectives to inform our work (Reay 1997a; Hey 1997).

Material constraints

In addition to possible constraints of entitlement and competence (discussed below), there are also associated material constraints, in part linked to class origins and to the delayed educational trajectories common amongst many working class accounts of access to higher education (Mahoney and Zmroczek 1997). We both identified a number of constraints of a material nature such as no recourse to parental financial support; having higher housing costs and caring responsibilities. It is indicative that we applied for fully funded full-time studentships rather than attempt to self-fund. For one of us the PhD studentship for those with dependents was more than the previous income, for the other, it was less.

Access to affordable and accessible childcare is crucial in enabling many to access doctoral research. For Harriet, the institutional policy and provision for childcare was favourable. In particular, the cost of childcare was income related, something which may not be so readily available with moves to cut university nursery funding (Jones 2002). As a PhD student, the fees were at the lowest rate (about half the average local rate for full-time nursery childcare). There was an on-site nursery close to the departmental offices. With the ability to relocate a couple of months before the beginning of the PhD, there was also the advantage of the nursery policy to gradually build up towards full-time attendance over a few weeks, thus potentially easing the transition for child and parent. Relocation to a new city, which was a considerable distance from where Harriet previously lived, also involved moving away from locally based peer support networks and generating these afresh. For Kathryn, access to childcare was also crucial but subsidised University nursery places were heavily over-subscribed. Kathryn already had nursery provision arranged and thus made the choice to balance costs through juggling studying (on a lower income) and childcare. This 'juggling' was made far easier by co-parenting during these years which reduced her individual burden of childcare costs.

Getting started

Key aspects in the first year of undertaking a PhD can be relocating, settling into a new university and academic role; establishing a research focus; designing and getting started with the research; fulfilling university regulations; undertaking research training; establishing supervision and developing support networks. Our shared reflections highlighted factors operating at the personal and institutional level but the ways in which our experiences can be viewed as embedded in habitus and field are also significant. Below we set out the key issues from our individual experiences of 'getting started' and discuss the theoretical implications of these experiences.

Kathryn

A key aspect to getting started was a shifting social positioning. I had moved out of a work environment where I was known and my work respected to being a student in an unfamiliar environment where no one knew me. I experienced this as a downward shift in status (power) and so it was interesting that some of my PhD colleagues who had moved straight from undergraduate to post-graduate study felt the opposite – an upward shift in status. Further complexities came in relation to how I perceived my own positioning/status in contrast to how others – and particular family members – saw me as having a higher (and more powerful) social positioning. Seeing myself through their eyes made me realise how privileged I was while simultaneously feeling a pervading sense of inferiority, paradoxes which others have written about (Reay 1997b; Morley 1999). I also struggled with the subject matter of my PhD – related to domestic violence. I had not anticipated that studying rather than front-line work in this field could be just as difficult and I decided I could not pursue this line of study. My supervisors encouraged me to think of an alternative topic. I submitted a proposal which connected to previous research interests about the experiences of working out different ways 'to do' family. While the support and renegotiation was empowering (I got to keep the studentship funding) it also left me with a sense of having got in 'through the back door' and raised anxieties about my academic capabilities as I had more confidence in being a practitioner than being an academic. Indeed initially I lost confidence. I had previously felt competent writing committee reports or funding applications but struggled to find an academic voice, which, in part, involved learning a new way of writing. My supervisors were tremendously supportive and expressed confidence in my abilities throughout to produce the drafts, take on board their feedback and comments, and rewrite work but this was an alien and new way of working. While I suspect that is not an uncommon experience, this was exacerbated by feelings that I was after all an impostor!

Harriet

On starting my PhD research, I had quite a lot of scope to determine my central research questions and was allocated supervisors experienced in the methodological and theoretical approaches I wanted to develop. In many ways I began with a level of autonomy and choice in establishing my subject area, the methodological aspects of the research and my everyday research activities. Such self directed research has been a defining feature of social science doctorates in the UK. However, at the outset I felt quite overwhelmed with the whole task, uncertain about direction and unconfident. In hindsight, uncertainty and doubt preoccupied my concerns rather than working out options and taking ownership of the study. Entries in my research journal from this time strongly reflect self-doubts about my academic competence, dismissing ideas quite quickly, feeling I couldn't contribute anything new to the area and general feelings of anxiety and panic (although there was also excitement and enthusiasm)! These perceptions were rarely voiced. I perceived peers as more competent and doubted my ability to express ideas to others either in writing or verbally using appropriate academic concepts. There were many stops and starts that later on became re-visited as what would have been fruitful lines of inquiry. I felt concerned about not having a focus and wasting supervisors' time. With hindsight I realise that my emotional responses were hindering my engagement with fundamental ethical and theoretical research issues. For example, one pertinent issue was the difficulty of finding space for mothers' experiences in academic research and in seeking to establish a research focus that fulfilled PhD requirements. Rather than set out my concerns systematically and investigate their nature, the early days of the research process included a myriad of emotional responses and anxieties.

Issues of competence and voice

We both experienced feelings of inadequacy and self-doubt (to greater or lesser degrees) which generated anxieties that were difficult to articulate within a generalised perception of seeing others as much more competent – and sometimes being seen to be more competent that we felt ourselves to be. These anxieties reflect a kind of cultural legacy of a subordinate status – one aspect of Bourdieu's concept of symbolic violence, which is representative of a 'habitualised element of the subconscious' (Connolly and Healy 2004). Symbolic violence operates as a force that encourages individuals to live according to the expectations of others, internalising ideas and structures which tend to subordinate them (Bourdieu and Passerson 1979). In this context, self-measurement of what one might be expected to achieve (or not achieve) forms a source of self-policing. The commonalties of our isolated experiences of insecurity, anxieties about competence and self-criticism could be seen to be an example of this kind of process.[2] One example of symbolic violence at play takes the form of insidious comparisons: the working class student who compares her performance to be inadequate in contrast to her perception of competent middle class others.

Our experiences of the anxieties provoked were different but dominated our initial stages of undertaking PhD research, leading to many stops and starts. Black (2005: 131) discusses the movement through social space for the working class female academic: 'The sense of movement or acquiring new skills ... are an additional burden arising from a marginalised position.' This 'burden' operated in ways that also inhibited, for example, articulating support and training needs, developing a voice as an academic authority, taking ownership of the research and developing strategies that would enhance personal and career development (Morley 1999). Such issues are often individualised and pathologised, attributed to personal failure, a key aspect of disempowerment (Hoggett 2000; Lawler 2005; Taylor 1995; Wisker 1996).

An alternative view of these kinds of difficulties could be to realise that such uncertainty could denote particular research training needs or avenues for critical inquiry. Indeed the recognition of the need to support PhD students in a more regulated way has led many universities to undertake annual training audits with students, in line with quality assurance recommendations (National Postgraduate Committee 2004; Quality Assurance Agency 2002).

Privilege, dislocation and exile

In sharing our experiences of 'getting started' as PhD students we both recounted ways that we experienced struggles as well as opportunities as 'non-traditional' students. Despite childcare, we experienced an almost daily trade off between being immersed in isolated study and attending seminars or social networking events. Yet the latter are crucial for immersion in institutional and disciplinary networks and cultures. Time pressures also manifested as anxiety over 'not doing enough'. However these experiences of motherhood became a rich source of critical inquiry, as well as an alternative set of commitments and more familiar social worlds through which to switch off from one's studies – marking some tensions between doctoral studies but also some complimentary aspects. Another aspect of our experiences was a feeling of increasing distance between different aspects of our identities and lives. Our experiences felt akin to a point made by Morley (1997). Morley (1997) cites Gardener (1993: 54) and describes how working class academics 'learn very early in their careers that their lifestyle, general interests and work are largely incomprehensible to their families'.

Reay notes how survival for working class women in an academic environment demands a voice to 'replace the one that has so often been silenced in educational contexts' (1997a: 20). This could be said to represent a shedding of the early habitus without having a new space to feel at home – thus continuing the sense of dislocation. The process of developing one's academic voice and becoming familiar with academic conventions and discourses for communicating knowledge formed a major site of resistance and conflict. A further implication of this new field and altering habitus at times led us to avoid, where possible, public defence of argument or critical appraisal of supervisors' suggestions in these early stages of the research – in favour of adopting a consensual approach rather than an authoritative one (Hoggett 2000; Wisker 1996).

In the first year of study, a feeling of being torn between different types of knowledge was strong. While our research motivations led us to be committed to unveiling marginal voices, recognising lay knowledges and producing theory grounded in women's experiences – we lived between the social worlds of academic knowledge and the lived experience – worlds that are far apart in many senses. While our own thoughts, ideas and theoretical conceptualisations excited us and were meaningful in academic settings, to our own family members, research participants and others in our social networks, these pre-occupations could be inaccessible. Ethically, we experienced a tension between being 'careerist', 'stealing' the experiences of those deemed marginal, and gaining academic recognition for such research. Mature students, women and working class groups, are less likely to directly engage in academic argumentation (Wisker 1996). However, becoming converse in academic disciplinary discourses is a must for student success (Wisker 1996). We both experienced ambivalence between representing the voices of our respondents in ways that we felt would be meaningful to them as well as satisfying the demands of producing an academic thesis and argument. These ambivalent feelings in taking up positions of academic authority contributed to delays and uncertainty in presenting our work to others and in publishing papers.

Conclusion

We recognise that there are many aspects of the PhD process not covered in this chapter. Areas worthy of further consideration include, for example, the constraints and benefits experienced between motherhood and our research areas, the role of social support and other aspects related to our delayed trajectories into academia. However, focusing on our experiences of the early stages of our PhDs, we have examined some of the complex interconnections between our biographies and the institutional settings of academia. In Bourdieu's terms, negotiating the PhD process meant operating in a different 'field' from our familial backgrounds and social locations as mothers. In the process we identify a shift from the conditions of our early habitus although, as discussed, these influences are too deeply ingrained to fully leave behind. In these new spaces we also experience a deficit of the right kinds and amounts of capital (cultural, social, and economic). The accumulative effect was a heightened sense of insecurity. We felt anxious about our perceived lack of knowledge about how things worked, time, energy and useful networks (as others emphasise in this volume; see Gillies and Alldred, Chapter 6). At the same time, it is important to recognise the many sources of agency and 'power' that we do possess by virtue of social location (being part of the majority ethnic group and of British nationality for example means we are not subject to some of the social disadvantages that minority groups are).

Reflecting on these experiences for this chapter, working collaboratively and with the Women's Workshop, and our access to different knowledges and theoretical perspectives has enabled us to develop an analysis of some of the ways in which power operates. This has been an empowering experience. Moving into academic spaces has given us the tools, space and time to locate our personal trajectories within a wider social and institutional context.

In the process of drawing on our personal journeys, we stress the need to move beyond a purely individualistic or subjective notion of power and disadvantage in order to analyse and challenge academic structures. A critical concern is the consideration of the ways in which we understand, resist and challenge the 'rules of the game' and processes of inequality. A collective response and vision is needed, which in itself requires time and effort. We value the Women's Workshop as a space seeking to create such collectivity as well as supporting individual theoretical development. At the same time as a PhD student one is learning how to become an academic, attempting to 'get on and get in' and in a vulnerable position to challenge power structures. Does one comply, learn to become an academic, or seek to challenge the 'rules of the game'? Some are sceptical of the possibilities. Wisker (1996) suggests that academia is a self-referring and regulating system, especially noting the legitimation of authoritative knowledge through academic peer review. Further, Morley (1997) notes the risks involved in seeking change from within. She argues that if one distances oneself from power games – one becomes out of touch and potentially isolated but to play them leads to daily negotiations and struggles that are tiring and depressing. But others suggest there is an empowering possibility.

While academia has given us now tools, space and time to do the work reflected in this chapter, we have had to work hard to value the influences of early habitus, the capitals we had access to – influences and resources that are not ascribed with a taken for granted value in academia but which crucially inform our work and our production of knowledge. It has been a journey – ongoing – into 'murky waters', of dislocation and disadvantage but also of privilege, resistance and empowerment.

Notes

1 Bourdieu observes that 'Just as no two individual histories re identical so no two individual habituses are identical' (Bourdieu 1990b: 46)
2 This does not imply a uniformity of experience – while there may be common themes, the intensity of self-policing and the effects of this operation of power is likely to vary at the intersections of gender with race, class, sexuality, disability and personal experience (of violence, abuse, poverty and so on).

References

Aldridge, A. (1998) Habitus and cultural capital in the field of personal finance, *The Sociological Review*, 46 (1) 1–23.
Black, P. (2005) Class matters in UK higher education, *Women's Studies International Forum*, 28 (2–3) 127–138.
Bourdieu, P. (1990a) *The Logic of Practice*, Cambridge: Polity Press.
Bourdieu, P. (1990b) *Sociology in Question*, Cambridge: Polity Press.
Bourdieu, P. and Passerson, J.L. (1979) *Reproduction in Education, Society and Culture*, London: Sage.
Bourdieu, P. and Wacquant, L. (1992) *An Invitation to Reflexive Sociology*, Chicago: University of Chicago Press.
Connolly, P. and Healy, J. (2004) Symbolic violence and the neighbourhood: the educational aspirations of 7–8 year old working-class girls, in *The British Journal of Sociology*, 55 (4) 511–530.
David, M. (2000) From Keighley to Keele: personal reflections on a circuitous journey through education, family, feminism and policy sociology, in *British Journal of Sociology of Education*, 23 (2) 249–267.
Edwards, R. (1993) *Mature Women Students*, London: Taylor and Francis.
Egerton, M. and Halsey, H.H. (1993) Trends by social class and gender in access to higher education in Britain, *Oxford Review of Education*, 19 (2) 183–196.
Hey, V. (1997) Northern accent and southern comfort: subjectivity and social class, in Mahoney, P. and Zmroczek, C. (eds) *op. cit.*, 140–151.
Hoggett, P. (2000) *Emotional Life and the Politics of Welfare*, Basingstoke: Macmillan.
Holloway, G. (1997) Finding a voice: on becoming a working-class feminist academic, in Mahoney, P. and Zmroczek, C. (eds) *op. cit.*, 190–199.
Hollway, W. and Jefferson, T. (2000) *Doing Qualitative Research Differently*, London: Sage.
Jenkins, R. (2002) *Pierre Bourdieu*, London: Taylor and Francis (Revised Edition, first edition published 1992).
Jones, J. (2002) *UK Childcare Support for Student Parents*, London: Nuffield Foundation.

Lawler, S. (2005) Rules of engagement: habitus, power and resistance, *Sociological Review*, 52 (Supplement 2, March 2005) 110–128.

Mahoney, P. and Zmroczek, C. (1997) (eds) *Class Matters: 'Working-Class' Women's Perspectives on Social Class*, London: Taylor and Francis.

McNay, L. (2000) *Gender and Agency: Reconfiguring the Subject in Feminist and Social Theory*, Cambridge: Polity Press.

Moi, T. (1999) Appropriating Bourdieu: feminist theory and Pierre Bourdieu's sociology of culture (1990), in Moi, T., *What is a Woman? And Other Ess*ays, Oxford: Oxford University Press, 264–299.

Morley, L. (1997) A class of one's own, in Mahoney, P. and Zmroczek, C. (eds) *op. cit.*, 109–122.

Morley, L. (1999) *Organising Feminisms: The Micropolitics of the Academy*, New York: St Martin's Press.

National Postgraduate Committee (2004) *Guidelines on Codes of Practice for Postgraduate Research*, http://www.npc.org.uk/page/1003801720.

Phillips, M.P. and Pugh, D.S. (3rd Edition) (2000) *How to Get a PhD: A Handbook for Students and Their Supervisors*, Buckingham: Open University Press.

Quality Assurance Agency (2002) *Institutional Audits Handbook*, http://www.qaa.ac.uk/reviews/InstitutionalAudit/handbook/audit_handbook.asp

Reay, D. (1997a) The double-bind of the 'working-class' feminist academic: the success of failure or the failure of success?, in Mahoney, P. and Zmroczek, C. (eds) *op. cit.*, 18–29.

Reay, D. (1997b) Feminist theory, habitus and social class: disrupting notions of classlessness, *Women's Studies International Forum*, 20 (2) 225–233.

Reay, D. (2002) Class, authenticity and the transition to higher education for mature students, *Sociological Review*, 50 (3) 398–418.

Reay, D. (2004) It's all becoming a habitus: beyond the habitual use of habitus in educational research, *British Journal of the Sociology of Education*, 25 (4) 431–444.

Reay, D., Ball, S. and David, M. (2002) 'It's taken me a long time but I'll get there in the end': mature students on access courses and higher education choice, *British Educational Research Journal*, 28 (1) 5–19.

Reay, D., David, M. and Ball, S. (2001) Making a difference? Institutional habituses and higher education choice, *Sociological Research* Online, 5 (4) <http://www.socresonline.org.uk/5/4/reay.html>

Skeggs, B. (1997) Classifying practices: representations, capitals and recognitions, in Mahoney, P. and Zmroczek, C. (eds) *op. cit.*, pp. 123–139.

Skeggs, B. (2005) Exchange, value and affect: Bourdieu and the self, *Sociological Review*, 52 (Supplement 2, March 2005) 75–95.

Steedman, C. (1986) *Landscape for a Good Woman: A Story of Two Lives*, London: Virago.

Taylor, M. (1995) *Unleashing the Potential: Bringing Residents to the Centre of Regeneration*, York: Joseph Rowntree Foundation.

Walkerdine, V. (1990) *Schoolgirl Fictions*, London: Verso.

Wisker, G. (1996) *Empowering Women in Higher Education*, London: Kogan Page.

3
Ambivalent Positions: Ethnicity and Working in our 'Own Communities'

Kanwal Mand and Susie Weller

Introduction

The role of ethnic identity in the composition and experiences of young (female) contract researchers has rarely been explored in the context of British academia (Burke *et al.* 2000; Fenton *et al.* 2000; Mirza, forthcoming). Figures suggest that minority ethnic groups are deterred from entering into an academic career. In 2004 only 6.3% of academics were Asian and 1.4% were Black (HEFCE 2004). Lower figures of minority ethnic academics have also been recorded in more senior positions (HEFCE 2004). Furthermore, women from all minority ethnic backgrounds are more likely to be in temporary positions (Fenton *et al.* 2000). As a result, identity politics as an unspoken force in an increasingly market driven higher education (HE) system remains unexplored yet fundamental. In this paper we borrow the concept of niche market from economics and marketing, given the increasing emphasis on competition, individualisation and specialism in HE. Niche markets refer to small specialised markets based on unique selling points and target audiences.

In this chapter we are interested in the intersection between power and niche markets within HE. Moreover we argue that niches are inherently gendered, raced and classed. In particular we illustrate the way in which many (women) researchers carve out a niche on the basis of identity politics often, although not exclusively, centred on working with and in their own ethnic and cultural communities. This frequently becomes a 'selling' point on the basis of authenticity in an HE market that increasingly relies on niches. We are, to some extent able to compare our experiences as an Asian/middle-class woman and a

White/working-class woman in addition to drawing on the stories of our colleagues[1] in the early stages of their careers. In this paper we ask what motivates women to work in their 'own communities' and whether women carve out such niches in response to constraints within the academy or because of opportunity factors. This chapter differs from other work in that it also focuses on the experiences of contract researchers who work within a particularised market.

Power and politicised identities in the academy

The arguments in this chapter have to be situated within the context of the power relations, particularly in relation to gender and ethnicity that exist within the British academy. It is important to recognise that global changes within academia have shifted focus towards internal markets, competitiveness and individualisation within the production and consumption of knowledge. Knowledge is created under the dominance of a relatively patriarchal, hierarchical and ethnocentric engrained system (see Sidaway 1997). In seeking a conceptual framework for our discussion we draw upon Sharp *et al.*'s (2000) work on the entanglements of power, whereby power is constructed of both dominating and resisting elements, where neither facet is independent and where entanglements may be metaphorical, material and/or symbolic (Sharp *et al.* 2000). These dominating and resisting elements are not simple power exchanges (see also Foucault 1977, 1979, 1980), and we are particularly interested in the unspoken encounters of power that impact upon a researcher's decisions vis-à-vis career development. As this chapter will show power relations and identities are politicised in different ways when ethnicity/race are either explicit or implicit foci of a study. Our experiences highlight how the intersection between our ethnic/gender identities and power relations in the academy are simultaneously enabling and disabling. We do, however, acknowledge that whilst ethnicity is significant we concurrently inhabit other niches either in terms of the research we conduct (with children, families, elderly and so on) or in relation to other aspects of our identities (for example, disability, sexuality and so on). Furthermore, in both our individual cases our research topics are highly gendered by association. We are both working broadly within the context of family. Whilst our experiences highlight that the rationale for working within our 'own communities' often centres upon both personal and political motivations, this is not always part of a conscious career strategy.

Given that our focus is on power relations in the context of British universities, we are interested in the inherent power associated with working in a 'niche' based on a researcher's ethnic, cultural or class background. Our experiences highlight the different factors that motivate or perhaps channel researchers into working within their 'own community'. Nonetheless, researchers recognise the constructed notion of 'community' (see, for example, Hillery 1955; Freie 1998; Ali 2003). In our reflections we found that we belong to different communities simultaneously and although these may stem from our cultural, racial and class backgrounds, over the life course we go on to develop associations with other communities based on our employment, education, and personal lifestyles. We find that the notion of communities needs to be fluid enough to acknowledge such historical shifts, but we must not lose sight of the fact that interactions between, within and outside communities operate within structures of power. Our terms of reference, therefore, lie in the notion that a researcher often has some commonality, shared identity, language, culture or geographical background with their participants, and that the power dynamics involved in this relationship and the consequent impact it has on a researcher's career often goes unspoken. We also acknowledge that in the transition to our professional lives we may actually have distanced ourselves from our 'own communities', for example, in terms of inhabiting a different class positioning or gender role (Reay 2001).

Hence, our experiences of working in our own 'community' can and do relate to power as a positive or negative experience, one that is relational and mediated by our social identities be they gender or generation and so forth. Our concern lies with the role and experiences of academic researchers in producing knowledge both explicitly and implicitly about race, ethnicity and culture. 'Ethnicity' and 'race' are constructed and contested terms; nonetheless the politics of 'race' and 'ethnicity' impact on women's experiences in the academy. However, this chapter differs from other studies in that we consider the majority and minority populations of Britain as socially positioned. This means that the authors, Susie and Kanwal, both form part of ethnic groups; however Susie, classified as white British, would not conventionally be seen as part of an 'ethnic' group. Kanwal, who would traditionally be categorised as an ethnic minority is a third generation migrant of South Asian origin. As we discuss below, these conventional categorisations fail to recognise the complexity of power relations inherent in working within HE and the significant role niche markets play in enabling/disabling careers (see Carter 2004).

Following postcolonial feminists we question privileging particular positions based on authenticity and an exclusive focus on lived experiences as it undermines the power of creativity and the larger political project of feminism (Carby 1982; Mohanty 1993). Like these authors we argue for a more nuanced approach and highlight women to be 'constituted' through legal, economic, religious, political and familial structures and call for a move away from 'ethnocentric universality' (Mohanty 1993). In doing this, we include class in our considerations and to some degree we can contrast our own experiences. Our encounters are shaped by working within one of the most ethnically diverse universities[2] in the UK, where 60% of students in 2003/04 were from a minority ethnic background (LSBU 2005).

Academic niches: enabling or disabling?

What follows is a discussion about how we have carved out a niche for ourselves in an environment that stresses particular outputs, namely the Research Assessment Exercise (RAE) (see chapter 8, this volume). Firstly, we want to stress our social identities and the resultant sense of expertise that this gives us particularly as our embodied knowledge is translated into qualification. The second way in which we feel that we have created a space for our work is based on the challenges we pose to disciplinary norms. We highlight these two aspects as being enabling although the proceeding discussion illustrates the slippage between what is enabling and disabling due to essentialist positionings, and the tensions inherent in terms of representation and authenticity that arise when working within our 'own communities'. In the section, 'the disabling niche' we draw attention to the context of research that stresses outputs with a result that researcher's latent talents, particularly linguistic skills, become an overriding factor and stress the need for more language training opportunities in qualitative research.

Carving out a niche: social and ethnic identities

Kanwal was born in Tanzania and is part of a South Asian migrant community in the British context as well as part of a transnational community of migrants. British colonial rule privileged minority migrant South Asians over the majority African and provided them (through overseas citizenship or protectorate passports) with an initial avenue to migrate to Britain (Mand 2004). Kanwal's migration was part of a family strategy related to perceptions about safety and aspirations for social mobility. Kanwal's education spanned state and private schools, prior to pursuing a BA from a 'polytechnic' and eventually a doctorate in social anthropology from a 'red brick' university. Through studying her 'own community' Kanwal has experienced social mobility and a rise in social status professionally and personally. Significantly, Kanwal found that women in her research also experienced social mobility and status enhancement through education, which was often translated into securing a good marriage alliance. Such overlaps and disjunctures sensitised Kanwal to issues such as marriage, education and employment and its relationship to migration (Mand 2004).

Although there were commonalities, Kanwal highlights that there were acute differences between her and the respondents drawn from her 'community' in terms of class, gender, generation, stage in the life course and geographic location. Firstly, education and social mobility has for Kanwal been in the realm of professional achievement and this generates a particular independence not experienced by the women of her research. Furthermore, unlike her respondents Kanwal was and is not married nor has children, a factor that was a central feature in the experiences of transnational mobility and her representation of women's lives. Kanwal experienced varying degrees of 'insider' and 'outsiderness' based on the geographic location, gender and generation. Kanwal says a common thread that enabled Sikh men and women, albeit in different ways, to understand her 'asking so many questions' was the close fit between her gender identity and interest in social networks, rituals and familial life as these are often perceived to be preoccupations of 'women's work' (Mand 2002).

Whilst Susie has taken a relatively conventional 'career path', moving straight from school to university and a job in academia this was, by no means conventional in relation to the norms of her family or community. Coming from the Isle of Wight, a predominantly white county of rural Britain she grew up in a white, working class family and she was the first in her family to go to university. Despite the rest of her family leaving school at 15/16 years, they are passionate learners and she grew up within a culture of curiosity and exploration that often centred upon learning about maps, the world and people. This, coupled with two inspirational geography teachers in what was then a failing comprehensive school sowed the seed for a future in geography. She commenced a geography degree at Brunel University, a cosmopolitan institution in West London in 1997. It was never her intention to pursue a career in academia and indeed she knew very little about those kinds of possibilities when she started university. In 2000 Susie completed a dissertation on social exclusion in rural communities having returned 'home' to undertake fieldwork. Loving research she gained a PhD studentship at Brunel and again returned 'home' to pursue fieldwork in order to explore teenagers' engagement with, and experiences of, citizenship (Weller 2004a). She shared an ethnic, class and age (young) background with many of her participants, affording her with a significant degree of cultural capital. At the time issues of power and ethnicity were not explicit in her research. Indeed, for her, class was much more of an issue. Working within her 'own community' was in many ways enabling as her social networks and cultural capital aided access. Her research agenda was received well by teenage participants as their exclusion from engagement in local decision-making was a cause that many held dear. Whilst several adults showed an interest in her project her new status as a non-resident and graduate[3] also rendered her as an 'outsider', thus highlighting the ambivalent and complex positioning she inhabited working within her 'own community'.

To date we have both occupied niches within academia that are heavily based upon our ethnic, cultural and class identities by returning to 'our communities' to pursue fieldwork. Other colleagues have also suggested that a fundamental motivation for working within their 'own communities' rested on the notion of being a representative particularly in relation to challenging negative stereotypes in, for example, the media. Not only did we seek to study and promote the experiences of 'our communities' but in a sense our research has also been a process of self-discovery and empowerment.

Carving out a niche: disciplinary identities

Kanwal feels that doctoral research enabled her to creatively explore migration and women's lives that had been absent from anthropological studies. Having undertaken fieldwork in Tanzania, Punjab and Britain, Kanwal's thesis argued the centrality of women and their networks for the establishment and maintenance of transnational households (Mand 2004). Kanwal found her discipline's mode of investigation was overlain with power relations, since social anthropology has historical links with colonialism and through the practice of fieldwork entailing 'being there' and living with the 'natives' masks ideological assumptions. These assumptions result in powerful messages that related to the 'civilising' West as opposed to the 'primitive' rest. Responding to critiques made by feminists and postcolonial theorists, of traditional anthropological practices, Kanwal adopted new methods and ways of framing contexts for enquiry (Fog-Olwig and Hastrup 1997; Marcus 1995). These critiques mean that migration has become incorporated into the anthropological gaze. Kanwal found she held a unique position and her connections were imperative for gaining access and understanding informants' perceptions and experiences of movement.

Susie's career has developed within the field of geography, which by definition involves studying human (although not exclusively) interaction with local, national, global and imagined spaces. Like anthropology, the production of knowledge within geography has been inherently bound to the exploration of places and peoples which, traditionally had an uncomfortable connection with imperialism and colonialism. Indeed, in both disciplines postcolonial feminist theories have been significant in critiquing the dominance of white-masculinity which not only viewed research as objective and rational but also dichotomised 'home/colonizers' as superior and 'other/colonized' as inferior (Gregson *et al.* 1997). Moving away from this, during the 1960s many Geographers were at the forefront of studying ethnic segregation in urban areas (Johnston *et al.* 2000). Much of this work was based on quantitative data and subsequently heavily criticised for its reliance on rigid ethnic categories. More recently, Geographers have been concerned with examining ethnicity in relation to discrimination and lack of access to jobs and services. Many have also been engaged in exploring the interface between ethnicity, class and gender (Johnston *et al.* 2000).

For us, pursuing a PhD was both an opportunity to be engaged in a creative venture, as well as to seek a qualification. Doctoral research may be seen as an apprenticeship and whilst it is often a time when postgraduate researchers feel relatively powerless it was, for us, a creative exercise during which we had relative freedom to pursue our own interests. Nevertheless, doctoral research is ridden with complex power relations (see chapters 1 and 2, this volume) and the pursuit of creativity is mediated by the practicalities of the research process, for example gaining access, language skills and funds.

In choosing to work within our own communities we were, in the main, from similar ethnic, cultural and often class backgrounds to our participants. We also shared experience and familiarity of local places, rituals and norms. Being viewed as an 'insider' brings to the fore assumptions about guaranteed access to participants, authenticity and privileged knowledge. Nevertheless, our identities are differentiated by gender, age and other aspects of selfhood which render us partial insiders. We believe that despite our junior positioning in the academy this 'insider status'; our knowledge and experiences of the way ethnicity and culture is played out within our research sites almost certainly aided our entry onto a PhD programme. Our ethnic and cultural identities and experiences enabled us to exert a level of expertise; to claim some degree of authority and thus power over the participants' lives we sought to explore. Rather than occupying a subordinate position within the academy we deployed our personal expertise almost as a substitute for our deficit in research experience. This knowledge can, for example, be particularly powerful in interviews for doctoral studentships and entry into the HE marketplace. With emphasis on PhD completion times and submission rates threatening academic departments with blacklisting,[4] networks and relationships, access, and language, as well as a deep-seated connection with the locale was likely to be advantageous in gaining funding to pursue doctoral research.

Although on one level we felt a greater sense of expertise and power through our knowledge of 'our communities' it has occasionally been drawn to our attention that such research is regarded as easier. Fieldwork is perceived as something akin to a holiday and this fails to acknowledge the complex insider/outsider power relations that have to be contended with. For example, Susie was taught by some of the teachers involved in her PhD research. The translation from former pupil to researcher was challenging and teachers often viewed interactions as conversations rather than research tasks by attempting to seek information that pupils disclosed, thus potentially breaching anonymity and confidentiality (Weller 2004b).

Both Kanwal and Susie are now employed as Research Fellows in the 'Families and Social Capital ESRC Research Group'[5] at London South Bank University. The group comprises three strands: ethnicity, intimacy, education and employment. Kanwal works in the 'ethnicity' strand whilst Susie is based in the 'education and employment' strand. Research participants in the 'intimacy' and 'education and employment' strands are from a variety of ethnic groups although in the 'ethnicity' strand the focus is on pre-defined groups, for example African-Caribbeans and South Asians. Kanwal's study focuses on a topic that has been featured extensively in the literature about South Asians furthering an association between people and practices albeit in a migratory location (Appadurai 1988). Susie, however, is working on a cross-cultural research project which explores children's experiences of moving to secondary school, within a conceptual framework based around the notion of social capital. Susie's project looks more implicitly at ethnicity considering the experiences of many ethnic groups in relation to one key issue. Despite the emphasis on ethnicity in the project Susie certainly does not feel like an expert in the area, a point we will return to later in this chapter.

The enabling niche

Successfully developing, inhabiting and promoting a niche based, in part, on a researcher's identity or community can be enabling. Indeed, for some this approach may be one of the only routes into academia allowing researchers to use their ethnic and cultural identities and experiences as a form of authority through which expertise are exerted. Furthermore, according to Kobayashi (1994), a researcher's identity, particularly in relation to their ethnicity, can determine who they speak for. Importantly it may be used to validate who can speak in authority and who may legitimately represent whom (Kobayashi

1994). Indeed, Kanwal's work makes a more explicit link to being an expert on 'ethnicity', whereas Susie's implicit focus on the experiences of different ethnic groups does not render her an expert in the field of ethnicity per se. Moreover, she is seldom seen as part of an ethnic group.

One colleague, Lorna, applied to work on a research project exploring the experiences of Deaf Chinese young people. A criterion for the position was a Chinese language. This opportunity enabled Lorna to use her newly acquired academic skills, she felt akin to the participants as a young person of Chinese origin and to some degree this empowered her as commonalities of 'culture' were beneficial for her and the respondents. Although the criteria of holding relevant linguistic skill is significant and useful, particularly in the context of transnational research, Lorna's experience touches on the power inherent and unspoken through the codification of knowledge into a qualification and resultant notion of 'expertise' that are based on social identity. Power relations are, however, inherently entangled and whilst working within your 'own community' may provide openings into the academy there is the danger that this approach may reinforce inequalities within the system by confining researchers into particular niches.

For Susie, shared ethnicity with the research participants in her PhD was important. Rural Britain, the context for Susie's doctoral research, is overwhelmingly white and in her research participants discussed the presence of racist attitudes in the area. Whilst this would not be the case in all contexts, the way participants viewed her ethnic and cultural background may have impacted upon their willingness to engage in the project. Although as Carter (2004) argues there are many advantages to cross-cultural research and a researcher may successfully work with participants from a different cultural or ethnic background, local context is important (cf. Archer 2002). To some extent conducting long-term research is likely to provide a solution as researchers would be able to establish rapport and develop relations.

Working within your 'own community' may also be enabling, particularly if members of that community have been underrepresented in research. One colleague, Karen discussed feeling like a representative of her 'community', as a way to begin countering dominant negative images. Moreover, emphasis on previously neglected ethnic and cultural groups, by those who have connections with the community may go some way to provide the anti-essentialist critique of white-male research that many (postcolonial) feminists have sought (Gregson *et al.* 1997). In the past 'objective' research only portrayed one truth and emphasis on anti-essentialism is particularly important in subjects such as geography and anthropology, which to some extent are still criticised for elements of colonialism (Gregson *et al.* 1997). It is questionable, however, whether a researcher may speak with more authority on their 'own community'. It is likely that they will be more aware of hidden norms, values and rituals but all research is subject to interpretation on the part of the researcher.

Formal procedures have been put in place in some institutions, including our own, to encourage undergraduate and postgraduate students to engage in research in their own communities, as part of a process of empowerment. One colleague, Faith, who has pioneered such a scheme, described her traumatic progression through academia, highlighting the oppression, constraints, challenges and self-silencing she had experienced as a Black woman (see Bravette 1994). Having spent much of her career researching woman, race and higher education she actively chose to move beyond 'just surviving' in the academy to working with integrity and authenticity. Faith described feeling ambivalent; between believing she could bring about change and a lack of belonging. Having accumulated a great deal of research knowledge she encouraged students to conduct research in their own communities through Academically-Based Community Service. She now works as a mediator between students and their communities and feels that this approach not only has the potential to be empowering; to engage in issues surrounding race but it also enables a body of knowledge to be built in relation to different communities. Faith's experiences reflect the historicity behind marginalisation of black men and women from particular spaces which leads to a process of self exclusion as they 'don't feel they belong in particular spaces'. At the same time, 'black' academics are often 'pigeon-holed' into an ethnically-aligned topic area and are 'seen as less capable of being in authority' resulting in overt surveillance and monitoring (Mirza, forthcoming).

One way to overcome institutional disadvantage has been tackled through the Race Relations (Amendment) Act 2000 that compelled universities to adopt policies and strategies which promote racial equality (HEFCE 2005). Despite such initiatives researchers with a similar ethnic background to the research participants are often recruited because of their shared identities. There is, therefore, often an overlap between the skills you have and your ethnic or cultural identity. Shared identity is often the 'unspoken' subtext of many recruitment advertisements. Being an 'expert' of your own ethnic and cultural identity and having experiences of places and practices may be beneficial in gaining funding in an era of short-term research projects, although this is likely to be subject to trends within research funding and policy. In our experience, unless research is cross-cultural there is often a 'matching' between the researcher hired and the ethnic and cultural identity of participants.

The minefield surrounding identity politics in research means those in more senior positions, heading projects may feel uncomfortable or unconfident given their own ethnic and class positions and so engage in 'matching' when recruiting more junior staff. Obviously if more work is funded with previously neglected groups this may be positive for individual minority ethnic researchers. Whilst we do not fundamentally disagree with positive discrimination our criticism is when it occurs at an unspoken level and there is no reflection surrounding the ways in which this is enabling/disabling given the employees' position in hierarchical institutions.

The disabling niche

The arrival of large numbers of migrants to Britain from former commonwealth countries and recently new migration from Eastern Europe have ultimately shaped and fuelled the growth in ethnicity and race-related research projects, publications and degree courses. Despite common representations of academia as liberal, racism is indeed institutionalised, in terms of inequalities in pay, status and permanency of contract (Crace 2004). Examining data from the Higher Education Statistics Agency (HESA), Fenton *et al.* (2000) found that 93% of research posts held by those from minority ethnic groups were fixed term contracts and were overwhelmingly in post 1992 universities. Contract researchers occupy a precarious position due to changing markets. Those working in highly specialist fields or with small minority groups are likely to be the most vulnerable given the prevalence of niche markets and vogues.

The convergence between being a female academic drawn from an ethnic minority whose 'expertise' lies in working within her own 'community' and the junior position held in the academy can potentially lead to 'social closure' that results in restricted access on the basis of an essentialised notion of identity and employment (Fenton *et al.* 2000). For example, being an 'expert' on ethnicity could result in a lack of experience and consequently employment prospects in working with a broader range of groups. Inversely, therefore Kanwal's status as an expert on ethnicity results in her being confined to study groups of people rather than issues that are likely to affect people on a more universal level. Such a specialist position has obvious repercussions, as the pool of minority ethnic participants is far less than the dominant population.

Whilst in many ways Susie's PhD research has presented many opportunities working within her 'own community' has also been a constraint, as she is likely to have been viewed as someone with expertise in rural, white Britain, rather than cosmopolitan Britain. Whilst completing her PhD, Susie worked as a research assistant on a project exploring out-of-school clubs in a number of diverse areas. On applying for full-time research positions Susie experienced the constraint of her expert niche when she applied to work on a project looking at the 'underachievement' of a specific ethnic group, different from her own. Although a link between her lack of shared ethnic background and failure to secure the position can never be proven, she couldn't help feeling not sharing an ethnic background was an important factor. This echoes Carter's (2004) experiences. His 'cross cultural' research was frowned upon during job interviews for academic positions:

> In some cases it became clear that my research was regarded by some members of the academic community as worthless because of my identity as a white male researching ethnic minority women (Carter 2004: 346).

Karen also noted such experiences, and having applied for other research posts on projects exploring 'family' she feels she is viewed as an expert on Black families rather than families more generally. Working within your 'own community' may therefore be disabling if the dominant perception is that this is all you can do.

In Lorna's employment on the project focusing on young Deaf Chinese migrants, the ability to communicate using sign language (not one of her skills) was considered less important than her ethnic identity in the eyes of her employers, thus highlighting ethnicity as a highly politicised industry. Similarly, this echoes the experiences of a colleague at another university who felt written out of a proposal that was centred on a different ethnic group to her own/studied previously, despite being viewed as an expert on ethnicity. Moreover, there are implicit language and cultural skills and knowledge which, in a time of short term contracts, mean that researchers often don't have the time and/or opportunities to gain new language skills to a high enough level to conduct interviews. Whilst language is not necessarily tied to ethnicity or culture, there are greater opportunities to learn certain languages in school. Susie, for example, only had the option of learning either French or German at school. Few staff development units appear to offer such courses. Current systems within HE represent a marked shift from conventional notions of academia where scholars were able to pursue more diverse and often more creative explorations of subject areas. A lack of opportunity to develop language skills not only influences who researchers are able to work with but it also disadvantages those from educational backgrounds where there were limited opportunities for the development of languages. In part, this reflects increasing specialisation and the speeding up of research in the quest for productivity. Significantly we note that the Economic and Social Research Council who fund doctoral students has begun in the 2005 competition for doctoral studentships a model of funding that gives the opportunity for language training.

A different illustration about identity politics and employment prospects comes from our colleague, Hilda, who is working within a very small niche group not conventionally recognised as an ethnic group owing to their European heritage. As discussed above this highlights some of the unspoken assumptions in social research and the essentialisation of identities. Hilda's work with this 'invisible' group renders her in a vulnerable position as she is subject to funding trends and a narrow job market. This contrasts with being part of a majority group, or working in an arena where identities are not politicised along ethnic lines. Being part of a majority ethnic group may provide researchers with more employment opportunities across different topic areas. Susie has, for example, moved from conducting research in her 'own community' to undertaking cross-cultural research around key educational issues. In her current research she has been exploring the perceptions of parents and children drawn from different ethnic and socio-economic positions on secondary school transition; a passionate and controversial subject area where race and ethnicity are implicit. Susie's project and associated identity became de-raced in this scenario. Parents may hold different responses based upon their economic status or socio-cultural networks, however, the centring of the research around a (perceived) common issue[6] made inter-ethnic differences less apparent. Fundamentally, we argue for more cross-cultural research which we believe would go some way to tackling the challenges of being 'stuck' in a niche.

Discussions with our colleagues also drew attention to the notion of a glass ceiling in relation to career progression. Karen believed that such a ceiling existed but wasn't sure where its boundaries lay. Linking her ethnic identity with her career given the changing nature of the marketplace leaves researchers like Karen in a precarious position. In particular she highlighted the scarcity of Black women professors and questioned whether she would ever be taken seriously if she did become a professor or whether people would see it as a tokenistic gesture. Karen felt that working in a 'women-family' environment was enabling in terms of her career progression and questioned whether she would have been able to progress so far in another field of research. Moreover, Faith describes the constraints she has faced as a concrete ceiling and argued that many women have migrated to the US where there are more opportunities for career progression.

The disabling aspects of working within a niche based on your 'own community' are fuelled by current drives for high quality and speed in the production of knowledge in academia. This coupled with burgeoning commitments to teaching and administration means that academics rarely have time to creatively explore arenas outside of their niche(s).

Conclusions

Whilst working within your 'own community' may provide openings into the academy there is the danger that inequalities within the system may be upheld, confining researchers into particular niches. Such niches may be simultaneously enabling and disabling but the dynamic HE market renders those on short-term contracts in a precarious position. As junior researchers we have highlighted that commonalities between researchers and participants based on minority/majority ethnic groups, gender and class are situational and operate in networks of power. These are all the more significant given the structure of British academia, where the stress is on particular outputs of academic knowledge that at times demand an essentialist position on social identities. These power dynamics ultimately influence who is employed.

We have discussed the process of essentialism around social identities in relation to niches that enable and disable in different ways as we seek to realise our professional ambitions. Reflexivity has been a dominant theme in our discussions surrounding processes of exclusion and inclusion and how these are implicated in reproducing power relations. Nonetheless, we acknowledge the very real barriers to entering academic careers according to gender, class or ethnic background. One avenue to overcome the obstruction to gaining meaningful employment in academia is to work within our own 'communities', however translating this knowledge for an academic 'community' leaves researchers in an ambivalent position given the significance of representation and authenticity. The enabling and disabling elements of our social identities and resultant work are, therefore, complex and fluid.

It is perhaps the trend towards competition and outputs that renders inter disciplinary and collective work difficult. Arguably, collective work may be more empowering, curtailing the disadvantages of working within one niche. Furthermore, collective work may foster possibilities for researchers to move within and between niches. As Karen stated, a fundamental shift away from the idea that *'Black women can only do research in Black communities'* is both essential and needed. Furthermore, there is a danger that individualisation, specialisation and the pressure to continue working and publishing within one niche, as fuelled by the RAE will exacerbate the compartmentalisation of different studies of ethnicity and culture which may indeed be disabling for the academy as a whole, as well as having policy implications. Issues and needs that cross-cut different groups within society may be neglected and there is a danger of over-emphasising culture. This issue may be overcome through the encouragement of more cross-cultural research. Moreover, a better system for career progression is needed for those working on short-term contracts, which would allow more women and minority ethnic researchers to reach senior positions. More practically speaking language training for researchers would draw in further possibilities to carry out cross-cultural research both in terms of cross-cultural comparisons and for researchers from different cultural groups.

Notes

1 We draw on the experiences of colleagues working throughout the UK in the social sciences. Some have been given a pseudonym.
2 London South Bank University.
3 Only 15% of residents on the Isle of Wight have a qualification at degree level or equivalent, compared to 20% in England and Wales and 31% in London (ONS 2005).
4 The ESRC require university departments to achieve a 60% submission rate where students must submit their thesis within four years of receiving funding (ESRC 2005).
5 For more details please see the research group website: www.lsbu.ac.uk/families.
6 The fact that the majority of parents felt they were being conned by the Government into believing they could choose which secondary school to send their child to.

References

Ali, S. (2003) *Mixed-Race, Post-Race: Gender, New Ethnicities and Cultural Practices*, London: BERG.
Appadurai, A. (1988) Putting hierarchy in its place, *Cultural Anthropology*, 3(1) 36–49.
Archer, L. (2002) 'It's easier that you're a girl and that you're Asian': interactions of 'race' and gender between researchers and participants, *Feminist Review*, 72, 108–132.
Bravette, G. (1994) Black Women Managers and Participatory Action Research, *World Congress 3 on Action: Learning Research and Process Management*, University of Bath.
Burke, B., Cropper, A. and Hamson, P. (2000) Real or imagined – Black women's experiences in the academy, *Community, Work and Family*, 3 (3) 297–320.
Carby, H. (1982) 'White woman listen! Black feminism and the boundaries of sisterhood', in *The Empire Strikes Back* (CCS), London: Hutchinson.

Carter, J. (2004) Research note: reflections on interviewing across the ethnic divide, *International Journal of Social Research Methodology*, 7 (4) 345–353.

Crace, J. (2004) 'We remain almost invisible', *The Guardian*, Tuesday 14th December 2004, http://education.guardian.co.uk/egweekly/story/0,1372658,00.html (accessed 13th January 2005).

ESRC (2005) *Submission Rates*, http://www.esrcsocietytoday.ac.uk/ESRCInfoCentre/opportunities/postgraduate/FactsandFigures/index7.aspx (accessed 9th August 2005).

Fenton, S., Carter, J. and Modood, T. (2000) Ethnicity and academia: closure models, racism models and market models, in *Sociological Research Online*, Vol. 5, No. 2. http://www.socresonline.org.uk/5/2/fenton.html (accessed 12th June 2005)

Fog-Olwig, K. and Hastrup, F. (1997) *Siting Culture: The Shifting Anthropological Object*, London: Routledge.

Foucault, M. (1977) *Discipline and Punishment*, London: Allen Lane.

Foucault, M. (1979) *The History of Sexuality Vol. 1*, New York: Vintage Books.

Foucault, M. (1980) 'Two lectures', in C. Gordon (ed.), *Michel Foucault: Power/Knowledge: Selected Interviews and Other Writings, 1972–1977*, Brighton: Harvester.

Freie, J.F. (1998) *Counterfeit Community: The Exploration of Our Longings for Connectedness*, Maryland: Rowman & Littlefield.

Gregson, N., Kothari, U., Cream, J., Dwyer, C., Holloway, S., Maddrell, A. and Rose, G. (1997) Gender in feminist geography, in Women and geography Study Group (eds), *Feminist Geographies: Explorations in Diversity and Difference*, Harlow, Essex: Addison Wesley Longman, 49–85.

HEFCE (2004) *Equal Opportunities Monitoring: Staff Tables*, http://www.hefce.ac.uk/lgm/divers/eomonitor.asp (accessed 31st August 2005)

HEFCE (2005) *HEFCE Race Equality Scheme* – January 2005, http://www.hefce.ac.uk/lgm/divers/res.asp (accessed 16th August 2005)

Hillery, G.A. (1955) Definitions of community: areas of agreement, *Rural Sociology*, 20, 111–123.

Johnston, R.J., Gregory, D., Pratt, G. and Watts, M. (2000) *The Dictionary of Human Geography*, Oxford: Blackwell.

Kobayashi, A. (1994) Colouring the field: gender, 'race' and the politics of fieldwork, *Professional Geographer*, 46 (1) 73–80.

LSBU (2005) *About London South Bank University*, http://www.lsbu.ac.uk/about/factsAndFigures.shtml (accessed 16th August 2005)

Mand, K. (2002) 'Place, gender, power in transnational Sikh marriages', in *Global Networks. A Journal of Transnational Affairs*, 2 (3) 233–248.

Mand, K. (2004). Gendered places, transnational lives: Sikh women in Tanzania, Britain and Indian Punjab. *PhD dissertation*, The University of Sussex.

Marcus, G.E. (1995) 'Ethnography in/of the world system: the emergence of multi-sited ethnography', *Annual Review of Anthropology*, 24, 95–117.

Mirza, H. (forthcoming) *The In/Visible Journey: Black Women's Life-Long Lessons in Higher Education*.

Mohanty, C.T. (1993) Under Western eyes: feminists, scholarship and colonial discourses, in P. Williams and L. Chrisman (eds) *Colonial Discourse and Post-Colonial Theory: A Reader*, London: Harvester Wheatsheaf, 196–220.

ONS (2005) *Neighbourhood Statistics: Isle of Wight*, http://neighbourhood.statistics.gov.uk/dissemination/AreaProfile2.do?tab=6 (accessed 14th March 2005).

Reay, D. (2001) Finding or losing yourself?: working-class relationships to education, *Journal of Education Policy*, 16 (4) 333–346.

Sharp, J.P., Routledge, P., Philo, C. and Paddison, R. (2000) *Entanglements of Power: Geographies of Domination and Resistance*, London: Routledge.

Sidaway, J. (1997) The production of British geography, *Transactions, Institute of British Geographers*, 22 (4) 488–504.

Weller, S. (2004a) *'Teenage Citizenship Geographies: Rural Spaces of Exclusion, Education and Creativity'*, Unpublished PhD Thesis, Brunel University, July 2004.

Weller, S. (2004b) Researching the familiar: age, place and social capital in the field, in Edwards, R. (ed.), *Social Capital in the Field. Researchers' Stories*. Families & Social Capital ESRC Research Group Working Paper. London: London South Bank University.

4
Interweaving Academic and Professional Power in Higher Education

Linda Bell and Maxine Birch

Introduction

In this chapter we trace the strands of academic and professional power that we have experienced when working in higher education. These strands interweave within the academy and with our own sense of academic identity in many complex ways. From our initial entry to higher education (HE) and completing PhDs to working as lecturers on professional and other programmes, we explore how these changing roles and identities influence our notions of being an academic and how this shapes our work. The teaching, research, scholarly and managerial roles we have undertaken involve negotiating an intricate mix of academic and professional demands that can result in us feeling more or less powerful at different times and in different contexts.

The analysis of power we adopt here follows Louise Morley's work to examine how these issues are interwoven with the micropolitics in the academy (Morley 1999, 2003). This touches on the sometimes competing discourses of power between academic learning and practice learning (which usually occurs in the workplace). At times this academic, practitioner mix involves different aspects of social, cultural and economic capital (Bourdieu 1993; Adkins & Skeggs 2004), resulting in varying opportunities to take part in decision making processes (Elias 1991). Ultimately, we locate these different analyses of power within the processes of 'writing' as a key site for academic activity and identity. The process of writing is examined with reference to Judith Butler's understanding of power as a form of subjection (Butler 1997).

Here the regulatory and productive effects of power form the restrictive processes where academic subjectivity is performed. By examining our different pathways into university education and subsequently our work as lecturers and researchers across social science disciplines in relation to health and social care practices, we find that our ability to be an 'academic' is judged through our writing and we continue to reproduce this judgment on other forms of writing by students and colleagues. Here the tensions of academic and professional power interweave and become more easily observed.

We find that our notions of being academic or professional are challenged by the expansion of universities over the past two decades. 'The university' now incorporates many new groups of students, for example those who study for professional qualifications in health, education and social care. The awards of diploma and degree gained in HE no longer solely represent the completion of a set of studies but can also represent the acquisition of a set of professional competencies. The professional roles we are concerned with here are distinctly defined through registration and regulation that give a specific licence to practice the relevant professional knowledge and skills, underpinned by professional codes of practice and acknowledged 'values'. As we will argue later, our original identities involved having a specific profession and being involved in the public sector, which has shaped our subsequent academic careers, placing us on the margins of some parts of academia. Linda's recent academic work with health or social care professionals has, she feels, distanced her from both her original profession as a librarian and equally from her students' professions. The inclusion of professional education programmes within HE can suggest that as 'academics' we are moving into a 'new' form of HE and away from old forms. However, as our own career trajectories show, we can easily find ourselves between an 'old' world focused on writing and scholarship and a 'new' world that we may not recognise *as* new – it was always 'there' (defined as 'vocational studies') but it was previously located outside the university. We are therefore attempting to interrogate our experiences of becoming and being academics within this academic, practitioner mix. We reflexively analyse how our own career trajectories interweave these shifting dimensions of power. We examine how academic feminism has aided or ignored the gender and class dimensions of these new groups of practitioner students and we question how different forms of learning are incorporated within university academic standards. We start with our first thoughts of embarking on a university education.

Becoming 'academic': exploring our career trajectories

Like many young women in the 1970s we were the first members of our respective families to take advantage of the extended secondary education and complete A levels. At this time this educational advantage set the seeds for getting each of us a 'good professional job' rather than embarking on degree level studies at a university.

Maxine

I was the first member of my immediate family and previous generations to stay on at school until 18. My mother had left school at 14 and in later life admitted to never reading 'a book'. I achieved one (low grade) A level in 1974 but left school with a great feeling of optimism. University entry and other forms of continuing education did not feel my only recourse to demonstrate my abilities. Only a small number (less than 6.5% in England in 1975) of my cohort went to study at university. However after three years of different 'jobs' I soon realised that an educational qualification beyond A level was necessary to secure employment that interested me and offered career prospects. I had good people skills and wanted to work with people. I was more attracted to careers in the public sector rather than profitable enterprises. I embarked on A level studies once more (now part-time) and gained entry to an Occupational Therapy (OT) college. The three year 'diploma' in OT, at a professionally accredited college, involved learning in the workplace as well as demonstrating knowledge of the relevant academic disciplines. At this time I was blissfully unaware of distinctions between 'training and education', 'knowledge and skills', 'theory and practice'. To me it was all part of becoming an OT. And a good OT I was as well! As a young woman my achievement of the OT diploma, the associated professional accreditation and subsequent positions I held, confirmed my sense of being a very able therapist. I recall feeling more powerful in my chosen professional career, a feeling I had never achieved in previous jobs. I could make decisions that influenced and changed working practices. I received feedback that recommended my abilities to do so. Whether OT education should constitute degree level or not was already debated by the educators and professional bodies at this time. The allocation of study time in practice settings appeared to be a major stumbling block. To some 'practice' did not warrant academic levels of study. For some at this time the academic standing of OT education had already entered a power struggle of acceptability and credibility.

Linda

I was also the first member of my family to take A levels and to then to contemplate a 'professional' (rather than immediately an 'academic' career).

However I had always wanted to write, but I was unsure whether I could 'make a living' by writing. Becoming a librarian seemed a good choice in these circumstances. Once I embarked on this path, first taking on a trainee post for a year in a large public library, and then a professional diploma course at a technical college in the Midlands, I realised that librarianship was less about books and more about people. A central idea at that time was the ideal of 'public service', and this is something that has remained with me throughout my career. This realisation did great things for my (underdeveloped) social life and 'people' skills but left a gap; I decided I would still become a writer 'one day', but that a 'professional' career was what I wanted. My idea of 'professional' at that time combined the notion of public service with individualised expertise. In terms of HE policy at the time that I took my diploma course (early 1970s), I think that it was accepted that some people would follow a 'vocational' diploma route to a professional career as I had done, and others would follow a more academic route: interestingly librarians were split between these paths – some people took a degree in an academic subject and then a postgraduate diploma in librarianship, and might for example aim to work in academic or specialist libraries. Most of my fellow students on the diploma course aimed for a public library career, although the idea of a librarianship degree with a central component of public sector management was undeveloped at that time.

During the 1970s other students were following more 'traditional' paths to academic success and once I had obtained my professional qualifications I also followed this path. This meant taking time 'out' from a professional career, with the ensuing personal financial implications. However, since university fees were not payable at that time and some state support was available, it could be argued that it was 'easier' to choose to go to university in the 1970s/1980s. (This highlights an important and developing conflict between state reduction in financial support and a higher education agenda for widening participation which opened up during the 1990s.)

Whilst at technical college, it was the male tutors in particular who encouraged me to think of doing a 'subject' degree course, something I had not considered up to that point. The idea that I was being judged favourably via 'academic' forms of written text seemed to be part of the reason for this encouragement. Equally, my own reasons for not previously having considered doing a degree had a lot to do with wanting to 'get on with' a professional career, rather than 'wasting time' on academic pursuits. What academic interests did I have? Despite the librarianship, a disappointing result in 'A' level English had discouraged me from studying literature. History at that time seemed boring. I settled on anthropology as it brought together many of my different interests, and after working for a year as a librarian in a government department (in order to acquire my formal professional qualification) I accepted the place that I was offered, much to my surprise, at London University. Once I had embarked on an anthropology degree, I found that this wide-ranging course 'opened my eyes' to such an extent that looking back it was a decision I have never regretted. I did return to librarianship for a few years after graduation, mainly working in academic libraries, but my sights were now set on taking a PhD in anthropology.

The 1980s continued this shift towards increasing access and flexibility in higher education. A broadening curriculum that included the social sciences was increasingly popular and was recognised as a good knowledge base for many professional roles in the public sector. Feminist theories and debates also played an important part in broadening this curriculum and in encouraging women into the new higher education market. Degrees appeared no longer as the preserve of traditional university pomp and ceremony. They could be accessed in ordinary buildings at 'the poly', alongside students who studied subjects like building construction and quantity surveying. Although state funding criteria for educational grants became more restricted new opportunities for study provided more flexible part-time routes that offered alternative support. For both of us our new roles of parenting and family life were conducive to developing our university study and work.

Maxine
In the 1980s marriage and children brought me to reconsider the now distinct possibility of doing a degree. In 1985 I was a mature, female, part-time graduate studying social science at a polytechnic that symbolised many aspects of the shift towards increasing access and flexibility in higher education. I found I was a capable student. I struggled but I learnt how to write well enough to demonstrate my knowledge successfully. My degree studies established my desire to teach. I wanted to enable others, like me into this fascinating world of learning. I also thought that I would become a good teacher. Already I recognised that the future of teaching in HE was by going to be governed by PhD.

Linda
Following my son's birth and my resignation from a library post, I was able to take up a part-time job as a university research assistant, and worked with academic colleagues I had met during my time in the library. Despite feeling a push towards becoming 'an academic' I also began to experience a tentative sense of being 'out of place' in directly 'academic' settings. I found I was good

at the practical research tasks, especially anything to do with literature searching or indexing, and developed something of a reputation for being 'reliable' and 'keeping things going'. Only later would I recognise the double-edged nature of this sense of power being linked to mundane expectations (see Chapter 5, this volume). Meanwhile my PhD research was progressing (slowly) and I experienced a fairly confused sense of identity at that time as a 'professional academic student'. The librarian tag was something I hung onto (along with my identity as a 'mother') as evidence that I had retained at least one foot in the 'real' (professional) world.

The 1990s brought even more change to higher education, and preparing students for undergraduate and postgraduate degrees allowed previously diverse institutions to achieve university status. Universities were an ever expanding business, from the growth of 'red brick' institutions in the 1960s, absorption of the polytechnics in the early 1990s, to a proliferation of university colleges in the later part of the decade; all contributed to a hegemony of the university. If this had occurred in the private business sector, the university sector could have been charged with monopolising our educational diversity. Increasing opportunities for part-time study and work brought forward many more women into the university world. Whilst this diversity supported our personally different objectives in taking a PhD, the growth of universities meant that the traditional academic role of the university lecturer was challenged at the same time. The university world now required academics to be teachers and researchers, but also managers in areas such as quality assurance or marketing.

All these new and confusing roles were emerging around us as our work on our PhDs continued. More opportunities were thus available for future work, but how was doing a PhD providing a route to being 'an academic'? Our feminist, qualitative research studies already posed many dilemmas for us when trying to place ourselves in this academic world (Bell 1998; Birch 1998). Furthermore, our involvement with the 'Women's workshop' at this stage in our careers suggested we were not alone in feeling that we were 'on the margins' in some respects as female academics.

Maxine
While I completed my PhD the institution I was registered at changed from Polytechnic to University. This had very little effect on my feelings about doing the research and neither encouraged nor discouraged my feelings of academic acceptability. It was only when I sought employment that I felt the true force of what a PhD could mean to others and their perceptions of me

being an academic and my ability to be a university teacher. I initially gained a lecturing position at one of the new university colleges, one built upon the foundations of further education, with a very strong teaching tradition. Here the teaching role was prioritised and indeed reflected my main interest in working at this institution. I worked on a new degree course for child-care in the early years. This new course of studies reflected the policy to create better qualified childcare workers and built on courses previously identified as vocational and skill based. I found that my academic award of PhD quickly established my ability to teach the subjects associated with the degree level 'early years'. At the same time my OT background gave me certain credibility as someone who could work with children (even though I had no particular expertise). This recent placement of child care knowledge and skills within academic standards gave me the opportunity to use my PhD in sociology combined with my OT background to influence in many decision making processes. Marking out my ability in this way often took precedence over my colleagues who had far more skills and knowledge to actually work with children.

Professional education for health, social care and education sectors brought large groups of new students to the widening HE market during the 1990s. In 1994 there were 8,669 full-time students studying subjects allied to medicine for their first degree. By 2004/5 this had increased to 27,880 (www.hesa.ac.uk accessed 25/04/06). The 'academicisation' of professional programmes like nursing, physiotherapy, occupational therapy, social work, and earlier incorporation of professional programmes involving primary and secondary school teaching or librarianship, added a large professional enterprise into university life. A vast legacy from this growth of the university sector is currently founded on the incorporation of nurse education into HE diploma and degree programmes. In 2001, 21% of all full-time students in universities in England were studying nursing and 89% of these student nurses were women (www.hesa.ac.uk accessed 25/04/06).

Maxine
The University I worked in adopted ways to cope with the different academic and professional standing of the staff working in the' early years' department. Amongst the teaching staff there was a no title policy so that the status of Dr was not noted on office doors or minutes of meetings. This attempt to respect all teaching staff regardless of academic qualification was soon challenged when the college tried to present academic kudos at more public meetings. Here my title of Dr was welcome and presented to give an academic flavour to degree awards, validation, QAA and research

meetings. This shifting celebration and acknowledgement of my academic title gave me different resources to influence my teaching role. With my colleagues and students on the 'shop floor' I still had to prove myself as a teacher. With my managers my academic standing was welcomed. These shifting acknowledgements that place me within different understandings of practitioner and academic credibility still pervade my work today. As a lecturer on a nursing programme at an established university, I am often introduced as the Occupational Therapist to improve standing on interprofessional education. With a history of being an OT, I also achieve more standing amongst my colleagues within the nursing programme as I can understand practice, I am not just an academic. Very rarely am I acknowledged for any disciplinary expertise in sociology or for continued professional development in pedagogy. This changes yet again when I move out of the nursing programme area into the Faculty and wider university environment.

Linda
My career had formalised from part time research posts into consultancy work and then into a full time senior lectureship in a new university by the mid-1990s. I became drawn into teaching, which unexpectedly I found I enjoyed, and was able to specialise not in my own area of 'subject' expertise but in the area of research methods, particularly as relevant to students on professional programmes. Despite my academic label and post-doctoral status, once again my practical and 'librarian' skills seemed to have come to the fore. There followed several years of uneasy shifting within and between different 'academic' and 'professional' programmes as I developed my skills and expertise in teaching others about 'doing research'. My career was moving towards postgraduate teaching and research supervision (which was welcomed by colleagues) whilst at the same time I was trying to remain neutral and even-handed in my work with various professionals involved in academia. This was difficult to maintain; I have often felt that my motives for taking a broader perspective were misunderstood, and so I was pressurised or blocked from taking up certain activities, whilst being encouraged in other directions.

Our focus on teaching students who seek professional roles and accreditation currently gives us differing positions of being 'on the margins' of academia; positions that adapt and shift daily, in the corridor, in meetings and when moving from one part of the university to another. Linda's focus on teaching research methods has resulted in her feeling 'in between' 'the academic' and 'the professional' as she has struggled to get professional students and colleagues to take research seriously. But she also acknowledges that she is happier working with 'professional' students who seem to have a least one foot in the 'real world' instead of being 'ivory tower' academics. She still sometimes feels she is trying to go in both directions at once, between what appears to be the 'old' world of academia and the (apparently) 'new' world of professional education; yet she had already experienced this familiar world as 'vocational studies' located in FE. Maxine depends upon her disciplinary knowledge of the social sciences and pedagogic experience to deliver her teaching, but with her nurse academic colleagues she experiences more power to influence and shape decisions in becoming the representative from another health care profession. This identity can easily shift to and from social scientist or teacher at other points around the university.

Writing, professional education and power

Central to our feelings about being 'an academic' and teaching/researching within this academic practitioner mix we identify the process of writing as one of the key sites where many dimensions of power are demonstrated, for ourselves and for our students.

> There is a widespread belief that academic discourse is a unique form of argument because it depends upon the demonstration of absolute truth, empirical evidence or flawless logic. Its persuasive potency is seen grounded in rationality and based on exacting methodologies, dispassionate observation and informed reflection. Academic writing, in other words, represents discourses of truth (Hyland 2004: 87).

Academic standards in assessing both skill and knowledge have traditionally been judged and assessed through written documents. Making judgements on written work is vital for all educational systems; it is seen as the key to demonstrating rational knowledge, and to an extent written work has often been judged as 'value free' or academically neutral. These judgements are what constitute higher education awards. Student assignments usually take the format of a written document and are assessed to classify abilities, decide entry to education institutions and determine how you progress once you are there. In this way assessing written work in academia can perpetuate a constant striving for power through the constant recognition of 'less' ability or 'more' ability. The widening participation agenda has brought together different groups of learners with different expectations and needs, but this learning has still been observed through the production of texts.

Linda
Once I began to undertake research in HE, I had also begun to 'write', but in different forms than I had anticipated. I wrote my first publication (a book review for a senior colleague) and was told I was 'a good writer'. Then came the writing of the PhD, there were methodological/feminist papers in which I found I could 'let my hair' down to an extent, and research papers or administrative reports which had to be formal and (re)produced information in ways which were prescribed by others. 'Real' (non-academic) creative writing seemed ever more elusive yet remained a possible 'escape' now that I was using my writing as part of an academic career. Writing is therefore something I have avoided and wanted to do by turns, and it is an activity which inevitably feels very personal: almost self indulgent, yet recognisably part of the academic persona that I have assumed. Nevertheless my professional library background (representing a 'practical' as opposed to a 'textual' orientation) seems to be something which is ingrained into my work (particularly my experience in a 'service' occupation). These two professional/academic elements appear to have allowed me to construct a recognisably 'academic' career whilst also feeling that I am often on the margins, especially when working with people who have their own 'professional' identities operating alongside their 'academic' ones e.g. social workers or nurses. However, whilst the tide seems to be turning in favour of 'professionals' in HE, which ought to work in my favour, I also understand the views of colleagues who think this may be undermining academic (textual?) standards and authority. Perhaps the truth is that I don't really want to take sides in this debate.

At the current stage in my career I also struggle like many academics to have 'more time for my own research'. What does this mean exactly? Getting research funding seems to have become the key goal that would apparently allow greater freedom to write; but I suspect that especially for me, the administrative responsibilities involved in running a research project would encourage or perhaps give me an excuse to put off that writing opportunity for more mundane research tasks. I sometimes suspect that colleagues who may be unaware of my career trajectory assume I have come from a 'purely academic' background because of my research interests; yet this position is something I have struggled with. I recognise I have presented my 'professional' or 'academic' self publicly as 'foreground' and 'background' at different stages in my career. I have used my identity as a 'professional' librarian or an 'academic' more visibly in my overall career at some times than at other times.

Maxine
Now 15 years on, after working primarily in a teaching role at universities of all guises (red brick universities, former polytechnics, new university status

colleges, partnerships between professional colleges and universities) I have observed how many professional programmes are transformed into degree studies. One of the key tensions that remains unresolved is how to place professional practice into the academic standards to preserve credibility. For me this tension centres on how written documents dominate the indicators of ability in any academic work. The different academic roles and responsibilities I undertake, teacher, researcher, scholar and manager, all converge on my performance of writing. From informal emails to published papers and books the recognition of being successful, being invited to take part in decisions, having opportunities to enable others, depend on the production of written documents. It doesn't matter about the different abilities perhaps acquired to teach students, research or manage staff, the processes of asserting power depend on the judgements on the written documents I produce and the judgements I impose on the written work of others. This is how power is performed and this performance subjects a person to the specific indicators of ability. So, if my demonstration of knowledge as presented in written work is used to establish my ability I am subjected to this power while at the same time reproducing this restriction of my ability to the act of writing. I continue this process as I work with students and other colleagues.

Current Government policy demands that the qualification standards of many public sector careers should improve and this fits with the calls for widening participation and a rapidly expanding higher education market. It is no surprise that improving educational standards in the public sector and offering wider access to higher education results in many tensions (Allen 2003). As shown by our narratives above, these are being played out within the academic and practitioner mix, and affect all the staff working with professional programmes and the learning demands placed upon the student.

When practitioner education became integrated into HE the problem of how to provide teaching for the relevant applied knowledge and skills became more visible. University based education was often seen to remove the student from the work place and this distance did little to prepare the future practitioner for the realities of work. This raised several questions. What knowledge and skills were required to produce competent practitioners and (how) could you demonstrate this knowledge and skill in the classroom? How were these skills (once identified as the important difference between learning for professional practice and for academic degrees) to be approached within an overarching 'academic' framework? How could practice skills be developed and academic skills achieved within the equivalent of a 3-year full time degree programme? What place would 'writing' have within these approaches to learning?

Feminist academics often share the commitment to empowerment in bringing forward the voices of people who experience fewer opportunities to be heard. But what happens when the voices of this new group of predominantly female, health and social care students are expressed through the written document? And does this textual medium adequately reflect the commitment to listen? *'Helping such students speak in their own voice through their writing has been a vital pedagogic task'* (Hoggett 2000: 115). This brings forward not only the problem of who is speaking and who is listening as identified by bell hooks (hooks 2000) but places this exchange firmly in the expert system of the academic community as initially posed by Anthony Giddens' theories on modernity (Hoggett 2000). Practitioners are asked to articulate their practice but can articulation easily fit with academic writing? Being 'a good writer' may not necessarily demonstrate skill as a good practitioner and vice versa. One of the criticisms of nursing degrees is that, degree educated nurses become 'too posh to wash' and 'too clever to care'. Such statements express the perceived tensions between 'doing' and 'academic writing'. When the power dimensions are observed between the interplay of practice skills, disciplinary knowledge and professional values, it is hard to see how to achieve appropriate status for all areas through the site of academic writing. Academia may be perceived not to value the traditions of professional care involved in working with people. Conversely, those in health and social care practice settings may not be seen as valuing academic knowledge. The combination of proficiencies set by regulatory professional bodies and quality assurance measures of teaching and learning have all aimed to produce standardised learning outcomes within higher education that can deliver a qualified practitioner who is successful, competent, effective and safe. This is particularly important where practitioners such as social workers expect to be working with 'vulnerable' people.

Professional qualification has usually incorporated learning in the work place. Combining learning and practice in the work place is perceived as the only way to assure competent and safe practitioners. When Linda took her librarianship diploma in the 1970s, professional practice was equally important but it occurred prior to and following the diploma course; the professional qualification was only achieved after a designated amount of time in practice following the college-based award. Maxine's diploma course in occupational therapy included one year spent 'in practice' that had to be successfully completed for the completion of the award. Work based placements are thus nothing new but are perhaps newer in occurring firmly *within* degree studies, thus challenging traditional notions of being 'academic'. New systems of delivering courses in academia aim to address concerns about practice and academic balance by combining periods of learning in the work place. Terms like mixed mode delivery, practice based or work based learning now receive increasing pedagogic attention. Increasingly, some students take professional education programmes at university whilst employed. Often known as 'employment route' or sponsored students, in this sometimes uneasy mix even the identity of being a student is altered, whilst the university has a guaranteed source of employer custom and income.

Irrespective of how programmes and courses are delivered, academic writing continues to dominate methods of assessing academic standards. It was our production of academic texts that ultimately provided the evidence for the graduate and postgraduate awards bestowed on us. Even when some 'academic' learning is transformed from the usual notions of studying at university (such as in the relatively new professional doctorate) these new processes still involve 'writing' as a central component of learning. Assessment methods linked to learning objectives and outcomes provide access to observable measures that incorporate new demands of professional competencies, quality assurance and the diversity of teaching and learning strategies. Academic standards are thus increasingly determined by these measurable outcomes, although demands for academic writing remain, while academic and educational identities become linked into a wider mix of staff development and workbased learning (Bell 2005; Birch *et al.* 2005).

The 'portfolio' is often viewed as an appropriate assessment tool for learning in the work place and argued to offer an alternative to the traditional essay format. This can easily be transported back into the academic world for further scrutiny of learning that took place. At the same time moving away from familiar written styles can encourage some academics to suggest that this academic and practitioner mix is part of a 'dumbing' down of academic standards and the loss of the intellectual knowledge.

> Academia has accepted that subjective emotional insights and skills-based training should be labelled 'knowledges', while accreditation of prior learning puts life skills on a par with academic qualifications and work related training and vocationalism on a par with scholarship (Furedi 2004: 68).

To counter this proposition of academic 'dumbing' down, it could also be argued that university education had not changed *enough* to incorporate different learning needs. While diversity in learning is encouraged by these recent developments, the use of writing as the means to assess learning has not. A mix of professional and academic skills and knowledge are challenged as they become restricted through the performance of writing. The portfolio is still a written document where all the usual expectations of academic writing prevail. The production of an academic text is still perceived as the central form of evidence.

In higher education today academic traditions are in flux. No longer can an academic identity rely on established disciplinary subject boundaries (Morley 1999, 2003; Deem 2002, 2003). Now the pursuit of knowledge at university can involve consideration of business acumen, marketing success, media production, practice competence and post-qualifying reflection as well as 'academic' skills such as writing. The previous boundaries of academic studies are now permeable to whichever subjects can formally constitute a degree that fits with the employment market. Knowledge now constitutes its own economy. It could be argued that feminist academics have influenced and continue to welcome this move towards interdisciplinary knowledge. Feminist academics have fiercely sought the role of mediating different knowledge worlds (David 2003).

> Transformations in knowledge economy and in family lives, and how we have been transforming our identities and subjectivity in relation to these wider contextual shifts is a critical part of feminist methodology and pedagogy (David 2003: 160).

But has this feminist endeavour failed to provide the right sort of mediation processes for this academic, practitioner mix? Practitioner students who experience new ways to learn may not be fully aware of the academic writing skills required. While some feminist academics have challenged traditions of academic writing and encouraged alternative pedagogies like autobiographical and creative writing (Ribbens 1993; Richardson 1990) these challenges have made little impact on currently expected student assessments. When the written essay, as the main demonstration of acquired skill and knowledge, is analysed with reference to Judith Butler's theories on the subjection of power, this performance is restricted by judgements about how a person achieves required academic standards in the written document; these position some people as being 'less able' or 'more able' than others. Here power is exerted through the restriction and subjection of ability.

> Hence, subjection is neither simply the domination of a subject nor its production, but designates a certain kind of restriction in production, a restriction without which the production of the subject cannot take place (Butler 1997: 84).

Feminist pedagogy was initially wedded to notions of empowerment (Lather 1991) but it now appears that such ideals have to fit with the regulations of quality assurance (Morley 2003). As Morley points out we are having to 'reinvent' ourselves in response to managerialism and 'performativity'. In many ways the links between performativity and managerialism are strengthened as performance indicators, just like learning outcomes for students, are seen to rationally tell the truth about someone's ability to work in academia. For Lyotard, the notion of performativity has broad links to managerialism, and in his division between 'science' and 'narrative based' knowledge, there is also the more abstract suggestion that science is currently dominant as performativity/performance in the job connects to 'science' in the guise of performance indicators to which academics have become subject. As Dent & Whitehead's (2002) discussion of Lyotard notes: 'there is no escape from performativity' (Dent & Whitehead 7–8; see also Cowen 1996).

So is 'writing' the ultimate bastion of academic identity? Equally, does 'scholarship' (based on written texts) still have a place in professional education? What are we doing to balance the needs of students and colleagues who, like Maxine, do not enter higher education to write, with those of people like Linda who has always been drawn to scholarship and writing?

Conclusion

Our own career trajectories have led us to observe that different contexts of academic and practitioner knowledge can provide different resources, or cultural capital as theorised by Bourdieu (1993; Adkins & Skeggs 2004), within higher education. We have experienced how tensions in the dualities of 'skill and knowledge', 'practice and theory', 'training and education' become heightened within professional education programmes. The career trajectories illustrated here demonstrate how higher education has been transformed in trying to adapt to the learning needs of health, social care and education professionals. They also show the impact these transformations have had on individual academic staff and how over time we have had to modify our ways of working and thinking about our careers. Our attitudes towards the place of 'writing text' are therefore central to these processes. That in turn permitted our entry into the world of academia.

Acquiring professional programmes and transforming them into university degree studies has certainly increased numbers of women students and staff in HE institutions. This gender dimension adds more complexity to how power relations are performed. So this complex matrix of gender, academic and practitioner identities combines to construct a particular student; the 'competent practitioner' may also respond to the demands of being an academic, take on analytical research, provide evidence, and perform other forms of academic action. For us as lecturers this also includes imperatives to be entrepreneurial, innovative and 'add value' to the organisation (Morley 2003: 68). We have to conclude that the academic identities of teacher and writer or practitioner and academic may no longer be as separable or as sufficient as we once thought. As Morley notes:

> Traditionally, universities have been able to assign individuals with a ready-made identity embedded in notions of social hierarchy. Now professional identities are constantly in flux. It is not enough simply to reproduce the skills and knowledges for which one was originally appointed. There is an imperative to be entrepreneurial, innovative and to add value to one's organisation. Multiskilling creates anxieties about maintaining expertise ... Academics are being asked to reinvent themselves, their courses, their cultural capital, and their research as marketable commodities (Morley 2003, 68).

Perhaps practitioner/academics are reinventing themselves differently from other academics (who are used to relying solely on texts/academic writing) and/or they are bringing back different aspects of their professionalism (with a focus on skills, competencies and professional values) into academia. Where we fit into these processes is confusing and we find ourselves subjected to all the different strands of power we have identified. Due to the constant circulation of these power dimensions we find that we cannot very easily decide if 'broadening the boundaries' etc is a 'good thing' for us or for academia. Should we as feminist academics continue to challenge 'academic' writing to show how power interweaves here to restrict potential processes of empowerment? Or do we also feel that widening the notion of what constitutes the 'ability to write' takes too much away from our resources of being an academic?

References

Adkins, L. & Skeggs, B. (eds) (2004) *Feminism after Bourdieu*, Oxford: Blackwell/Sociological Review.

Allen, D.K. (2003) Organisational climate and strategic change in higher education: organisational insecurity, *Higher Education*, 46 (1) 61–92.

Bell, L. (1998) Public and private meanings, in Diaries: researching family and childcare, in J. Ribbens and R. Edwards (eds), *Feminist Dilemmas in Qualitative Research*, London: Sage.

Bell, L. (2005) 'We're getting there ... it's like British Rail, but we will get there'; concepts of process, outcomes and performativity in the narratives of male and female health & social services workforce development (training) managers. Paper presented at the *9th International Dilemmas for the Human Services Conference*, London, September.

Birch, M. (1998) Reconstructing research narratives: self and sociological identity in alternative settings, in J. Ribbens and R. Edwards (eds), *Feminist Dilemmas in Qualitative Research*, London: Sage.

Birch, M., Gallagher A. & Finlay L. (2005) Positioning the learner: how work based, open and distance learning can develop professional competencies in pre-registration mental health nurse education, in K. Rounce and B. Workman, *Work-based Learning in Health Care: Applications and Innovations*, Kingsham and Work Based Learning and Accreditation Unit, Middlesex University.

Bourdieu, P. (1993) *Sociology in Question*, London: Sage.

Butler, J. (1997) *The Psychic Life of Power: Theories in Subjection*, Chicago: Stanford University Press.

Cowen, R. (1996) Performativity, post-modernity and the university, *Comparative Education*, 32 (2) 245–258.

David, M. (2003) *Personal & Political: Feminisms, Sociology and Family Lives*, Stoke on Trent: Trentham Books.

Deem, R. (2002) Talking to manager-academics; methodological dilemmas and feminist research strategies, *Sociology*, 36 (4) 835–855.

Deem, R. (2003) Gender, organizational cultures and the practices of manager-academics in UK universities, *Gender, Work and Organization*, 10 (2): 239–259.

Dent, M. & Whitehead, S. (2002) Introduction: Configuring the 'New' Professional in Dent, M. & Whitehead, S. (eds), *Managing Professional Identities: Knowledge, Performativity & the 'New' Professional*, London: Routledge.

Elias, N. (1991) *The Society of Individuals*, London: Continuum.

Furedi, F. (2004) *Where Have All The Intellectuals Gone?* London: Continuum. hesa.ac.uk/holisdocs/pubinfo/student/quals9495.htm (accessed 23.04.06).

Hoggett, P. (2000) *Emotional Life and the Politics of Welfare*, London: Palgrave Macmillan.

hooks, bell (2000) Feminist theory: from margin to centre, 2nd edition, London: Pluto Press.

Hyland, K. (2004) *A Convincing Argument: Corpus Analysis and Academic Persuasion*, Section II in Discourse in U. Connor and T.A. Upton the Professions: perspectives from corpus linguistics. Amsterdam/Philadelphia: John Benjamins.

Lather, P. (1991) *Getting Smart: Feminist Research and Pedagogy with/in the Postmodern*, New York: Routledge.

Morley, L. (1999) *Organising Feminisms: The Micropolitics of the Academy*, London: Palgrave Macmillan.

Morley, L. (2003) *Quality and Power in Higher Education*, Milton Keynes: SRHE & Open University.

Ribbens, J. (1993) Facts or fictions? Aspects of the use of autobiographical writing in undergraduate sociology, *Sociology*, 27 (1) 81–92.

Richardson, L. (1990) *Writing Strategies: Reaching Diverse Audiences*, Newbury Park CA: Sage. hesa.ac.uk/holisdocs/pubinfo/student/quals9495.htm (accessed 23.04.06).

Table 14a – Qualifications Obtained in the United Kingdom by Mode of Study, Domicile, Gender and Subject Area 1994/95. *hesa.ac.uk/holisdocs/pubinfo/student/quals0405.htm (accessed 23.04.06)* Table 14 – HE qualifications obtained in the UK by level, mode of study, domicile, gender, class of first degree and subject area(#6) 2004/05.

5
Power Relationships in Research Teams
Melanie Mauthner and Linda Bell

Introduction

This is our first collaborative writing together even though our 'we' voice might suggest that we have previously belonged to the same research teams. We use 'we' as a device in this chapter to describe the range of our teamwork experiences in an anonymous way. We write from a position of feeling marginal inside academic institutions, even though we are surrounded by female, often 'feminist', colleagues (Reay 2000; Morley 1999). In common with other feminist academics, we feel more acknowledged and valued as researchers outside our institutions than within them. Partly, we realise this is linked to different discourses of performativity that dominate in specific settings.

Our history as researchers and members of research teams reflects our multi-disciplinary backgrounds. Melanie trained initially as a linguist and journalist. She became a sociologist after studying Women's Studies and has carried out empirical research on family relationships for over ten years. She has studied contemporary family life as part of teams in a range of settings including health, social welfare and education. Her main interest is in lateral intimate ties especially sibling cultures and friendship. Recently she researched children's relationships with their sisters and brothers; and in her current work she is moving from a focus on siblings towards an exploration of migration and family history. Linda trained first in library and information work and then studied anthropology. She has carried out empirical research for over a decade which included work on mothering and social support, neighbourhood development, domestic violence and aspects of professionalism, health and social care. Her most recent studies consider professionals and bereavement support, and social support for mothers in Tehran (Iran).

Our working notion of power is informed by post-structuralist theory (Weedon 1987). This perspective assumes that power is diffuse, shifting and fragmented. Power is not fixed in one location in contrast with modernist understandings but resides in various places. We are interested in three aspects of power: the power to define, the power that certain people have over others, for example in relation to leadership or management, and power as embodied in personal and social relationships. Drawing on previous studies where researchers conceptualise power relations in social groups such as siblings and intimate relationships (Holland *et al*. 1998; Mauthner 2002) or in relation to the negotiation of professional or occupational research responsibilities (Bell & Nutt 2002), we suggest that power in the context of research teams is located in four sites.

The first site relates to structured, institutionalised power relations and in this context corresponds to the institution of *academia* (Morley 1999). Academic institutions themselves as organisations play a key role in producing the social contexts where research teams are located. The organisation as made up of ideas, processes, discourses and social relationships plays a large part here. This stems from the way that institutions socially construct the micro-politics within them. Therefore, we can ask: 'do organisations 'exist' except as 'places and spaces inscribed upon, collapsed into, defined by and constitutive of psyches and bodies' (Ford & Harding 2005: 828). The nature of the organisation as an amorphous entity that fosters or hinders research work is significant. Our research is circumscribed by the academic groups and centres that we are attached to: these create a local and intellectual sense of belonging for us with cultural and geographical boundaries. This is in spite of the fact that 'research' always appears as the last item on the staff meeting agenda in some teaching focused academic departments.

The second site where power comes alive is in *enacted practices and experiences*. In research teams this manifests itself through the social interactions of the group: talking, emotions, caring, silences, tensions, surveilling and policing as well as conflicts. This site corresponds to the interpersonal dynamics in the team and to the different kinds of belonging that we are part of. The space and location we work in, the fieldwork we carry out, the participants we interview, the documents we produce: all inform these enacted practices. How we think and make sense of a particular moment of working in a team shapes our empirical experience of it in the present as well as the memories of it that linger once a project ends.

The third site where power is present is in specific *discourses* at the level of ideas and ways of thinking about teamwork. Examples here might include: an emphasis on evidence-based research, on performativity and managerialism; an ethos of collaborative working; collective working; positioned or fixed power dynamics where power explicitly resides in a leader; and shifting positions where intellectual and managerial leadership reside in more than one person or fluctuate over the life of the research project. Ethical issues such as consultation about how to divide up the labour in a team and negotiating authorship of various publications may form part of a particular ethos or ethic of teamwork (Hey 2001).

Lastly, power is located in individual agency and action. This form of power enables team members to interpret, question, resist and modify their teamwork and manage their belonging to the team, to forge a new team and also to leave it. This dimension allows researchers to adopt more powerful, less powerful or reciprocal positions. Here we are thinking of ways to initiate and refuse to take on specific tasks such as: writing ourselves in as principal investigators on a research proposal, the amount of fieldwork and data analysis we carry out, and presenting papers at conferences.

We shall refer to these four sites throughout our discussion by thinking about the context in which knowledge is generated, the learning this may lead to, the processes of creativity involved, the presence or absence of reflexivity and of a (feminist) collective ethos, as well as opportunities for agency and resistance. The first site, institutionalised power relations, forms the bedrock of the environment in which research occurs; indeed the power of grant holders and team leaders is built into the funding and institutional structure of universities so it is hard to share this out.

These four sites are reflected in the social context of funded research that we address in section 1. In section 2, we look at the learning opportunities for ourselves as researchers in the other sites; practices and experiences on the one hand, and discourses on the other, in relation to methods training and processes of creativity in intellectual work. In section 3, we consider the synergies between creativity and reflexivity. Lastly, we consider the scope for agency and resistance at the end of the chapter through a number of questions that we suggest are useful to ask ourselves before initiating, joining or declining to participate in teamwork.

The social context of funded research

We start off by considering the social and recent historical context of funded research as our joint experience of social science research extends back more than a decade. We have conducted research during different epochs when one type of research was more in vogue than others, from exploratory and descriptive research in the 1980s to projects with more 'managerialist' agendas in the first decade of the twenty first century.

The context of belonging to research teams includes a gamut of statuses, experience and expertise. Teams may contain a professor, research assistant, academic staff and professionals from outside academia (e.g. social workers, teachers, counsellors). Some research assistants will also be carrying out doctoral research part-time. Increasingly, the intellectual and methodological training of research students is more controlled and managed than in past decades. We have witnessed the development of a more formalised role of the leader in university based research teams. This arguably ranges from being a mainly 'intellectual' leader, to the leader becoming a 'principal applicant' for funding purposes (which is consistent with the rise of 'managerialist' agendas in higher education) (see Natasha Mauthner and Rosalind Edwards, this volume).

Alongside the overall development of these managerialist discourses within higher education,[1] we argue that the implications of these for academics who are researchers have been profound (David 2004). Morley (2003) sees a clearly gendered division opening up in higher education between male, higher status researchers who may be concentrated in research based universities and women who 'are already disproportionately concentrated in areas and institutions with the lowest levels of research funding' (p. 155). Furthermore 'women are too busy teaching or administrating, too junior and too precariously employed to gain major research grants' (p. 155). Morley suggests that women are therefore drawn into the 'domestic labour of teaching and administration' (p. 156) in universities, which, paradoxically, can then become their major sources of power within the institution.

However Trowler (2001) further suggests that: 'the dialogical nature of universities means that the impact of NHE (New Higher Education) discourse on organizational practices is mitigated as it is read and reacted to in varied ways, that academics are not fundamentally "captured" by this discursive form.' This indicates that it would be useful to look in more detail at research performance/

performativity in order to unpick some key themes from our own research experiences relevant to the social context of funded research. By performance we mean presentation (i.e. 'a performance') although this can also imply outcomes; by performativity we imply productivity. As Louise Morley (2003: 72) notes: 'New managerialism has reinforced performance discourses. Staff have performance reviews, individuals and departments are required to have performance targets ...'. We are working with Morley's definitions since she usefully interprets Judith Butler's ideas in an organisational way. There are aspects of performativity that are gendered displays of activity such as carrying out routine tasks much like housekeeping. Part of the task is to present the self as female, behaving in a feminine way, for example, through behaviours such as ways of dressing.

The sense of performativity being linked to the 'presentation' or performance of self, such as Morley's (2003) description of the female academic who 'dressed up' and 'performed' for the 'audience' at a QAA review (p. 158), reflects the way that some women are prepared to use dress in order to conform to certain expectations and displays of femininity despite their misgivings:

> Performativity, in this case, is highly gendered. The language that this informant used was evocative of narratives of violence against women. Violence in organisations is often subtle and confusing...She felt 'soiled' by what she felt as the dishonesty of the gendered performance. (Morley 2003: 158)

Doing what is expected in order to keep the show on the road is a task-centred approach that conforms to gender stereotypes. Often this work brings no acknowledgement. Strategy and vision usually come from men who are more successful in obtaining professional accolades.

A historical case exemplifies this gendered divide between mundane routine tasks and an over-arching vision. A fraught episode in scientific laboratories illustrates this division of labour and intellectual ownership of ideas in research teams at the University of London over fifty years ago. It is a sad and famous tale that epitomises struggles over definitions and meanings of working collaboratively versus working alone in the race to understand the biochemical structure of DNA in 1951 at Kings College, London. This excerpt from a biography of scientist Rosalind Franklin reveals the costs of collaborative work for her in a story of scientific discovery where she, the solitary biochemist was only recognised for her achievements half a century after her death.

> Collaborate? She exploded. It was the only time that [Maurice] Wilkins saw her completely lose control. 'How dare you interpret my data for me!' Rosalind had good reason. Her work was her life, the core of her identity. Undervalued at Kings, she had just achieved extraordinary results by working in virtual isolation. Now what she saw as a less able colleague of higher rank was proposing to elbow in and spoil the clarity of her investigation. (Maddox 2003: 154)

This example highlights the invisibility of concentrated feminine activity in a laboratory over many years, and of the low regard accorded to practical and experimental work carried out through inductive methodology. It clearly applies to other settings beyond merely scientific teams. It reminds us of how rife rivalry and competitiveness have always been in research as well as the gendered aspects of experimental versus deductive ways of working. It also alerts us to the potential for power relations to contaminate exploratory research even in the case of the lone investigator such as Rosalind Franklin, for one cannot escape the dynamics of the broader institutional environment.

In terms of persuading funders to support research projects, we have become aware over the past two decades of greater importance being placed on evidence-based discourses. This has been accompanied by a developing emphasis on research findings generating specific outcomes and performance indicators. To an extent, this suggests that intellectually exploratory processes are becoming squeezed in favour of research teams meeting funders' pre-specified outcomes. This process is evident in the very detailed specifications that are set out for researchers who apply to many competitive research programmes.

Picking up Morley's point about the gendered divisions of labour within academia, and her earlier discussion of the gendered micropolitics of research (Morley 1999: 178–183) our own research experiences suggest that even under an 'exploratory' ethos, it is often female researchers who take responsibility for the tangible and 'domestic' aspects of research activities. Keeping up to date records and making detailed analyses of findings may appear grounded and therefore potentially powerful activities in terms of the research process. Conversely, these tangible activities can also be monitored which can make those carrying them out liable to greater accountability than other members of the team.

The 'thinking' (and therefore intangible and unaccountable) aspects of research work may nevertheless carry more weight, especially with funders. This may be compounded in situations where the 'leader' expects to do most of the thinking and reporting to outside bodies (including funders) and where those involved in the tangible research processes are subtly taken for granted or rendered invisible, for example, as potential authors of publications. If this happens then members of the research team may perceive that they are 'poorly managed' and this can lead to rapid staff turnover as team members leave to pursue better careers which give them more of an acknowledged share in the research they undertake. These processes can also reinforce potential inequalities between women who are involved at different levels of authority within academic research (as noted by Morley 1999: 181), as well as between women and men in similar contexts.

Learning in research teams

In this section we weigh up the different kinds of learning that working in research teams offers. We contrast two types of skills that researchers learn from the teams they contribute to: the methods component and the broader processes of visionary thinking or creativity that underlie intellectual work. Indeed, over the past decade we have noted another change in the increased development of, and emphasis given to, formalised training in research methodology for research assistants or postgraduate students.

There has, in our view, been a complex yet uneasy tension between this 'training' which is often aimed at learning techniques involved in undertaking the more tangible aspects of research processes and the 'education' that researchers depend on for developing their subject expertise that underpins the'thinking or intangible aspects of research projects. There is a risk of these techniques turning researchers into technicians and a danger of stultification at the level of the imagination. Institutionalised regimes of quality assurance, the material aspects of methodology training, and other elements such as money, time, equipment, housekeeping and data management resources are all viewed as tangible and thus measurable outcomes of research. However, we wonder whether this emphasis on the 'tangible' privileges disciplinary training rather than creativity, method and planning more than imagination, identity as a scholar/researcher or visionary thinking.

In their review of research on networks and mentoring amongst women academics, O'Leary and Mitchell (1990) note how 'specialising in an area of research' was very productive for women researchers and enabled them to develop more effective networks than their peers who were less well 'connected'. Our own training as doctoral researchers was structured around taking part in projects on a range of topics. Gradually, we learned to integrate the tangible and (in some instances) intangible subject 'expertise' underpinning the research into our identities as professional researchers. As we completed our doctoral research we slowly started to define our own specialisms to ourselves.

Next we give a brief example of a moment in the process of learning while working in a scientific team that contributed to our own methodological and epistemological training and skills as social researchers. This experience also made us aware of a particular set of research management practices that construct the process of producing knowledge in a complex scientific team:

Scientific team
I acquired a rigorous approach to assessing the link between theory, methodology and findings in a large complex study. I felt oppressed in this team by its scientific approach to research and ruthless management of research staff. I wanted to quit and stuck it out because I knew I was learning a lot intellectually even though I felt miserable at the human level at the way I was being treated. I felt 'minoritised' or marginalised because I was one of the few on the team without a scientific background. Also because I was assigned to the qualitative element of the project that was being fitted in or tagged on to the larger quantitative whole. So, marginalised at two levels: in terms of my disciplinary training and my epistemological standpoint. This was a project I felt completely at odds with in every aspect except that methodologically I learned a tremendous amount. I was glad to have at least one experience of working on a quantitative scientific project.

This example concerns a health education project that one of us worked on during the 1990s that epitomised the sudden turn to evidence-based research. We worked in an over-managed team that was structured very much like the hierarchical teams that conduct research in the natural sciences. Indeed, the epistemological stance of this team and research was positivist. The research was not intellectually exciting yet it provided a rigorous training for us as research assistants (some of whom were carrying out our part-time doctoral research at the same time). It also developed our critical stance towards understanding the link between epistemology and methodology even though this was not one of the aims of the project. This learning occurred outside the confines of the team and project. We experienced the research process as one-dimensional with little awareness of how social and cultural issues can affect the content or processes of research and teamwork.

So there is a risk in some projects that the leader may not fully acknowledge, value or integrate the expertise of other team members. The learning may only be visible to the researcher over time from the mundane and routine tasks performed. The labour of junior researchers, attention to detail in filing, liaising with respondents or other researchers, collecting and analysing data can often be subsumed in the final stages of writing up and disseminating results. Tensions can arise over commitment to the team as opposed to the demands of doctoral research, project workload versus thesis completion and claims to authorship versus erasure in the publication of findings.

Other struggles ensue around institutional monitoring and surveillance when research training is organised separately from subject expertise around prescribed learning outcomes with an emphasis on statistical and other tangible skills. Although the contemporary approach may seem to provide 'better' research skills in the long run, it is open to question whether this does effectively prepare junior researchers for research leadership and creativity or mainly for the tangible aspects of research housekeeping (Hey 2001; Oakley 1995).

Attention to detail and tight deadlines, rigour, productivity and reliability can contribute to our professional reputation as efficient and dependable researchers. Yet a fine line exists between having power as reliable and being exploited for this trait. When women move away from housekeeping tasks and into administration and management, they can gain recognition: yet they are less likely than men to move into research management (Sagaria and Rychener 2004). How do good housekeeping, tangible technical skills, hyper-productivity and frenetic activity in research teams impact on our capacity to generate new ideas?

Creativity, motivation and resistance in teamwork

In this section, we turn to a crucial component of knowledge production that is affected by power relations in teams, that of creativity, motivation and resistance, all necessary for intellectual endeavour. We identify several elements that are required for creative intellectual work. First, a strong vision of the team's goal and the aim of the research. Second, for the team leader to see themselves as catalyst and mentor with an ability to involve team members intellectually in the project. Third, a recognition that intellectual and managerial leadership do not necessarily have to reside in the same team member. Fourth, we signal the importance of achieving a balance between an individual and a collective ethos and way of working and between belonging to both its internal and external fabric and identity.

We want to contrast several of our own examples of working in teams, one from a mixed methodology project in the 1990s and two different feminist teams. This links to our previously discussed notion of the second site of power in *enacted practices and experiences*. Issues to highlight are the importance of achieving balance between the individual and the collective, and between the internal and external notions of belonging to a team, research practices and expectations (i.e. as in the next example). We compare feeling valued inside the mixed methodology team and yet devalued and exposed outside it in the public realm. In the feminist team on the other hand, experiences of belonging to both the internal private entity of the team as well as to its external public stakeholders or representatives were more connected. We expand on this from our own histories as researchers:

Mixed methodology team
I worked several years ago in a project team using a 'mixed' methodology which was very creative and where everyone was involved in regular discussions about what we were trying to achieve. This allowed the more junior staff to contribute ideas, for example about what should be included in questionnaires and interview schedules. This appears to be a productive approach, but these ideas were not necessarily followed through, nor even acknowledged as originating with junior staff by team leaders (for example, in later publications). Much of the day to day work ('performativity') in this team was left to the more junior (female) staff, who were tacitly relied upon to produce the actual results. Male colleagues who did not wish to 'get their hands dirty' with mundane tasks, who were not producing their promised results, although they continued to contribute ideas, were allowed to get away with excuses which female colleagues would have felt guilty about using. Whilst 'being reliable' made female staff feel powerful in some situations, the authority to present the research to the outside world in specific ways remained with the team leaders (female and male).

This raises the issue of resistance to more powerful forces that threaten to damage our work and our own sense of self-esteem within research work. These forms of resistance can occur in a third site of power (as mentioned in our introduction) at the level of *ideas and ways of thinking about teamwork* as well as within the fourth site, *individual agency and action*, which may be difficult to achieve in a team setting. By participating in collaborative or collective working at all we may appear to allow ourselves to experience a loss of personal power, especially if that power is seen to reside mainly in individual agency. For example, situations may occur where conference invitations are issued to senior research team members, but not to the more junior members who are responsible for the actual data generation and analysis. Resistance by 'junior' individuals in this situation may bring more equitable results, especially if senior staff, support other colleagues.

However, in some situations this kind of resistance is more difficult. Resistance to bullying tactics aimed at an individual, can show strength in holding on to our own intellectual ideals and ways of thinking rather than weakness in 'allowing ourselves' to be bullied. Yet this form of resistance brings isolation when colleagues distance themselves from us in these scenarios, perhaps believing us to be 'weak'. It is sometimes only when the bully goes too far in widening the argument to involve others, or if the problem is played out as a clear cut gendered situation, that colleagues will be prepared to offer support. It can be very hard to hold on to our dignity and inner strength in such instances.

In contrast to this, we can also draw on rewarding experiences of participating in collective teamwork informed by an explicit feminist ethos. In the first of the following examples of feminist research teams, the team leader displayed intellectual and managerial leadership in a collective context.

Feminist team i)
I worked in an all female team which was 'mixed' in terms of the members' own methodological orientations, as well as in the research methods applied to the project. I felt that it was due to the mutual respect between team members, that we were able to divide amicably into two methodological areas and carry out the project work in parallel; regular team meetings allowed us to (re)connect the two 'halves' of the project. This also allowed us to learn more about different methodological approaches with which we were not so familiar. As a team, we did not feel oppressed by either approach being dominant. Interestingly, at the writing up stage the funders took a more

critical interest in the quantitative results obtained from one part of the project, and tended to ignore our other data, so we had to defend our overall mixed methodological approach as a team.

In a second feminist team ii) two managers acted as co-leaders of an interdisciplinary team based outside academia in the voluntary sector. They sought and fostered the intellectual impetus of the research from all team members from a collective standpoint. The team included two social researchers, three health professionals, and two consultant academics. The team acknowledged and worked creatively with a tension regarding the disciplinary and methodological direction of the research. There was a risk of one theoretical perspective dominating and this was successfully tempered by the collective multidisciplinary stance which, informed by principles of feminist methodology decided to privilege participants' standpoints.

Feminist team ii)
One of the most rewarding research teams that I have belonged to stands out for its openness to divergence and disagreement for the sake of exploring disciplinary boundaries, for reflecting on where these collide and where the points of commonality lie. This way of working in this health research team enabled us to constantly remind ourselves of our commitment to remaining close and faithful to participants' perspectives in the final report. This occurred in a context fraught with tension when these voices risked being overshadowed by the voice of expertise that some of the professionals involved in managing the project wanted to predominate.

Another feature here was the creativity of multi-disciplinary thinking, a merging of theoretical and methodological stances that rarely encounter each other in a research setting. In this case it was psychoanalytical clinical practice meets feminist sociology in conjunction with clinical psychology. The pre-eminence and explicit adherence to principles of feminist methodology was a guiding force in the research process. These principles enabled the team to make sense of the tensions during the trajectory of the research process in a positive way.

The tensions in the group dynamics of this team were resolved through the team's decision to give pre-eminence to the lay perspectives in the representation of the published findings. So the researchers' advocacy and struggle to privilege respondents' traditionally silenced voices in this field swayed the outcome in this highly reflexive team. This case illuminates researchers' power to influence how data are presented and disseminated, and here to resist the pressure of senior experts in the team who wanted to couch the findings in a more theoretical language.

Developing resistance to blocked creativity

In two of the teams that we have belonged to, the scientific one and the mixed methodology one, the vision of intellectual work implicitly led to an amalgamation of ideas rather than to a creative exchange of ideas. This was driven by a strong commitment in one case to a positivist epistemology; and an interpretive one in another. There was little interest in building on previous work of some team members. There was little explicit recognition or valuing of the disparate provenance of ideas. The leader in these instances often espoused a definite intellectual agenda (effectiveness in evidence-based research, for example) and saw the breadth of intellectual contribution fitting into a pre-ordained framework. The agenda did not extend to engaging with the framework or challenging it in any critical way. In the interpretive team, a pragmatic outlook imposed by managerialist funders contributed to the completion of the research according to the timetable and delivery of expected outputs, and neglect of potentially creative team work.

Reflecting on power relations in research teams we wonder whether as women we are being diverted into busyness or being busy bees (hyper-productivity) in order to slow down our thinking. Mary Evans outlines this idea in *Killing Thinking* (2005a and b). We succumb to pressure to be useful, to acquire a reputation of being helpful and of taking on tasks and activities. This can be seen as a negative aspect of performativity.

Authoritarian leaders or team members are not always aware that they are imposing their views or theoretical perspectives on others. How can leaders foster synergy and avoid an imbalance created by an authoritarian team member? We acknowledge that senior women managers with authority who perhaps feel more uncertain than men in their identity as intellectuals can be oppressive to other women (hooks 1996). We wonder whether when men display oppressive behaviour we are more likely to resist it than when women display it (especially ostensibly feminist managers). Another element includes the tyranny of workload allocation monitoring whereby work programme hours are recorded through transparency and accountability exercises. Indeed, audit can be seen as both a form of collective identity and of violence according to some (Morley 2003; Deem 2002, 2004). Paradoxically, the managerial and quality assurance culture gives some women opportunities to rise through the ranks. Morley argues that this leads to a divide between managers and researchers, and between teaching and research universities. Thus the structure of workloads can also militate against creative thinking, especially for team managers with more institutional bureaucratic tasks to shoulder. This heightened control and surveillance can act as a break on creativity (Ford and Harding 2005).

We deduce from our experiential knowledge that reflexivity is necessary for, and an intrinsic part of, creative intellectual thinking. Its absence, we suggest, can have a considerable impact on the way that teams operate. A number of questions occur to us concerning the links between gender, creativity and teamwork in research. We need to consider how we might capitalise on our creativity when working in research teams. In particular, how can we gain recognition for our ideas as well as for our practical efficiency?

We have already noted that there are situations in which some female colleagues have their ideas accepted, whilst those of others are ignored. This raises issues about the circumstances in which we can challenge inflexible actions and attitudes that threaten to block our full participation in research. Spending some time working alone in order to develop one's ideas and pursue a personal intellectual agenda is one, perhaps obvious, way of gaining the strength to continue our participation in research teams. However, for our own intellectual development as much as for the contributions we can make, we also need to work through collaborative situations. These include giving or receiving mentoring, directing the work of peers, doctoral supervision, or setting up or joining a research group. Above all, our experiences suggest that we need to create or find intellectual spaces to belong to where we feel valued and respected. This has often involved, for each of us, increasing our academic visibility outside our own immediate academic institution.

Conclusion

Co-writing this chapter made us aware of our similar experiences as members of research teams despite our location in distinct institutions and research settings. At the outset we planned this piece by reflecting in some depth on our research training and our skills as researchers. Gradually, we moved away from the detail of our research backgrounds and membership of specific funded projects in order to explore broader themes relevant to other researchers. The issues of performance and power relations that arise when working in teams extend beyond the life of particular teams. Our collaboration led us to interrogate our experiences and develop our ideas in the context of our reading. We found it useful to pursue this iterative process in dialogue with each other away from the larger group (of the Women's Workshop) to see where our ideas took us, without having to respond during this gestation period to concerns or anxieties of colleagues.

We wanted to consider some collective lessons by drawing on literature from health on 'what makes teams work well' (but found this is relatively pragmatic e.g. having your own office space) or from organisational management and therapeutic research on group and institutional dynamics. We identify the need for a combination of technical and organisational elements as well as intellectual and creative aspects. We end by raising several questions for ourselves as researchers to ask when deciding what types of teams we wish to work in, whether to join them and how well they are operating once we belong to them, and also how to manage them. We recognise that in many circumstances we actually have little choice however as often we are hurled into teams with little prior knowledge about their make-up. These questions go some way towards articulating elements of resistance and agency.

1. What kind of team and leader will I be working with? Collective/collaborative; large/small; mono versus multi-disciplinary; exploratory research versus evidence-based research?
2. What kind of team and leader bring out the best in me: the positivist, the interpretive, the post-structuralist? The mentor, the catalyst, the authoritarian?
3. What is the social and cultural make-up of the team (including differences in status)?
4. What scope does this team offer for intellectual creativity?
5. What range of skills will I acquire or develop in this team (methodological, theoretical, managerial)?
6. How do we each feel about how well our team is functioning (intellectually, inter-personally, financially, in terms of workload and time management)?
7. What kind of team do I want to create and what type of leader do I want to become in the teams that I lead?

In this chapter we addressed in turn the social context of funded research, the learning that occurs in teams including skills, techniques, disciplinary expertise and imaginative thinking and the conditions that foster intellectual creativity in teamwork. We have acknowledged through this exploratory process how power in the context of research teams can be located in different sites. By drawing upon our own experiences as team members we reflect that different types of teams and leadership styles may be appropriate in specific research contexts, at certain stages of the research process and according to the aims of the research (exploratory, policy driven, evidence-based). However, we conclude by recognising, since our notion of power is diffuse, shifting and fragmented, the value of taking a collective (and feminist) ethos for making sense of how teams function.

Notes

1 This is termed by some e.g. Trowler as the 'New Higher Education' (NHE) discourse.

References

Bell, L. and Nutt, L. (2002) Divided loyalties, divided expectations: research ethics, professional and occupational responsibilities, in Mauthner, M., Birch, M., Jessop, J. and Miller, T. (eds), *Ethics in Qualitative Research*, London: Sage.

David, M. (2004) A feminist critique of public policy discourses about educational effectiveness, in Ali, S., Benjamin, S. and Mauthner, M. (eds), *The Politics of Gender and Education: Critical Perspectives*, Basingstoke: Palgrave.

Deem, R. (2002) Talking to university managers – methodological dilemmas and feminist research strategies, *Sociology* 36 (4) 835–855.

Deem, R. (2004) Gender, organisational cultures and the practices of manager-academics in UK Universities, *Gender, Work and Organisation*, 10 (2) 239–259.

Evans, M. (2005a) *Killing Thinking: Death of the University*, London/New York: Continuum International Publishing Group.

Evans, M. (2005b) Too bad, 'good girl', *The Times Higher Education*, 22 July.

Ford, H. & Harding, N. (2005) We went looking for the organisation but could find only the metaphysics of its presence, *Sociology* 38 (4) 815–830.

Hey, V. (2001) The construction of academic time: sub/contracting academic labour in research, *Journal of Education Policy*, 16 (1) 67–84.

Holland, J., Ramazanoglu, C., Sharpe, S. and Thomson, R. (with Rhodes, T.) (1998) *The Male in the Head: Heterosexuality and Power*, London: Tufnell Press.

hooks, b. (1996) Sisterhood, in Penny Weiss and Marilyn Friedman (eds), *Feminism and Community*, Philadelphia: Temple University Press.

Maddox, B. (2003) *Rosalind Franklin: The Dark Lady of DNA*, Glasgow: HarperCollins.

Mauthner, M. (2002) *Sistering: Power and Change in Female Relationships*, Basingstoke: Palgrave.

Morley, L. (1999) *Organising Feminisms. The Micropolitics of the Academy*, New York: St Martins Press.

Morley, L. (2003) *Quality and Power in Higher Education*, Buckingham: Open SRHE and University Press.

Oakley, A. (1995) Women and children first and last: parallels and differences between children's and women's studies, in B. Mayall (ed.), *Children's Childhoods*, Sussex: Falmer Press, pp. 13–32.

O'Leary, V. and Mitchell, J. (1990) Women connecting with women: networks and mentors, in S.S. Lie and V. O'Leary (eds), *Storming the Tower: Women in the Academic World*, London: Kogan Page.

Reay, D. (2000) 'Dim dross': marginalised women both inside and outside the academy, *Women's Studies International Forum*, 23 (1) 13–21.

Sagaria, M.A.D. and Rychener, M.A. (2004) Inside leadership circles and the managerial quagmire: key influences on women administrators' mobility and opportunity in US Higher Education, in Ali, S., Benjamin, S. and Mauthner, M. (eds), *The Politics of Gender and Education: Critical Perspectives*, Palgrave: Basingstoke.

Trowler, P. (2001) Captured by the discourse? The socially constitutive power of new higher education discourse in the UK, *Organization*, 8 (2) 183–202.

Weedon, C. (1987) *Feminist Practice and Poststructuralist Theory*, Oxford: Blackwell.

6
Making the Right Connections: 'Knowledge' and Power in Academic Networking

Val Gillies and Pam Alldred

Introduction

Academic survival demands far more than the obvious vocational skills of researching, publishing and teaching. In order to succeed (or even hang on in) you are required to 'be' as well as 'do'. By this we mean there is a hidden but potent ontological pressure to embrace particular values about who you are and how you relate to others. Such values emphasise individuality, independence, rationality and merit, and form the cornerstones of the educational establishment. Reflecting and reinforcing the lives and experiences of the dominant and powerful these values invariably underpin academic achievement at both school and university. Those who are successful in exams and become teachers or academics themselves have either been brought up to take these values as given, or must internalise them in order to progress. This chapter explores the social process of academic assimilation, focusing particularly on the practice of social networking in universities.

Becoming an academic is not an uncomplicated process for those who grew up outside of dominant cultural value systems. Statistics highlight the consistently low numbers of working class students entering university (HFCE 2005) and the continuing under representation of ethnic minority and/or women in academic positions of power (Abbott, Sapsford and Molloy 2005). The institutional disadvantage faced by those who fit awkwardly into the white, male, middle class defined conventions of academic life is rarely overt or easily identifiable. Instead it is silently and subtly maintained within university social hierarchies. This covert exercise of power depends upon a social art practiced at the level of everyday interactions. The rules and expectations of academic socialising are never made explicit, but their significance is crucial in making possible and determining academic career trajectories. Concepts of networking, collaboration and mentoring are often positively depicted and encouraged as integral to the academic experience. Yet, as previous work on 'old boy networks' has illustrated, such practices reproduce entrenched frameworks of power, privilege and patronage (Stiver Lie and O'Leary 1990).

In this chapter we seek to deconstruct the practice of academic networking. By social networking we mean the social niceties and events which might appear to the untrained eye as incidental to the job. We argue that this subtle interaction works its own powerful magic, masking the significance of seemingly mundane social encounters to preserve an ethos of meritocracy. We speak from the perspectives of those who have had to adapt to academic culture from white, working class backgrounds. Our efforts to fit in and withstand social norms which can operate to exclude people like ourselves informs our account, as does our experience of becoming networkers ourselves. Our aim is to identify the raw workings of power concealed by ideals of collegiality. Although we make no accusations of conscious scheming, we argue that much academic networking is a self serving practice, pursued for individual promotion often at the expense of others. Using our own experiences as networkers we highlight the ways in which power is operating to particular exclusionary effects through everyday moments and interactions.

However, we also point to the significance of a more collective feminist tradition of networking associated with solidarity and support. This form of networking has been crucial to our academic trajectories. We have been lucky in working with supportive and encouraging feminist supervisors and managers, and in having had the opportunity through the Women's Workshop to network in a way that allows us to admit and explore our differences rather than concealing or trying to eliminate them. Those less fortunate litter the academic wayside or find themselves permanently consigned to the margins through short term contracts. But as we will demonstrate such feminist networking practices are undermined by the increasingly competitive demands of academia, while their language and credibility is co-opted for more mainstream institutional purposes.

From 'old boy networks' to social capital

Social networking has always underpinned career development but was traditionally associated with the practices of rich and powerful men.

The phrase 'old boy network' emerged in the mid 19th century to describe the social bonds deriving from membership of particular elite educational institutions (McCarthy 2004). Such shared affiliation was capitalised on to access favours, support and patronage, thereby shoring up and protecting the privilege of the ruling classes. This systematic but invisible culture of inherited advantage formed the target of social class critiques throughout the last century. The ability of some to exploit influential connections was generally viewed as an obstacle to creating a just and meritocratic society. The concept of the 'old boy network' eventually came to symbolise a more general tendency for men to construct systems of social support to the exclusion and disadvantage of women (Currie and Thiele 2001).

While the feminist led battle for equal opportunities in the workplace challenged these practices and succeeded in implementing legislation and guidelines designed to counter discrimination, influence gained through the exploitation of social contacts within organisations is not easily regulated. The cultivation of valuable social relationships thrives on commonality of experience, culture and worldviews ensuring the continuing dominance of white, middle class men in positions of power. This is particularly the case in the academic world where the exchange of ideas and opinions is prized and built into institutional practices.

The inequalities faced by women and ethnic minorities in the university sector are well documented and enduring (Wilson 2003; NATFHE 2003; Abbot, Sapsford and Molloy 2005). Most institutions adhere to anti-discriminatory guidelines, but as Helen Brown (1997) notes equal opportunities polices can be looked to as a technical fix absolving institutions of responsibility while inequality thrives. Aspirational statements of policy and procedure can deflect attention from the responsibility of institutions for scrutinising their ongoing practices and their effects.

Instead of waiting for the balance of power to shift, feminists academics pursued more active and dynamic solutions, harnessing their own networking resources. With few female academics in positions of power, they were united by a shared sense of marginalisation and a responsibility to support and nurture fellow members. These aims characterise the thinking behind the original setting up of the Women's Workshop as a PhD support group, as well as feminist academic journals and collectives. Women academics began a slow trickle into positions power during a period of dramatic upheaval in the UK higher education sector. Universities in the 1980s and 90s were forced to compete to meet new political and market demands, creating the current context of scarce resources, job insecurity and intense pressure to publish and secure external funding (Davies and Holloway 1995). As a result feminist academics often find themselves compromised by the investments needed to survive in a highly competitive environment (Burman 1996; Hey 2004; Skeggs 1995).

Strategic networking has become ever more central to achieving professional goals in two key respects. Firstly, the pressure to maximise student numbers leads to last minute decisions about funding for staffing and this means greater reliance on word of mouth for hearing about job opportunities. With the increasingly common use of casual, short-term and fractional 'contract' workers employers can exempt themselves from their own equal opportunities practices. Secondly, the peer review system which determines publication and funding success is, by definition, a reflection of social visibility within particular disciplinary networks. In this hard-pressed environment many feminist alliances have come to more closely reflect the culture of male networking, constituting what has been termed in the business world as 'new girl networks' (McCarthy 2004). In an effort to challenge male dominance in academia, women have set up associations with the intention of 'breaking through the glass ceiling' by promoting opportunities and advancement within the sector (King 1997). Meanwhile, the practice of networking has attracted broader political attention through the popularity of social capital theory. Conceptualised as the resources that can be derived from social groups and relationships, social capital has been valorised in government policy circles (Edwards, Franklin and Holland 2003). Networking is generative of social capital, which is turn is viewed as a vital resource underpinning personal well being and national economic growth. From this perspective, social relationships are intrinsically valuable and can and should be capitalised on for mutual gain. The ability to form and cultivate social networks for personal advantage is regarded as the antidote to disadvantage, with the onus placed on individuals to develop appropriate social skills. Therefore having the 'right' connections is now commonly represented as a marker of personal competence rather than an unfair advantage conferred by birth.

This notion appears to have inspired a new approach to equal opportunities in universities, where emphasis is placed on encouraging marginalised groups in the workplace to network their way out of disadvantage. For example, in several universities specific networks for women employees have been set up in order to promote 'equity, fairness and inclusion'. In the introductory literature at one university it is stated that networks play an important 'role in providing women with an opportunity to exchange knowledge and experience, develop effective career development and progression strategies'. This theme was followed up at a launch event during which a panel of 'successful' women, including a Pro Vice Chancellor, a managing director, and a Chief Executive gave biographical accounts of their achievement. Obstacles and discrimination were downplayed for an emphasis on individual determination and confidence, with the event resembling a motivational self-help session. A question from the audience about the significance of luck was met with the sarcastic response 'it's funny but the harder I work the luckier I get'. The event was itself was followed by a networking reception where audience members were provided with canapés, champagne and chocolates and encouraged to mingle. While good intentions clearly lie behind such initiatives they draw on feminist language of solidarity and collaboration to promote a highly individualistic ideology that attributes structural discrimination to a lack of social capital on the part of the individual. The concept of equal opportunity is thus re-framed through a concern to ensure all individuals are skilled at forming advantageous social networks.

In the repackaging of networking as a legitimate rather than an ethically dubious means of conferring advantage in universities, there is little acknowledgement that this advantage may depend on the exclusion of those outside of particular networks or groups. The influence gained from accessing social contacts necessarily disadvantages those not in the loop and ensures that those with access to powerful friends and family gain at the expense of those lacking patronage. This focus on social skills as a way of overcoming structural disadvantage mirrors a more general cultural reconstruction of class inequality. Theories of the reflexive, late modern agent have generated a new language to explain disadvantage at the level of the individual rather than in terms of a particular group or class (Gillies 2005; Skeggs 2004). For a while this approach was successful in levering the issue of class off the academic agenda during a period of unprecedented inequality in the UK (Savage 2000).

However, feminist sociologists have challenged this silence by drawing out the real lived experience of class and reasserting its contemporary relevance (Skeggs 1997, 2004; Reay 1998, 2000, 2005; Lawler 2000; Walkerdine, Lucey and Melody 2001; Lareau 2003). Such understandings of class have shifted away from dominant fixations on structure and stratification towards a more complex engagement with culture, subjectivity and power. This research continues to points to the way social relationships are grounded in a material reality (Gillies 2005, 2006). Instrumental networking for personal gain is most associated with those who have greater access to resources and influence (Gillies and Edwards 2006). As work by Pat Allatt (1993) demonstrates, middle class families work hard to instil in their children the principles and practices of instrumental networking by instituting widely sourced beneficial social links and emphasising social competence. Less privileged families are more likely to value a core network of tightly bonded and highly reciprocal relationships which allow them to get by on a day to day basis (Gillies and Edwards 2006). While networking is presented as a tool allowing individual mobility, this belies its highly classed, exclusionary nature.

Yet, as Pierre Bourdieu (2001) has argued this kind of exclusion and distinction is the driving force of academic life. While education is almost always regarded as a positive social good, benefiting individuals and communities, it has a much less benign purpose of exerting what Bourdieu has termed 'symbolic violence'. From this perspective, knowledge and learning are not neutral practices in that they inscribe legitimacy through the imposition of a 'cultural arbitrary' (Bourdieu and Passerson 1977). Knowledge is socially constructed and has no authenticity beyond its own terms of reference. In his detailed analysis of the French higher education system, Bourdieu (2001) demonstrates how universities work to reproduce and reinforce wider social class distinctions. Academics are the foot soldiers in this process. When we teach, our aim is for our students to demonstrate their grasp of middle class cultural arbitraries. We use all the power we have to ensure this occurs (recording, assessing, classifying, giving feedback etc.). The content of our teaching might seem uncontroversial or even, at times, radically progressive, but we are still complicit in reproducing and justifying a system in which particular ways of being and knowing are enforced. When we teach we reward those who conform, while in effect we marginalise those who don't from academia.

To be a successful academic particular values and ways of being must be internalised and practiced, through the generation of what Bourdieu terms an academic 'habitus'. The requirement to develop an 'academic self' in order to progress through the university hierarchy operates as a homeostatic mechanism, ensuring a shared interest in maintaining the *status quo*. In other words, personal investments in the academic mode of production de-radicalise and demand an intimate familiarity with the expectations of White, male middle class culture (Gillies and

Alldred 2002). Social networking is an informal but highly effective method of enforcing this cultural bias. Those who are proficient at the art of academic networking build their social capital at the expense of those who are less experienced, less confident or have less in common to connect them to powerful individuals.

Learning the rules and playing the game

The social expectations associated with academia are tacit but extremely powerful. They are not specified in the job description nor taught in the induction process, but they must be met in order to build a career. It is the unacknowledged and unelaborated nature of these demands that make them so tricky for outsiders to navigate. Those of us who entered university without the traditional grounding in white, middle class culture have struggled to learn the codes, customs and etiquette in order to get by. We can now reflect on our own social learning curve in becoming academics, but are very aware of the potential for these unspoken expectations to act as impenetrable barriers for others. Particular social skills must be learnt and practised in order to play the academic 'game'. One person's gain is another's loss because of the competitive hierarchical structures of employment. As a result, sustaining an academic career invariably involves a crash course in assimilation for those with different (ie. non-white and/or working class) cultural values and practices.

Beneath an air of informality at conferences, seminars and book launches there is a strong functional undertone. As we have noted academic life is structured around peer review systems through which publications and research funding are adjudicated, and career progression is decided. It is often necessary to secure the support of influential colleagues in order to name them as potential referees. Given the extent of competition among academics, it pays to be known and liked by your colleagues. Social skills are also implicated in a range of academic credits that augment status, including membership of influential boards and committees, consultancies, invitations to speak at seminars and conferences or to contribute articles and chapters. These are almost invariably negotiated verbally and informally and spring out of opportunistic social exchanges. Job opportunities are also commonly accessed through social contacts made on the academic circuit. This is particularly important for contract researchers and those at the beginning of their careers, who might gain teaching work or short term posts by being written into research funding bids. Developing your social capital in this context may also help gain a 'shoe in' when permanent posts arise in the department. Aside from the importance of knowing who to approach how to approach them and what to say academic networking also relies on a strong instrumentalist ethos. This can seem can seem alien and calculating to those used to more tightly bonded social relationships. As such, learning to become an academic can challenge previously held values concerning sincerity and what constitutes exploitation or manipulative behaviour.

Academic networking skills also require a sophisticated appreciation of existing hierarchies of power and influence. Universities may have clear management structures defining authority and responsibility, but prestige and status operate as a more nuanced currency. As Louise Morley (1999) points out 'the exercise of power in organisations can be overt and identifiable, but also subtle, complex and confusing' (p. 5). At a broader level academic institutions are characterised by a hierarchical lattice work of disciplinary affiliations, 'pedigrees' and reputations within which individuals are positioned. Social events are among the most tangible manifestations of the academic pecking order, where you must know your place in order to participate. For low status members of staff such social occasions require the right mix of confidence and deference as well as a thick skin. Such occasions can be a jarring reminder of your position in the wider academic hierarchy. For example, when your usually friendly local professor heads towards you at a book launch, any comfort you took from a friendly face in the crowd can turn to embarrassment as they bustle past you to greet someone much more important. Most of us have experienced the sinking feeling of engaging a familiar face in conversation only to watch their eyes wander the room in search of someone more influential. For those unversed in the hierarchy and conventions surrounding the practice of academic networking such personal humiliations provide sharp correction.

By making these points we are not seeking to unconditionally condemn the practice of networking in universities. Developing social links is clearly an integral part of being an academic. Opportunities to discuss theory and share ideas drive the production of knowledge which universities depend on. We highly value our own networks, not least the Women's Workshop. We would also stress that strategic alliances can be used to challenge entrenched systems of power, privilege and patronage bringing about much needed reform. However, we argue that these positive attributes can obscure the deeply conservative and regulatory functions of networking in universities. It is this murkier side of academic socialising we are aiming to explore by drawing on some of the personal experiences of Women's Workshop members.

Power, values and social spaces

Conferences, seminars and book launches are designated academic networking opportunities, but these spaces rely on implicit shared values, common purpose and understandings. For example, the expectation that you will 'circulate' at academic events rather than sticking with your colleagues is not obvious to everyone. One of us remembers feeling distinctly abandoned and confused at her first conference when her more established co-author disappeared into the social foray. The experience of being left, invisible among a throng of seemingly self-assured conference veterans felt traumatic and left her scanning the room for the exit. She eventually struck up a conversation with another first time delegate, although a sense of allegiance and misplaced guilt sent her scuttling back to her co-author when ever she spotted her alone. The significance of 'circulating' was more explicitly articulated at a later date through a colleague's sneering dismissal of two huddled together PhD students as 'joined at the hip' and incapable of independent thought. She now speculates that her more working class and female prioritisation of personal connection and loyalty was ill-fitting in the individualistic academic arena.

The concept of working your way around a room full of semi acquaintances and strangers, often while balancing a wine glass and a plate of food, can feel daunting to many. However, for those with little sense of their right to be there in the first place the experience can provide a tangible confirmation that they do not belong. Academic careers are built upon a mastery of dominant 'cultural arbitraries' and, for those without the requisite grounding, this means perfecting a convincing performance. Many academics from working class backgrounds have discussed the anxieties and insecurities associated with learning to 'pass' as middle class in order to gain credibility (Hey 2003; Zmroczek and Mahoney 1997). This sense of 'faking it' is accompanied by feelings of disconnection, ambivalence and acute vulnerability. Networking is a highly embodied practice in which aspects of personal self and culture are on public display. Valerie Hey (2004) describes the intensity of conference-going in terms of the identity risks which can weigh on the nerves and be felt as physical symptoms. Risk of 'exposure' can appear overwhelming particularly when conversations precariously highlight your difference. For example, accents invariably betray social origin as do patterns of speech, phraseology and vocabulary (Hey 1997). One of us vividly remembers the shock and embarrassment of having her accent suddenly mocked (albeit in a friendly and non malicious way) by a group of well-spoken colleagues.

Several of us recall learning painful lessons in middle class nomenclature and etiquette when attending meals at academic events. As a Research Assistant, one of us gratefully accepted when delegates she met at a conference invited her to join them for dinner. Other than worrying about how to make interesting conversation she thought little more about it until one of them approached her at breakfast the next morning to ask where she had been. When they explained how they had waited then gone to a nearby restaurant, it suddenly dawned on her that 'dinner' meant evening meal. She had always understood 'dinner' to be eaten at midday. She felt mortified at having stood them up but cringed even more about being 'outed' as someone who ate 'dinner' at lunchtime and 'tea' in the evening. She mumbled 'oh, dinner!' as the others asked good-humouredly if 'she'd had a better offer'. Years later she still carries the sense of having been rude, stupid and ungrateful. Another of us recalls her confusion around napkins at the dinner table. At a formal conference meal she watched everyone delicately balance cloth squares on their knees, but left hers on the table because she wasn't sure how to fold it. Eventually an elderly professor placed the napkin in her lap as if she were a child. In both cases the opportunity to 'dine' with colleagues offered networking opportunities, but sharing particular understandings was necessary for smooth entry into the network.

Academic dress conventions can also be hard for the uninitiated to decipher, ranging as they do from relatively smart (and expensive) suits to an unkempt look that only the most secure in their authentic status can pull off. This apparent *laissez faire* approach conceals strongly classed codes around clothes, particularly for women. One of us recalls how a conference speaker dressed in a pink lycra top was later described by colleagues as an looking like she was on her way to bingo. Jokey references to 'chavs' and 'Essex girls'[1] are common even in the most politically aware academic departments and convey the strong message that certain clothes are contemptuous, essentially because of the status of the social groups who wear them. Determining which clothes mark us out as working class can generate deep insecurity, as can conversations that delve into personal subjects. Even seemingly innocuous discussions about plans for Christmas can invoke paralysing feelings of difference, when descriptions of formal family gatherings, with claret, goose and charades are contrasted with Cava, paper hats and TV specials.

We are not claiming that these differences necessarily provoke overt discrimination, but that they operate in a broader context in which working class culture is devalued. As we have suggested class has increasingly come to be understood in terms of mobility, with an emphasis on social and personal improvement (Gillies 2005; Skeggs 1997, 2004). The current glut of TV make-over shows in the UK highlights the extent to which lifestyles are constantly subject to value judgements which shame and pathologise those who do not meet middle class standards. Consequently, being identified as working class invariably means being positioned as inferior. In an academic environment a presumption of superiority exerts a powerful pressure on those aspiring to sustain a career. Conferences, seminars and other social events are where this superiority must be demonstrated.

The impact of this pressure is often at a self destructive, personal level, but we would not want to underestimate the extent to which academic exchanges can work to isolate and exclude those who challenge the dominant culture. The highly regulatory function of academic socialising is rarely overt and is often concealed beneath a façade of liberal tolerance. For example, one of us witnessed subtle but systematic discrimination levelled against a PhD student with a pronounced working class regional accent and prominent tattoos. While she (and her funding) was welcomed into the department she struggled to gain respect or support from its members and was often the butt of surreptitious jokes. Despite finding her colleagues to be generally polite and encouraging she was left out of meetings and social events, and overlooked when opportunities to teach arose. She eventually left after it was suggested she work from home on the day a prestigious guest was visiting the department.

As Naz Rassool (1995) highlights, these exclusionary practices, in the form of institutional racism, are familiar to many black and ethnic minority academics. But social class positioning also intersects with race to generate a more complex social positioning for black academics from working class backgrounds. For example, Tracey Reynolds (1997) reflects on the contradictions she personally experiences around class, race and gender. She describes how her ethnic identity enables her class background to go unmarked in the academy generally, but notes how when she is networking with other black women academics she becomes uncomfortably aware of her working-class positioning. This highlights the way in which networking mobilises senses of sameness and belonging tacitly, even by virtue of opposition to the mainstream, and forces us to acknowledge that in practice most successful black and ethnic minority academics are those with relative class advantage.

Western feminist politics was forced to learn a hard lesson about recognising diversity amongst an oppositional constituency, and feminist academics must take care not to assume class commonality through networking practices. Feminist networking practices can be as normatively middle class, and might even be experienced as more daunting for their presumption of commonality and for their tacit denial of difference. For example, awareness of feminist critiques of the public/private division, combined with a valiant effort to accommodate childcare needs, led some feminist academics to meet at each others' homes. This is compounded by the difficulty of finding a time-slot for several busy academic women, resulting in meetings of journal editors, co-authors and even research teams being arranged for weekends or evenings. The expectation that you will host such a meeting can come as a bit of a shock, particularly if you are struggling to maintain a 'credible' performance as an academic.

Visits to other academics homes can heighten this anxiety by revealing the extent of your cultural and economic differences. For example, some of us have been struck by the size of our colleagues houses, the fact they are spotless (possibly because they employ cleaners), or small details like matching crockery and 'tasteful' art. Although we have always been made to feel welcome, the idea of reciprocating this generosity can seem overwhelming. We have cringed at the thought of refined academics walking through large urban estates to our small messy council flats and felt embarrassed at not having a garden or anywhere comfortable to sit. These concerns have paralysed some of us when locations for meetings are being discussed. We have stared at the floor and desperately willed someone else to volunteer, but are aware that reticence risks being interpreted as laziness, rudeness or lack of collegiality.

Cultural difference is not the only barrier to successful academic networking. Practical and material constraints can seriously limit networking opportunities, particularly for women. The popularity of arranging seminars, book launches or social events for evenings can make them difficult or impossible for those with child-care responsibilities, and residential attendance at conferences or 'away-day' trainings can exclude those with any type of care commitments. Reimbursement for conference attendance is increasingly rationed by university departments, often leaving academics to pay part or all of the cost. Sometimes administrative hiccups or inefficiency mean conferences demand financial commitment before the department has agreed to meet the cost, and it is often assumed that staff can afford the initial outlay in advance of reimbursement. This highlights the significance of departmental influence and personal income in accessing crucial networking opportunities. The over-representation of women in low status, low income academic posts means they are more vulnerable to exclusion from core disciplinary conferences. Preference towards socialising in expensive restaurants and bars can also exclude or embarrass those on a low income, particularly when costly bottles of wine are ordered and the bill is split. Other practical concerns might further limit participation in networking opportunities. While it might be assumed that all members of a department or research team will feel equally at ease in a given social space, some bars or venues may be less comfortable for ethnic minorities, lesbian/gay colleagues or women. Muslim or Hindu academics may also feel excluded by the extent to which networking opportunities are based around alcohol consumption.

Networking and knowledge

Our focus on the negative aspects of socialising in universities is intended as a critique of its central role in reproducing privilege. We are arguing that the prevailing silence on the power dynamics structuring academic networking not only conceals the key significance of such events, it also contributes to the effective disadvantaging of non middle class, non White people (women in particular). This exclusionary mechanism extends further than just inequality of opportunity in HE. The confined circles of power and influence which constitute academia work to regulate 'knowledge' production, ensuring that academic research inevitably reflects the partial, invested and privileged viewpoints of those who conduct it. As Diane Reay (2000) notes, those from working class backgrounds who try to draw on their own experiences to counter elite representations are accused of failing to maintain a requisite theoretical distance. As she states: 'Academia is founded on exploitative hierarchies. It is little wonder that it has such a poor track record in challenging those beyond its portals when it has made virtually no headway on challenging those within' (p. 20).

Yet having built up our stock of middle class cultural capital in order to become academics we are ourselves heavily implicated in this reproduction of the academic and social order. Our reflections on learning to manage the networking demands of academia have led to a realisation that we now unconsciously reinforce many of the social boundaries we previously faced. Some of us take pleasure in our hard learned proficiency in networking, and have leant to enjoy academic 'smoozing' to some degree, or at least to find it less stressful. Even those of us who still dread such social occasions have developed strategies to cover up our vulnerabilities and enable us to cope. Through our compliance we become part of the regulatory establishment that we ourselves found so daunting. We realise how easy it is to unthinkingly reproduce conventions and hierarchies, sometimes while guiltily observing the travails of those lower in the academic 'food chain'.

As the Women's Workshop we have struggled with issues around accessibility, particularly as members have gained their PhDs and moved up the academic hierarchy. We have had countless discussions over the years about our purpose and membership base. New members are usually recruited through our personal networks, but despite the group's origins as a postgraduate support group some PhD students have said that they find us intimidating. Our image of the group as a safe space to discuss and develop ideas is not necessarily shared by others who might potentially view us an academic cabal. Our feminist roots have led us to emphasise our common experiences as women in academia, but this can encourage ignorance or naivety towards our differences in terms of power and status. In writing this chapter several questions have played on our minds. Can we network in a more ethical and inclusive way or are we ourselves too invested in preserving the *status quo* for personal advancement? What responsibilities do we have to others when we network? Is there scope to form more radical collectives to challenge the normative pull of academia?

Jo Stanley (1995) effectively highlights the potential for academic feminists to unwittingly marginalise those not sharing in their privilege. She has written about her alienating experience of attending a Women's Studies Network conference in the early 1990s, describing how she felt excluded and disempowered. However, rather than giving up or seeking to conform, her more creative and defiant response was to organise a workshop at the following years conference titled 'Feeling like a working class thicko at academic conferences'. While essentially self depreciating the title is highly subversive in naming and thereby challenging the naturalisation of academic values. Jo describes the powerful impact of the workshop and the alliances that were built as a result. The organisation of this workshop demonstrates the more radical form that networking can take and how it might be used to highlight and resist the exclusions and injustices perpetuated by current higher education systems.

Diane Reay (1997) also points to the subversive role academics from non traditional backgrounds might play in undermining institutional facades. As she states: 'Certainly, in academia and other middle class contexts there is a need for people who are prepared to strip away the denial and pretence, to unmask the dissimulation which we can see clearly because it was never part of our growing up' (p. 25). This brings us back to the questions about how we might challenge the more exclusory aspects of networking while harnessing its transformatory potential. There are, of course, no easy answers. Resisting the draw of the academic mainstream can feel like trying to defy gravity, particularly when so much energy is required just to stay in an HE orbit. However, many of us have a strong commitment to social justice, and as such are motivated by more than personal aspiration. In addition, there is a strong pleasure to be gained from helping and supporting colleagues without expecting or receiving anything in return. Despite all the pressures and constraints, generosity and altruism is still commonly found within the academic community.

Ultimately we are left with ambivalent feelings about the way we as individuals (and members of the Women's Workshop) network. On an individual level we can be reflexive about our actions and compromises. At the very least we recognise our responsibility to return the favours shown to us by supporting, encouraging and speaking out for those whose culture clashes with the academic norm. We can also take opportunities (as with this chapter) to illuminate the inconspicuous but powerful social spaces through which individuals are distinguished and excluded. Revealing the implicit value judgements governing the academic world enables a questioning of the validity of a system of privilege that so blatantly reproduces in its own image. These individual actions are crucial, but collectives bring significantly greater power and security. While networking can be employed to exclude and discriminate for personal gain, it can also be used to include, support and effect change. As academics we are inevitably implicated in the former, but we also actively do our best to pursue the later.

Notes

1 The terms Chav and Essex girl are UK slang used ridicule and stereotype working class individuals as stupid, tasteless and vulgar.

References

Abbott, P., Sapsford, R. and Molloy, L. (2005) *Statistics for Equal Opportunities in Higher Education: Report To HEFCE, SHEFC, HEFCW*, Glasgow, Caledonian Centre for Equality and Diversity.

Allatt, P. (1993) Becoming privileged: the role of family processes, in I. Bates and G. Risebourough (eds), *Youth and Inequality*, Buckingham: Open University.

Bourdieu, P. (2001) *Homo Academicus*, Oxford: Blackwell.

Bourdieu, P. and Passerson, J. (1977) *Reproduction in Education, Society and Culture*, London: Sage.

Brown H. (1997) Equal Opportunities Policy, in H. Eggins (ed.) *Women as Leaders and Managers in Higher Education*, Buckingham: Open University Press.

Burman, E. (1996) Introduction: contexts contests and interventions, in E. Burman, P. Alldred, C. Bewley, B. Goldberg, C. Heenan, D. Marks, J. Marshall, K. Taylor, R. Ullah and S. Warner, *Challenging Women: Psychology's Exclusion's, Feminist Possibilities*, Buckingham: Open University Press.

Currie, J. and Thiele, B. (2001) Globalisation and gendered work cultures in universities, pp. 90–115 in A. Brooks and A. Mackinnon (eds), *Gender and the Restructured University*, Buckingham: Open University Press.

Davies, C. and Holloway, P. (1995) Troubling transformations: gender regimes and organisational culture in the academy, in L. Morley and V. Walsh, *Feminist Academics: Creative Agents for Change*, London: Taylor and Francis.

Edwards, R., Franklin, J. and Holland, J. (2003) *Families and Social Capital: Exploring the Issues,* Families & Social Capital ESRC Research Group Working Paper No. 1, London: South Bank University.

Gillies, V. (2005) Raising the meritocracy: parenting and the individualisation of social class, *Sociology*, 39 (5) 835–852.

Gillies, V. (2006) Working class mothers and school life: exploring the role of emotional capital, *Gender and Education*, 18 (3) 281–293.

Gillies (in press) *Marginalised Mothers: Exploring Working Class Parenting*, London: Routledge.

Gillies, V. and Alldred, P. (2002) The ethics of intention: research as a political tool, in M. Mauthner, M. Birch, J. Jessop and T. Miller, *Ethics in Qualitative Research*, London: Sage.

Gillies, V. and Edwards (2006) A qualitative analysis of parenting and social capital: comparing the work of Coleman and Bourdieu, *Qualitative Sociology Review*, Vol II, Issue 2 (http://www.qualitativesociologyreview.org/ENG/archive_eng.php).

Hey, V. (1997) Northern accent and southern comfort: subjectivity and social class in P. Mahoney and C. Zmroczek, *Class Matters: 'Working Class' Women and Social Class*, London: Taylor Francis.

Hey, V. (2003) Joining the club? Academia and working-class femininities, *Gender and Education*, 15 (3) 319–335.

Hey, V. (2004) Perverse pleasures – identity work and the paradoxes of greedy institutions, *Journal of International Women's Studies*, 5 (3) 33–43.

HFCE (2005) Young participation in higher education, http://www.hefce.ac.uk/pubs/hefce/2005/05_03/05_03.pdf Accessed 31/8/05.

King, C. (1997) Through the glass ceiling: networking by women managers in higher education, in Heather Eggins (ed.) *Women as Leaders and Managers in Higher Education*, Buckingham: SRHE and Open University Press.

Lareau, A. (2003) *Unequal Childhoods, Class, Race and Family Life*, Berkeley: University of California Press.

Lawler, S. (2000) *Mothering the Self: Mothers, Daughters, Subjects*, London: Routledge.

McCarthy, H. (2004) Girlfriends in high places. *How Women's Networks are Changing the Workplace*, London: Demos.

NATFHE (National Association of Teachers in Further and Higher Education) (2003) *University Pay Survey Shows Failure to Tackle Gender Pay Gap*, Press Release, 27 May.

Morley, L. (1999) *Organising Feminisms. The Micropolitics of the Academy*, New York: St Martins Press.

Rassool, N. (1995) Black women as 'Other' in the academy, in L. Morley and V. Walsh, *Feminist Academics, Creative Agents for Change*, London: Taylor and Francis.

Reynolds, T. (1997) Class matters, 'race' matters, gender matters, in P. Mahoney and C. Zmroczek, *Class Matters: 'Working Class' Women and Social Class*, London: Taylor Francis.

Reay, D. (1997) The success of failure or the failure of success, in P. Mahoney and C. Zmroczek, *Class Matters: 'Working Class' Women and Social Class*, London: Taylor Francis.

Reay, D. (1998) *Class Work: Mother's Involvement in Their Children's Primary Schooling*, London: UCL Press.

Reay, D. (2000) A useful extension of Bourdieu's conceptual framework? Emotional capital as a way of understanding mother' involvement in their children's education? *Sociological Review*, 48 (4) 568–585.

Reay, D. (2005) Beyond consciousness? The psychic landscape of social class, *Sociology*, 39 (5) 911–929.

Savage, M. (2000) *Class Analysis and Social Transformation*, Buckinghamshire: Open University Press.

Stiver Lie, S. and O'Leary (1990) *Storming the Tower: Women in the Academic World*, London: Kogan Page.

Skeggs, B. (1995) Women's studies in Britain in the 1990's, *Women's Studies International Forum*, 18 (4) 4775–4788.

Skeggs, B. (1997) *Formations of Class and Gender*, London: Sage.

Skeggs, B. (2004) *Class, Self, Culture*, London: Routledge.

Stanley, J. (1995) Empowering working class women at academic conferences, in L. Morley and V. Walsh, *Feminist Academics, Creative Agents for Change*, London: Taylor and Francis.

Walkerdine, V., Lucey, H. and Melody, J. (2001) *Growing Up Girl: Psychosocial Explorations of Gender and Class*, Hampshire: Palgrave.

Wilson, T. (2003) A crisis of inequality, *The Guardian*, 23 May.

Zmroczek, C. and Mahoney, P. (1997) *Class Matters: 'Working Class' Women and Social Class*, London: Taylor Francis.

7
Representing Academic Knowledge: The Micro Politics of a Literature Review

Jane Ribbens McCarthy[1]

Introduction

One of the tasks that all researchers have to undertake, whether for postgraduate study or for funded research, is a literature review. Such reviews are particularly significant in the light of current policy and professional concern for 'evidence based practice' (Muir Gray 2001). At the same time, we have seen an explosion of academic and research publications in recent decades, making it an increasingly daunting task to develop and maintain a knowledge base in our areas of interest, so that we become reliant on other people's summaries. What is entailed in a literature review, however, may be quite variable, and has been the subject of considerable discussion, and a focus for increasingly 'sophisticated' guidance and instruction (e.g. see Hart 1998, 2001; Rowley and Farrow 2000). And, as with any piece of academic writing, the reviewer may feel able to take varying levels of control and authority in the process, in terms of what to select, how to critique it, and how to shape it into an argument.

Whenever we seek to represent the work of other people, however, there is always the potential for re-interpreting, mis-understanding or distorting their work (an issue to which I return below.) But here I am concerned with the bigger enterprise of presenting an overview of a field of work, which of course depends on the building blocks of 'accurately' understanding the work of individual authors, and then presenting a useful and insightful summary of the resulting overall structure and conclusions concerning the published arguments and evidence.

> [T]he key objective that all reviews share is to provide a clear and balanced picture of current leading concepts, theories and data

relevant to the topic of matter that is the subject of study.
(Hart 1998: 173)

A literature review is a summary of what is currently known about some issue or field on the basis of research evidence and/or what lines of argument there are in relation to that issue or field.
(Hammersley 2004a: 577)

The nature and procedures of literature reviews have become increasingly categorised and contested in recent years, with major lines sometimes drawn between different approaches. Some forms of review, particularly the systematic review, have been argued to drastically reduce the scope for the reviewer's decision making and control by requiring her or him to follow very specific instructions about how to undertake such a review. Such approaches have been the subject of major debates about their value and relevance: for example, in relation to research and practice in education, see Avis (2003), Evans and Benefield (2001), Hammersley (2001), Lather (1999), Livingston (1999), MacLure (2005), Meacham (1998), and Oakley (2003) (discussed further below). And, while part of MacLure's argument is that all reviews – including systematic reviews – inevitably in practice require interpretation and judgement (and thus, the exercise of power or influence) on the part of the reviewer, some writers also argue that such interpretation is not only inevitable but desirable, as with interpretive reviews, or meta-ethnographies (Noblit and Hare 1988).

But there are also other sources of variability between different sorts of literature reviews, and some carry more weight than others for reasons of institutional positioning. When the reviewer is a well-known and respected academic or professional, for example, undertaking a review that is presented as an overview and statement about the main state of the field at issue, her or his conclusions may be taken by others working in the area as representing a definitive picture of 'expert' 'knowledge' and debates as they stand at that point in time. Such a reviewer is thus in a very powerful position, to select and shape what counts as 'knowledge' and all the social and institutional processes that flow from that, whether in terms of the directions of future research activities, what is taught within academic institutions, or any policy and professional relevance.

When the literature review is commissioned and funded by a major research body, then that too lends it weight and a sense of authority to its writers. And this is the position I have been in with the funded literature review undertaken on the topic of 'Loss, bereavement and young people', on behalf of the Joseph Rowntree Foundation (Ribbens McCarthy with Jessop 2005; Ribbens McCarthy 2006). My intention in this project was to 'map' the contours of the knowledge available concerning young people and bereavement, to provide an overview rather than definitive conclusions on any particular more narrowly defined research question. The work probably falls closest therefore to the category of an academic or narrative review (although I consider its links with policy further below). This suited my own style of work, and hopefully brought a fresh perspective to an applied and practical field.

In the actual process of carrying out the work, however, I have found myself in shifting positions of feeling both powerful and powerless, and wanting to resist and challenge the power of others, who at times appear to have used their power carelessly or even irresponsibly, whether consciously or not. For the present discussion, then, I am not concerned with the content of the review itself, but with the processes by which it has been produced.

In many ways, what follows is an autobiographical account of my personal journey (at times almost amounting to a transition story[2]), of the transformations in my personal, 'intra-psychic' sense of power/lessness in undertaking this review.[3] Along the way I touch upon such issues as:

- deciding on the search terms
- dependence on electronic searches or on personal networking
- selection and framing of sources to cite
- working between different epistemological stances
- pursuing other people's citations
- finding that eminent authors may be seriously distorting the work of others, with the potential to exercise considerable power in mis/representing the evidence
- balancing out the different interest groups involved
- presenting the work to practitioners and policy makers
- finding the courage to speak up!

In discussing ideas about personal power/lessness, I am thinking about such features as the ability to make key decisions, and to project our own authority, which may be linked to our individual characteristics, but will also be intricately interwoven with wider inter-personal, cultural, structural and institutional processes of power. In presenting this discussion, then, I will start from my experiences of personal power in this enterprise, before moving on to consider relevant aspects of academic reviews in the public domain, and concluding with some of the implications that may flow from this discussion, including the need for greater reflexivity to enhance the credibility of this key aspect of academic work. It is interesting that I have not been able to find any other such accounts of the literature review process to draw upon,[4] given that reflexivity has now become standard practice in most discussions of high quality empirical fieldwork (Elliott 2005). Why, then, do we not similarly expect reflexivity in the reviewing process?

Finding my own (personal and academic) power

Claiming and asserting our individual power is something that I regard as a key aspect of the core academic training experience of undertaking a PhD. This may be exemplified through the frequent advice given to doctoral students to use fewer caveats in their writing, and to present their arguments and conclusions more assertively. And all sorts of features of our personal histories (e.g. our experience of the power relationships of child and parent in family lives, or of boss and employee in work situations) and structural positioning (e.g. our class, race, gender etc) may make it more or less difficult for individuals to take such an assertive stance in the public contexts of academic life. And ultimately, of course, whether student or funded staff, we need to be able to obtain acceptance of our individual claims to legitimate authority within the context of our relevant academic communities. But in undertaking a funded literature review as a professional task, I have felt that I have had to 'notch myself up' another level in asserting and claiming my authority as an academic reviewer and 'expert' in this field.

In considering academic authority and its links with personal power, I am thinking of an individual style that I believe crucially underpins one's ability to assert one's authority as an academic – to be able to present oneself and one's work, either in person or in writing, with confidence and flair, as well as with intellectual credibility. In this respect, it may not be so much a question of *what* you say, as *how* you say it, and I found this to be a particularly difficult process in developing the (self) presentation required for the project on young people and bereavement, as I have slowly developed a professional identity as an 'expert' in these areas. It is for this reason, I believe, that the only way I have felt able to write this present discussion is through an autobiographical style – which in itself, of course, raises the personal stakes higher again, in the public context of an academic publication.

At the same time, it is important to recognise the interpersonal context for this personal experience. While the literature review has felt a risky and difficult business for me as an individual, taking risks in the project overall, and in writing this piece here,[5] has been greatly eased by opportunities to share anxieties with colleagues and obtain feedback. At various stages the Women's Workshop itself has been enormously supportive, from its early inception to its tentative conclusions. Taking and asserting authority in this present discussion may represent the notching up of yet another level of personal power then, that may, perhaps, be translated into academic credibility, but social context, as ever, has been crucial in generating and energising any such power.

In order to describe this personal experience of 'notching up' my professional authority, it is necessary to explain the background to the work I undertook. As a family sociologist, I have regularly undertaken work with relevance to my personal life, so when I experienced the death of my 50-year-old husband in January 2000, leaving me with a 5-year old daughter to bring up without her father, I was very conscious that such a major life experience might be something that I would want to explore further through my academic work, although perhaps not immediately. However, when my attention was drawn to the call put out by the Joseph Rowntree Foundation (JRF) for a literature review on the topic of 'Loss, bereavement and young people', it seemed like an appropriate opportunity to develop my potential interest in bereavement issues without myself embarking – perhaps prematurely – on a major piece of new fieldwork in this area.

I was of course keenly aware that undertaking this work for the JRF would take me into a new academic field – since bereavement issues are not generally discussed within mainstream family studies – and it certainly felt that I was venturing into pastures new, as I found myself feeling an 'outsider' at unfamiliar conferences, encountering new networks, and often talking with those with more experience who looked at me with kindly concern and wished me luck in my undertaking. But my 'outsider' perspective also had the potential to bring a different disciplinary perspective to bear on the evidence, and to range broadly across the types of evidence available, relevant to the JRF's on-going programme of work around the lives of young people, particularly of those who are disadvantaged and at risk of social exclusion. But, while as an academic I was tempted to keep my focus to the theoretical and empirical work undertaken around young people and bereavement, the needs of the funders meant that it was also important to consider the implications for policy and practice. And, although I have had experience of such professional and policy contexts in my work life prior to my doctoral research (see, for example, Central Council for the Disabled 1975; Dorn *et al.* 1987/1994), I have always had some (hopefully realistic) anxiety about presuming to be able to advise professionals and policy makers about the relevance of academic research findings for policy and practice. After all, as Hammersley has argued (2004b), the goals and needs of academic research on the one hand, and professional and policy evidence on the other, may be driven by different epistemological, ethical and value relevances.

Within this particular project, then, it is perhaps not surprising that I found myself having to undertake a personal emotional journey to find my authority to speak about the academic evidence on young people and bereavement. A further reason, however, for my sense of insecurity concerns the various meanings of what it entails to be doing 'research'. My doctoral and subsequent funded research work had always involved the conduct of empirical fieldwork, leading to new data sets. When presenting such work, then, I felt that my authority lay in representing the perspectives of those we had interviewed in our fieldwork – taking an epistemological stance that depended on the credibility and relevance of my empirical data, but informed by a feminist/post-structural view of all such research data as socially produced and situated. In undertaking research in the form of a literature review, by contrast, I felt that my personal authority was more exposed and contestable, as the credibility of what I had to say would depend on my intellectual capacity to understand and analyse the evidence and arguments of existing authoritative academics and researchers – a sort of double-representational challenge. What is more, in the process of reviewing the evidence, I seemed to become positioned as an 'expert' in the field. While, at a philosophical level, the epistemological claims being made in a review are not different from those employed on behalf of the participants in my earlier studies, the structure of institutional power is different, and therefore raised my status as author.[6] Consequently I felt that my own 'voice' was more apparent – and exposed – than when I was presenting the 'voices' of others, leading to a new form of self-consciousness about my standing and presentation. But in this process, personal, intellectual and professional considerations are closely intertwined, including issues specific to this project, as well as more abstract considerations about the nature of the academic enterprise and 'knowledge production' in general.

Young people and bereavement – a personal view?

Family research often concerns sensitive and personal issues, about which we will have individual experiences and emotions that may be highly relevant to the ways in which we approach topics academically. Indeed, the personal significance of such issues may cause many academics to steer clear of them, perhaps focussing instead on more abstract and apparently less emotive areas of work – although here too the personal relevance may still be present, if less obvious. Similarly, researching and writing about death, dying and bereavement – particularly in relation to children – are areas in which quite a self-selecting set of people may want to be involved. Asserting academic authority in such areas, then, is also likely to make quite personal demands on the researchers concerned, in the face of such topics of everyday suffering and existential imponderables and uncertainties.

My family history of bereavement has, of course, meant that reading on the topic of young people and bereavement inevitably has major emotional and personal significance, for me as both a widow and a mother. Furthermore, others around me have noticed my daughter's unease at times, when she has heard me talk to friends with enthusiasm and interest about quite depersonalised academic and research debates on topics in which she knows her own experiences are deeply implicated.[7]

But my personal sense of 'taking power' on these topics has also been shaped by encounters with professionals around my family life. I have thus been on the receiving end of others' understandings of the evidence, and the associated professional implications of current research. For example, when I sought professional input for my daughter in the intensity of the first year of her father's death, the response was to provide support for me, but to exclude my daughter herself from this, much against her wishes. The reason given for this decision – doubtless made in good faith by the professionals concerned – was that I was the key support for my daughter, and that it would be most helpful for her to know that I could provide this, rather than look to others. Furthermore, it was suggested that she needed to know that she was a child, and allow adults to take power and control. Although I fundamentally disagreed with this view – given the absence of any other adults in our networks to whom she could express feelings she might find difficult to share with me – I was powerless to change this situation. Indeed, despite my frustration, I was required to justify the decision to her on behalf of the professionals.

When I later started reading the research evidence, then, about the needs of bereaved children in the context of their family relationships, it had great personal resonance to find that there was evidence to support both my own and the professionals' points of view. By supporting me, then, they were perhaps improving my own ability to cope and support my daughter, which the evidence certainly suggests would be a key factor for my daughter's responses to her father's death. However, at the same time, research evidence shows that children can be quite actively suppressing and masking their own feelings in their concern to 'protect' their surviving parent (Ribbens McCarthy; 2006). Nevertheless, even if I had been able to discuss this evidence at the time of the professional input into our lives, I was their 'client' or 'patient', and they were already apparently quite uneasy about my professional standing as a family sociologist, which perhaps threatened their own sense of power and professional authority. As it was, I often found myself keeping quiet about academic debates concerning the social construction of childhood and child development, while also making a personal judgement about the desirability of taking advantage of any support that they were prepared to provide on their own terms. I have no doubt, looking back, that I was not altogether an easy client to relate to!

The relevance of this history for my present discussion is that these professional encounters had placed me in the position of client, powerless to effectively challenge their decisions. In embarking on the funded literature review, then, I had to shift my personal sense of power away from such vulnerable passivity towards an active and assertive confidence. Such a positive state of mind was necessary to be able to subtly shape the inter-personal dynamics of my self-presentation in academic and professional encounters, and in my writing, to be able to project an identity of credibility and expertise, and to develop the authority necessary in author-ing[8] a review of the research evidence.

One such aspect of developing my author-ity has concerned how I position myself in terms of applying professional, de-personalised, methods for conducting the work. In discussing this personal history in the present academic context, then, I am of course very aware that I may be undermining the credibility of my literature review in the eyes of some readers (an issue to which I return below). Nevertheless, I suggest, adherence to apparently 'objective' or routinised techniques and methods of reviewing – as with all research – can be used to mask the input of the researcher as an individual (see, for example, the article by Judith Aldridge, and others in the 1993 special edition of *Sociology*, 27(1), also Becker 1986; Smith 1989). I turn next, then, to consider some of the social and personal processes behind the apparent impersonality of various elements of undertaking an academic literature review.

Professionalism and self-presentation in selecting our sources

In embarking on a literature review, as with any research project, the researcher is making key decisions from the outset, but such decisions may often not be explicated, and at times, reviewers may not even be aware of their significance themselves. Furthermore, increasing reliance on electronic tools for information searching and retrieval may give the appearance of a review as somehow disembodied and detached from personal decision.

An early decision, then, concerns which databases to search, and what search terms to input. It is now common practice to include this information in any resulting publication, but the basis for such decisions, and their unanticipated consequences, may not be acknowledged. It was thus only after a period of some time that it became apparent that the word 'bereavement', in itself, led towards certain types of literature, most notably a literature rooted in psychological and counselling perspectives (Ribbens McCarthy with Jessop 2005). And it was only at this point, then, that it was really possible to reflect upon some of the theoretical assumptions built into the concept itself (Ribbens McCarthy 2006), and the sorts of evidence to which it led us. Search terms are thus not just a matter of identifying a pre-given topic area or object, but may be tied to a particular orientation or disciplinary perspective. Furthermore, not only are concepts and empirical knowledge intricately inter-linked, but concepts have practical consequences (Sayers 1992).

But the apparent objectivity of the electronically facilitated literature search also has to be supplemented in practice by other, more serendipitous, methods of locating relevant materials. Such methods may involve some quite arbitrary decisions, and unexpected and even unlikely happenings. One important way of expanding the search, then, is to follow up the sources used by key authors, and this can indeed become quite an exhilarating pursuit, almost like a giant detective hunt, mapping out the history of a particular (set of) debates and research work, and the ways in which these have been constructed over time and within particular networks of academics and researchers.⁹

But, while such detective work might at least rely on published references, other important sources might not be identifiable by these means at all, for example, where a broadly focused study of young people's lives happened to include a consideration of bereavement issues. Locating such materials might depend on chance discussions with colleagues, if I started talking about the project and its themes and interests in various venues.

And then again, beside such chance encounters, themselves mediated by the social interactions of academic life (see chapter 6), other features of the power structures of public knowledge came into play. Thus, as my involvement increased over time in various settings and conferences concerned with bereavement issues, I became aware of which individuals were seen to be most respected and authoritative, and to have the highest standing among professional workers, perhaps indicating the operations of an 'invisible college' (Zuccala 2006) to which I might want to gain access. It thus seemed important to ensure I included the work of such individuals for my own writing to have authority, regardless of any other consideration of the worth of their work.[10] And, since reading one piece of literature took time away from reading others, such decisions inevitably meant, at a practical level, that the work of more obscure authors might be neglected. Indeed, I have been only too painfully aware, over the years since my PhD, of the exclusion of my own earlier work on mothering (Ribbens 1994) from reviews and debates where I would have seen this work as highly relevant.

In terms of my self-presentation as an independent, expert writer in the work on bereavement and young people, it has thus seemed important to ensure that the most eminent writers were indeed cited in the review. But it has also felt important that the frequent arbitrariness and chance factors, underlying such decisions of who should be included, should not be made apparent. At the same time, while I have thus been implicated in the reproduction of existing power structures of academic and professional standing, I have also been aware of the possibilities for being more subversive through the inclusion of more obscure authors who might be little known among professional circles. Nevertheless, at the end of the day, my scope for such (minor) power plays has also been limited by the power of the publishers, who told me I had too many references, and that I would have to make further decisions about who to exclude, in order to cut the word length of the bibliography.

Sorry personal tales of academic mis-representation

Having selected the sources, the next task of the literature review is of course to be able to summarise and re-present these sources. But, as mentioned earlier, the ability of academics to understand and represent others' work 'accurately' or 'faithfully' is not always evident. Some of this may be inevitable, and even desirable, as, for example, when major historical works in sociology are reconsidered and re-interpreted in the light of changing social contexts and academic debates. This in itself raises major issues about the practice of 'reading'. Any reader of a piece of text brings their own sets of concerns and perspectives to their reading, with the potential for creativity as well as distortion. And while we may have emotional investments in how we read and understand, some would suggest that there is no such thing as a 'correct reading' (Lather 1999: 4). Nevertheless, the academic enterprise does require that other authors' work is re-presented as faithfully as possible, and that any creative re-interpretation is acknowledged and explicitly argued for.

To summarise and re-present the work of another, then, puts the reviewer into a powerful position, one which arguably also carries an onus of responsibility. But the pressures under which contemporary academic life is carried out, along with the enormous proliferation of work that may be relevant to any particular review, perhaps increases the risk that literature will be read hastily, perhaps relying on abstracts only, and failing to take the time to really 'listen' to what is being written about, so that it can be understood on its own terms. In the early stages of reading in my new field of interest, I felt heavily daunted by, but also cautious about, the need to take my time and understand the thinking underpinning this unfamiliar area of study. But, as pressure grew towards completing my outputs, and my confidence increased that I had my own point of view to argue, my reading of others' work perhaps became more cursory and superficial.

And yet I have my own rather sorry experiences of having my work mis-represented by others. Once any publication is completed, I am aware that it takes on a life of its own, and it can be very pleasing to find that it is at least being cited in another's work. But the pleasure may turn to frustration if it then appears that my original intentions and arguments have been heavily subverted. I have had experience of this in two particular arenas: other people's (mis)representation of my work on typifications of children and appropriate maternal responses (Ribbens 1994), and, more starkly still, the complete inversion of the argument that Rosalind Edwards and I (1990) made about the **un**desirability of using the notion of 'strategy' in relation to women's lives as mothers. Such experiences would not seem to be unusual: some have even reported the fabrication of quotations by reviewers, causing the author to threaten legal action for gross mis-representation (Duncan 2006).

In approaching the review of the literature on bereavement and young people, then, I was very strongly aware of both my power and my responsibility towards the authors whose work I was re-presenting, in the context of a serious substantive issue that has major relevance and significance in the everyday lives of young people and those around them.

Taking an epistemological stand

In compiling that last sentence, however, I am aware that I am shifting my epistemological tone. Most of my discussion here so far, as in much of my academic work, has sought to explicate the limitations and social contexts of knowledge production, but in my last sentence of the preceding paragraph I am taking a more authoritative tone, concerning a 'factual representation' of real lives with practical import (i.e. that bereavement is a relevant and significant issue for young people). Sometimes, indeed, it becomes wearisome, and perhaps unhelpful, to refrain from asserting statements of fact.

How we regard the status of 'facts' in social life is, of course, the subject of major philosophical debate concerning the ontological and epistemological standing of the social sciences. In reviewing the literatures on bereavement and young people, I was reading works across the entire range of disciplinary, ontological and epistemological positions – although the predominant approach is founded (implicitly at least) on a realist or positivist perspective, based in psychology, and using largely quantitative methodologies that result in straightforward assertions of 'facts'. I made a decision early on that I would seek as far as possible to review each piece of research within its own epistemological terms, but I was aware that, in reviewing work from contradictory epistemological positions, I might find myself having to shift my epistemological tone in different parts of my discussion (Alldred 1998). This allowed me to avoid making judgements about which sorts of evidence, and their associated epistemologies, might be considered more credible or 'truthful', but at the same time, potentially undermined my own authority overall. My book from the review, then,

(Ribbens McCarthy 2006) contains extended methodological discussions and epistemological critiques, which overall risks making the entire academic and research enterprise appear to be too fraught with problems to be worth bothering with!

Nevertheless, I am certainly not advocating that we should turn to the sort of strictures used in many systematic reviews in order to improve the apparent credibility of academic research. As Hammersley discusses, the 'slogan' of 'evidence-based practice' may be 'formulated as implicitly to disqualify alternatives' (2001: 550), disguising the ways in which particular kinds of evidence get privileged. I was thus glad instead to be able to quote from Craib in the concluding chapter to my book (Ribbens McCarthy 2006):

> ...it is not all confusion; there is such a thing as morality, even if it is inevitably contested; such a thing as knowledge, even if it is not absolute; there are power differences between people that can be creative as well as destructive. (1994: 186)

In presenting the resulting review to various policy and professional audiences, however, such debates and epistemological nuances have had to be largely set aside, in the attempt to say something of clarity, relevance and usefulness to the pressing substantive issue at hand. Indeed, for such audiences the complexity and contradictory 'findings' of the research may cause considerable frustration, and I have struggled to maintain a balance between recognising the difficulties in the knowledge bases available, while also saying something useful. In doing so, I have been proceeding on the belief that robust academic research knowledge, even where it is inadequate and contradictory, is likely to have something particular to offer to the development of policy, and may provide a crucial input to professional decisions.[11]

One major section of my literature review, for example, has concerned the question of whether bereavement puts young people 'at risk' of particular (generally negative) 'outcomes' in their lives, either during their teenage years or later adulthood. Faced with the very contradictory and complex nature of the evidence available on these issues, in the applied contexts of presentations and publications for policy audiences (Ribbens McCarthy with Jessop 2005) I have limited my discussion to an attempt to make some sense of the evidence, without debating its epistemological foundations. Indeed, at times it has felt like a breath of fresh air to make a really clear-cut statement of 'fact' – in this case, about the greater risk of undesirable outcomes that the research agrees may occur for bereaved young people who experience several losses, or have other significant personal or social difficulties already present in their lives. In representing these findings, then, I have found myself sounding like – and being quoted as – an authoritative expert, and enjoying being able to make stronger arguments as a result.

Being an 'expert' – ambivalence and deconstruction

The relationship between academic research, political values, and policy and professional practice, has of course been keenly debated in various forums. While feminists have long argued for clear recognition, and valuing, of academic work that is explicit about its political commitments, others have been very concerned to maintain the values of 'objectivity' and 'detachment' in academic work (May 2001), if it is to be seen to have something particular to offer. And within policy and professional contexts, a well-accredited academic 'review of the evidence' may well, under some circumstances, carry considerable weight. Indeed, one of the main *raisons d'etre* for the JRF, the funder for my own project, is a belief in the value of research for political and policy ends (see http://www.jrf.org.uk/about/history.htm). One outcome from my own project was thus for the JRF to fund the Childhood Bereavement Network (CBN, an independent charitable organisation based at the National Children's Bureau in London) to organise a seminar for policy makers and professionals to hear some of the main findings of the literature review, as a basis for discussion and policy development with regard to young people and bereavement.

Controversies over the links between epistemology and political values thus present a real dilemma for academics wanting, or being asked, to offer an input into policy and professional debates. In some contexts, then, I may want to be listened to as an 'expert', offering clear findings and 'hard facts' based in a realist or positivist ontology. Am I, then, risking undermining my own 'expert authority' by writing this current piece here, advocating a more reflexive stance around the production of literature reviews, and exposing some of my personal history, which others might see as potential sources of 'bias' undermining my objectivity and academic credibility, and casting doubt on my findings and conclusions? Much depends, of course, on how readers receive what I've written here – some might (hopefully!) take the view that such reflexivity and open-ness enhances the credibility of my work. Perhaps somewhat ironically, I do myself believe quite passionately in the value of seeking some detachment for my literature review, including through the application of the standard practices of academic work (such as citing our sources, assessing the credibility of the research we cite, presenting logical arguments etc). In the context of the literature review on bereavement and young people, I have particularly felt the desirability of keeping a clear focus on the need for dispassionate discussion and judgement, in the context of such a difficult topic, where professional expertise may become clouded by personal and organisational positioning and hostilities (discussed further below).

The operation of power and authority in the public domain

These, then, are some of my autobiographical themes in undertaking a major literature review. But this personal experience is of course also intricately intertwined with features of the public domain in which the academic enterprise is set. A number of institutional and structural processes have thus helped to facilitate my work. Some of these have been apparent already in my discussion above: issues of funding, of institutionally based academic standing, of professional networks, of a coincidence of interests and shared agenda between funding and professional bodies (i.e. the JRF and the CBN), of the commercial interests of publishers (which favour the publication of a literature review that could be used as a professional text), and the drive towards RAE publications which encouraged my institution to provide support towards the completion of the book (see Chapter 8, this volume). In these respects, then, my personal search to develop a new sense of authority in the literature review has been enabled. However, authority perhaps also entails an obligation to act responsibly, and to exercise any associated power with careful consideration. This may not be an easy undertaking for any of us, for all the reasons of social and personal context discussed above, that underlie our academic work. But in this regard, it has been instructive to observe how the authority of experts may or may not appear to be well based. In the current project, this has been apparent with regard both to academic and practitioner representations of evidence and 'knowledge'.

The circulation of professional and policy rumours?

In the course of the project, I have become aware of the ways in which evidence may be cited to establish 'facts' that may be asserted and repeated verbally in professional and policy circles, but which, when investigated, appear rather to have the standing of 'rumours', without a firm research base. I experienced this, for example, in relation to statements that bereavement is a factor in school exclusion, and also in youth offending. With regard to both of these, when I have sought to pursue the sources for professional assertions, my emails have been met with a resounding silence from the originators (but see Ribbens McCarthy 2006, for a discussion of the published evidence that is available concerning bereavement and youth offending). Yet these ideas continue to circulate as established 'facts' at seminars and conferences.

Of course, as discussed throughout this present discussion, I would never see 'facts' as unequivocally independent of social context, but, equally, I do expect experts to be able to provide evidence for their assertions. I was thus considerably surprised by my experience following a bereavement conference for professionals, at which a question from the audience raised the subject of youth offending. To my delight, the speaker (a well-known and extensively published social work authority) referred to published evidence on this issue, and afterwards I emailed him to ask for details. However, once I traced the reference he gave, it was apparent that the article concerned people already in prison who had suffered a bereavement while incarcerated – it was thus not relevant to the establishment of bereavement as a factor behind youth offending. In perplexity, I returned to the social work authority to query whether this was indeed the reference intended, only to be told that it was. Yet practitioners attending the original conference will presumably have left with the belief that they had been given authoritative evidence of the importance of bereavement as a factor in youth offending.

The assertion of such apparent 'facts' concerning policy evidence may not only occur at professional conferences, but may also circulate in print and impact on policy at the highest levels. Hammersley (2004b) thus offers an extended discussion of how some 'facts' may appear to be 'too good to be false' in terms of their professional and practical relevance, while Duncan's (2005) review of research evidence concerning young parents casts serious doubt on the political view of such young people as a social problem at risk of social exclusion.

(Mis)representing the evidence?

While conference presentations, and media and political debates, may lend themselves to such unhelpful practices, can we expect publications in refereed journals to be more securely founded? However, just as it is possible for researchers to selectively report data from new empirical research to present those 'findings' that support the conclusions the authors want to make, so also can research publications be selectively cited in order to make particular arguments.[12] And in the case of young people and bereavement, the existing published evidence in many/most areas is extremely complex and often contradictory. It is thus very possible, for example, for writers to find a selection of apparently academically robust sources to cite either for and against the contention that childhood bereavement is a 'risk' factor for adult depression, according to the argument the particular authors want to make, ignoring those publications that don't 'fit' the argument being made.

Perhaps this apparent one-sided reporting of the evidence was a factor behind the controversial publication by two clinical psychiatrists, Harrington and Harrison, in which they asserted that there were unproven assumptions circulating about the implications of childhood bereavement, and the need for children to grieve. At first sight, this may sound like another example of the sort of professional rumours discussed above (in this case, among bereavement organisations and counsellors for the need for interventions), being effectively challenged by careful and responsible clinicians who had undertaken a more balanced review of the evidence. Citing several research studies in support of their case, then, Harrington and Harrison's argument appeared in an academic journal (1998), a professional therapy journal (1999), and was taken up by elements of the national press (see, for example, Doughty 1999; Langdon 1999; Norton 1999). At the same time, it caused consternation and dismay among many bereavement organisations and professionals, two of whom went into print to argue the case for the (non-clinical) 'interventions' that they were offering bereaved children (Winton 2002; Woodroffe 1999). However, neither of these 'rebuttals' sought to directly dispute the research evidence, but rather the ways in which it might relate to practice.

Certainly for me, as a family sociologist, such controversial debates, and complexities of evidence, generated great anxiety about how to write about this difficult but important area of my literature review, concerning the mental health implications of childhood bereavement, and how to draw any clear conclusions. For a long time I tried to steer clear of it, but eventually my perplexity at knowing what to say led me to start tracing sources used by Harrington and Harrison, only to find, to my astonishment, that these sources did not apparently support the arguments for which they were being cited. (Indeed, I was so surprised

Jane Ribbens McCarthy   139

at this situation that I had to read some articles several times to see if I had understood them correctly, or missed some vital part.)

For present purposes, by way of example, I will restrict my discussion to just one aspect of Harrington and Harrison's discussion, concerned with bereavement as a major risk factor for mental disorder in children. In this section, the authors make strong statements that:

> None of the large epidemiological surveys conducted in the past thirty years has shown bereavement to be a strong correlate of mental or behavioural disorder among the young (Offord *et al.* 1989; Rutter *et al.* 1970; Bird *et al.* 1989; Anderson *et al.* 1989; Velez *et al.* 1989). Systematic controlled studies of bereaved children have been few, but the data suggest that sadness, crying and withdrawal occur in less than 50% of cases (Van Eerdewegh *et al.* 1982; Gersten *et al.* 1991).... bereavement does not emerge as a strong predictor of depression, especially by comparison with, say, parental separation (Reinherz *et al.* 1989). (1998: 230)

However, in turning to the original sources cited here, several do not appear to contain information about bereavement per se at all (Anderson *et al.* 1989; Bird *et al.* 1989; Offord *et al.* 1989; Rutter *et al.* 1970; Velez *et al.* 1989). By contrast, the article by Gersten *et al.* (1991) is explicitly focused on parental death, which is used as a case example for studying factors in the epidemiology of children's mental health disorders. I have not, however, been able to find any evidence in this article relevant to the statement for which they are cited, concerning the prevalence of 'sadness, crying and withdrawal'. Rather, their data is focused on standardised composite measures of depression and conduct disorder. Furthermore, and much more seriously, their research appears to directly contradict Harrington and Harrison's main conclusion concerning the absence of epidemiological evidence for bereavement as a factor in depression, when they state, 'In this study, death of a parent was a strong risk factor for depression in children and early adolescents' (1991: 495). Similarly, Reinherz *et al.* (1989) report that death of a parent was one of three significant factors that they could identify for depression in girls at age 15 – again, in direct contradiction of the statement for which Harrington and Harrison cite this study.

I can only speculate as to how such an apparently complete misrepresentation of these works could have come about, whether through mis-reading, mis-understanding, or perhaps through involvement in professional agenda and boundary disputes between statutory clinical services and voluntary sector bereavement services. But the consequentiality of Harrington and Harrison's argument for service development, and how the public might view the needs of bereaved children and young people, render it highly significant at a practical level.

But it also has to be clearly acknowledged how difficult the task of reviewers can be, when 'findings' do not speak for themselves, and can even be used, quite validly, to provide opposite interpretations of the same data. For example, the study by Van Eerdewegh, cited by Harrington and Harrison (in the quote above) as showing low levels of 'sadness, crying and withdrawal' among bereaved children, is also cited by Lutzke *et al.* as evidence for, '...relatively large differences between bereaved and non-bereaved children... [concerning] overall negative affect (e.g sad, crying, irritable, and/or moody symptoms)' (1997: 221).

So, we may reasonably ask, how can the same study be used in support of such apparently opposite conclusions? In this instance, there does not appear to be any complete distortion of the source, but in the ways authors have attended to different parts of the evidence and its significance. Thus, overall we find that Van Eerdewegh and colleagues conclude, from their study of children of young widows and widowers compared with controls, that:

> There were no significant increases in behaviour problems and severe forms of depression... our results suggest that in children at least during the year following bereavement, there is little psychopathology and even less general impairment of health, aside from an early dysphoria that disappears over time and a mild depression that appears early or within the year following the death. (Van Eerdewegh *et al.* 1982: pp. 23 and 28)

This publication, then, appears supportive of Harrington and Harrison's overall argument. So is it Lutzke *et al.*, in this instance, who have mis-cited their evidence? In their case, the basis for their conclusions would appear to lie in the detailed results of the study, and the ways in which these are interpreted. Notwithstanding the overall conclusions reached by Van Eerdewegh *et al.*, then, we also find in the body of the article, the following statement about their data:

> A severe depressive syndrome, using criteria similar to those used in adults (Kuperman and Stewart 1979), (i.e. presence of dysphoria and

at least four depressive related symptoms), was not significantly more frequent. However, when a depressive syndrome was *defined using only three positive symptoms* from the depression checklist, in addition to having a dsyphoric mood, the group of bereaved children showed a frequency of 14 per cent compared with 4 per cent for the controls (significant at the .03 level). (1982: 26, emphasis added)

This, then, points to key issues about how measures are defined and data interpreted: is it open to others, when citing sources, to attend to some aspects of the data rather than others and/or should they always adhere to the interpretations made of the data by the original researchers? Is it open to others to dispute the conclusions reached by authors themselves? If so, it would seem important to explicate and justify this to the reader.

Personal and academic implications: Are we all wasting our time?

There may be a real danger here of undermining the credibility of the whole academic exercise, by suggesting that evidence, like statistics, can always be manipulated to make particular arguments, and that this manipulation may reflect personal or professional biases and agenda as well as straightforward errors. While we can see some of the public mistrust of statistics, for example, in the discrediting of criminal statistics, nevertheless, as a society we do continue to rely very heavily on statistical information. Similarly, the answer here cannot be to ignore research evidence or to abandon the art of reviewing. Instead, it must be to find better ways to review and re-present evidence within well-accredited and explicit academic processes, without resorting to the mind-numbing strictures of systematic reviews. As Hammersley reminds us, the scientific process does not require us simply to follow a set of rules:

> ...judgement is involved, it cannot be eradicated; and attempting to eradicate it is unlikely to serve the task of research well. It is important to remember that we are not faced with a dichotomy between rational rule-following and irrational judgement. (2001: 545–546)

Indeed, a major *raison d'etre* of academic procedures is to allow us to scrutinise the evidence in just the way I have considered the discussion by Harrington and Harrison. But it seems likely that the difficulties in their article may not be all that unusual – taking into account the experience of mis-representation experienced by myself and others (discussed earlier). Such occurrences may indeed proliferate given current pressures to produce work at high speed, and consequently to find reasons at times to ignore much of the evidence (MacLure 2005). Perhaps one requirement in the academic process is for us to slow down, work carefully and thoroughly, to read with respect, to really try to listen/hear other writers' ideas and engage in constructive dialogue, and to explicate our doubts and difficulties where these occur in reading other people's research. But there is no institutional support for taking such an approach, when quantity rather than quality of output is so often taken as the criterion of academic success. And yet it is precisely its 'unhastened quality' that Pels (2003) argues both has been, and should be, the hallmark of the scientific endeavour.

Autobiography and reflexivity

The issues I have discussed here, in relation to my personal journey in undertaking a funded literature review, are not just a matter of personal challenge or angst, but are intended to illustrate the need for greater reflexivity about the reviewing process. In current practice, discussion of the 'methodology' of such a review is generally limited to an account of what databases have been selected, what search terms have been used, and what criteria applied for deciding the academic credibility of any particular publication. As well as higher standards of reading and representing others' work, then, we also need to be more explicit about how we undertake reviews, and the choices and perspectives we bring to this.

Such reflexive and personal approaches may of course feel risky to individual researchers.[13] But if we are prepared to take such risks, is any associated vulnerability to be regarded as being made possible through a well-rooted sense of personal security and power? And, in the other direction, is a more traditional assertion of academic power sometimes used as a cover for one's hidden vulnerabilities? In taking what feels to me to be quite risky decisions here, you may not be surprised to know that I hope readers/you will interpret this, not as foolhardiness or pointless subversion, but as indeed reflecting a secure and well-balanced psyche! But, clearly, how you receive this piece is beyond my power to shape.

I suggest, then, that the academic endeavour will be enhanced if we recognise that – as with empirical work – reviewing is not produced by disembodied detached individuals who are simply following procedural rules of how to select, evaluate and present the evidence. We thus need to explicate the intellectual judgements, the personal issues and social contexts that inform our reviews in order to improve their credibility and trustworthiness. While research knowledge is never perfect, and 'truth' always involves matters of judgement, such judgements are made within the practices and debates of academic communities (Hammersley 2004b). And such communities are themselves suffused with power dynamics, including interwoven institutional, cultural, interpersonal and intra-psychic processes. Whatever the nature of any particular literature review – whether systematic, narrative, interpretive or something else – it will be embedded in such power dynamics, and we need to open this up to reflexivity in order to enhance its credibility. And, as Lather (1999) argues, we may need to be prepared at times to admit, 'we don't know', while also saying how knowledge is still possible.

Notes

1. Although this chapter represents my views alone, I would particularly like to acknowledge my indebtedness to Julie Jessop, another member of the Women's Workshop, who worked with me on aspects of the literature review, and who made the original suggestion for writing this particular piece from it.
2. With thanks to Martyn Hammersley for suggesting this thought to me.
3. See Ribbens McCarthy (2006) for information about the individual researchers who were involved with the project over time. The particular personal histories of those involved, and the power dynamics between the team itself, are not included in the present discussion, but I would like to acknowledge the extent to which the current autobiographical discussion is self-centred, and neglects to analyse my own position of power within the team. See chapter 9, this volume, for discussion of the power dynamics of managing research teams.
4. One unusually explicit account, however, is that of Atkinson's (1982) justification for his review of research on suicide (discussed by Hart 1998).
5. I would also like to thank Simon Duncan and Martyn Hammersley for their very thoughtful and helpful comments on an earlier version of this chapter.
6. I am indebted to Pam Alldred for explicating this point.
7. Indeed, in writing autobiographically here I also risk implicating my daughter's personal history more directly in this public-ation, and have had to make some key decisions about what I will refrain from writing here, as well as what I will include. But at present, in relation to my daughter (now aged 11), I have very substantial power to shape any such representation of her.

8 The use of the hyphen is intended to draw attention to the link between authoring (as the activity of writing and publishing) and authority (as the effective claim to legitimated power).
9 Hart (1998) provides explicit guidance about how to trace the historical development of particular academic debates.
10 Nevertheless, work which did not meet acceptable criteria for academic publications (citing of sources and evidence etc) were excluded as sources for the literature review, regardless of the professional standing of any authors concerned. But see chapter 4, this volume, for further discussion of the criteria by which academic standards focus on the central act of 'writing'.
11 The application of research knowledge to practice inevitably requires personal and professional judgements implicating various institutional and epistemological tensions (Avis 2003), and may indeed entail different 'truth' claims (Hammersley 2004b). Evans and Benefield (2001) discuss Weiss's (1979) consideration of the various ways in which policy makers may use research evidence, while Hill Collins' (1990) offers a useful and thoughtful discussion of practical knowledge as 'wisdom'.
12 Indeed, this is a key argument made for the advantages of systematic reviews, which require clear criteria for including or excluding studies, and joint reviewing to reduce bias (but see earlier discussion and references cited on the requirements and drawbacks of systematic reviews).
13 Indeed, with regard to issues of reflexivity in the conduct of empirical research, some writers take brave personal risks, for example, in exploring their own intrapsychic processes that may shape the fieldwork undertaken. See, for example, Lucey *et al.* (2003).

References

Aldridge, J. (1993) The textual embodiment of knowledge in research account writing, *Sociology*, 27 (1) 53–66.

Alldred, P. (1998) Ethnography and discourse analysis: dilemmas in representing the voices of children, in J. Ribbens and R. Edwards (eds), *Feminist Dilemmas in Qualitative Research: Public Knowledge and Private Lives*, London: Sage.

Anderson, J., Williams, S., McGee, R. and Silva, P. (1989) Cognitive and social correlates of DSM-III disorders in preadolescent children, *Journal of the American Academy of Child and Adolescent Psychiatry*, 29, 842–846.

Avis, J. (2003) Work-based knowledge, evidence-informed practice and education, *British Journal of Educational Studies*, 51 (4) 369–389.

Becker, H. (1986) *Writing for Social Scientists: How to Start and Finish Your Thesis, Book or Article*, Chicago: University of Chicago Press.

Bird, H.R., Gould, M.S., Yager, T., Staghezza, B. and Canino, G. (1989) Risk factors for maladjustment in Puerto Rico children, *Journal of the American Academy of Child and Adolescent Psychiatry*, 28, 847–850.

Central Council for the Disabled (1975) *Towards a Housing Policy for Disabled People: Report of the Working Party on Housing for Disabled People*, London.

Craib, I. (1994) *The Importance of Disappointment*, London: Routledge.

Dorn, N., Ribbens, J. and South, N. (1987) *Coping with a Nightmare: Family Feelings About Long-Term Drug Abuse*, London: Institute for the Study of Drug Dependence (2nd ed 1994).

Doughty, S. (1999) Leading Psychiatrist Attacks Industry that 'Feeds on Tragedy', *Daily Mail*, May 10th, p. 19.
Duncan, S. (2005) *What's the Problem? Teenage Parents: A Critical Review*. Families and Social Capital Working Paper, London: London South Bank University.
Duncan, S. (2006) Personal communication, University of Durham.
Edwards, R. and Ribbens, J. (1990) Meanderings around 'strategy': a research note on strategic discourse in the lives of women, *Sociology*, 25 (3) 477–489.
Elliott, J. (2005) *Using Narrative in Social Research: Qualitative and Quantitative Approaches*, London: Sage.
Evans, J. and Benefield, P. (2001) Systematic reviews of educational research: does the medical model fit?, *British Educational Research Journal*, 27 (5) 527–541.
Gersten, J.C., Beals, J., Kallgren, C.A. (1991) Epidemiology and preventive interventions: parental death in childhood as a case example, *American Journal of Community Psychiatry*, 19, 491–498.
Hammersley, M. (2001) On 'systematic' reviews of research literatures: a 'narrative' response to Evans and Benefield, *British Educational Research Journal*, 27 (5) 543–554.
Hammersley, M. (2004a) Literature review, in M. Lewis-Beck, A.E. Bryman, and T. Liao Futing (eds), *The Sage Encyclopedia of Social Science Research Methods*, Vol. 2, Thousand Oaks CA: Sage.
Hammersley, M. (2004b) Too good to be false? The ethics of belief and its implications for the evidence-based character of educational research, policymaking and practice. Unpublished manuscript, Open University.
Harrington, R. and Harrison, L. (1998) Unproven assumptions about the impact of bereavement on children, *Journal of the Royal Society of Medicine*, 92, 230–233.
Harrington, R. and Harrison, L. (1999) Do children need to grieve?, *The New Therapist*, 6 (4) 40–42.
Hart, C. (1998) *Doing a Literature Review: Releasing the Social Science Research Imagination*, London: Sage.
Hart, C. (2001) *Doing a Literature Search: A Comprehensive Guide for the Social Sciences*, London: Sage.
Hill Collins, P. (1990) *Black Feminist Thought: Knowledge, Consciousness, and the Politics of Empowerment*, London: HarperCollins.
Langdon, J. (1999) 'Byline', *Mail on Sunday*, May 16th, p. 41.
Lather, P. (1999) To be of use: the work of reviewing, *Review of Educational Research*, 69 (1) 2–7.
Livingston, G. (1999) Beyond watching over established ways: a review as recasting the literature, recasting the lived, *Review of Educational Research*, 69 (1) 9–19.
Lucey, H., Melody, J. and Walkerdine, V. (2003) Project 4: 21 transitions to womanhood: developing a psychosocial perspective in one longitudinal study, *International Journal of Social Research Methodology*, 6 (3) 279–284.
Lutzke, J.R., Ayers, T.S., Sandler, I.N. and Barr, A. (1997) Risks and interventions for the parentally bereaved child, in A. Sharlene, S. Wolchik and I.N. Sandler (eds), *Handbook of Children's Coping: Linking Theory and Intervention*, New York: Plenum Press.
MacLure, M. (2005) 'Clarity bordering on stupidity': where's the quality in systematic review?, *Journal of Education Policy*, 20 (4) 393–416.

May, T. (2001) (3rd ed.) *Social Research: Issues, Methods and Process*, Milton Keynes: Open University Press.

Meacham, S.J. (1998) Threads of a new language: a response to Eisenhart's 'On the subject of interpretive review', *Review of Educational Research*, 68 (4) 401–407.

Muir Gray, J.A. (2001) *Evidence-Based Healthcare*, Edinburgh: Churchill Livingstone.

Noblit, G.W. and Hare, R.D. (1988) *Meta-Ethnography: Synthesizing Qualitative Studies*, Newbury Park: Sage.

Norton, C. (1999) Counselling Children 'Can Add to Grief', *The Independent*, May 10th, p. 6.

Oakley, A. (2003) Research evidence, knowledge management and educational practice: early lessons from a systematic approach, *London Review of Education*, 1 (1) 21–33.

Offord, D.R., Boyle, M.H. and Racine, Y. (1989) Ontario child health study: correlates of disorder, *Journal of the American Academy of Child and Adolescent Psychiatry*, 28, 856–864.

Pels, D. (2003) Unhastening science: temporal demarcations in the 'social triangle', *European Journal of Social Theory*, 6 (2) 209–231.

Reinherz, H.Z., Stewart-Berghauer, G., Pakiz, B., Frost, A.K., Moeykins, B.A. and Holmes, W.M. (1989) The relationships of early risk and current mediators to depressive symptomology in adolescence, *Journal of the American Academy of Child and Adolescent Psychiatry*, 28, 942–947.

Ribbens, J. (1994) *Mothers and Their Children: A Feminist Sociology of Childrearing*, London: Sage.

Ribbens McCarthy, J. with Jessop, J. (2005) *Young People, Bereavement and Loss: Disruptive Transitions?*, London: National Children's Bureau.

Ribbens McCarthy, J. (2006) *Young People's Experiences of Loss and Bereavement: Towards an Inter-Disciplinary Approach*, Buckingham: Open University Press.

Rowley, J. and Farrow, J. (2000) *Organizing Knowledge: An Introduction to Managing Access to Information*, Aldershot: Gower, 3rd ed.

Rutter, M., Tizard, J. and Whitmore, K. (1970) *Education, Health and Behaviour*, London: Longman.

Sayers, A. (1992) *Method in Social Science: A Realist Approach*, London: Routledge, 2nd ed.

Smith, D.E. (1989) Sociological theory: methods of writing patriarchy, in R. Wallace (ed.), *Feminism and Sociological Theory: Key Issues in Sociological Theory*, London: Sage.

Van Eerdewegh, M.M., Bieri, M.D., Parrilla, R.H. and Clayton, P.J. (1982) The bereaved child, *British Journal of Psychiatry*, 140, 23–29.

Velez, C.N., Johnson, J. and Cohen, P. (1989) A longitudinal analysis of selected risk factors for childhood psychopathology, *Journal of the American Academy of Child and Adolescent Psychiatry*, 28, 861–884.

Winton, P. (2002) A personal perspective, *Childhood Bereavement Network Bulletin*, October, 3, 3–4.

Woodroffe, I. (1999) Children need to grieve, *New Therapist*, 6 (4) 42–43.

Zuccala, A. (2006) Modeling the invisible college, *Journal of the American Society for Information Science and Technology*, 57 (2) 152–168.

8
Measuring What's Valued or Valuing What's Measured? Knowledge Production and the Research Assessment Exercise

Pam Alldred and Tina Miller

Introduction

The final Research Assessment Exercise (RAE) is being implemented midst rancour and debate about what counts as knowledge, and who will do the counting. This mechanism for measuring research productivity has created imperatives for most lecturers in the UK – intensifying the pressure on academics not just to produce 'research outputs' but to produce certain types of knowledge in certain types of publication. Its demise is not grounds for celebration, however, since a metrics-based alternative looks set to entrench existing funding success more deeply and make it even harder to do research that has no customer (e.g. Bekhradnia 2006). This chapter does not address which mechanism provides a more truthful account of the value of a set of 'research outputs'. Instead, it is concerned with the power of such a mechanism to reinforce particular values and to inscribe resulting hierarchies regarding knowledge. We will argue that, regardless of what replaces it, the RAE process will have been productive, not just reflective of academic values. We will examine some of the consequences of the RAE for UK academic life, focusing on two themes, both of which highlight the operation of power through processes of knowledge production.

First, we will consider ways in which practices intended merely to measure research productivity themselves create particular dynamics of power and produce or sustain particular hierarchies regarding types of research and models of knowledge production. In addition, we will argue that what, at one level, appears a rational, if overly-bureaucratic, measuring exercise is, in practice, a variable and shifting endeavour that rests on highly subjective 'measures'. We suspect that, not only does it fail to live up to its promise of transparency and clarity, but, as more is written about the criteria in the name of clarity, the closer we get to MacLure's use of Breton's 'clarity bordering on stupidity' (2005: 1).

Second, we will explore the impact of these dynamics and status hierarchies for individual academics. As academics become increasingly self-conscious of performance indicators and, individually more visible through them, we are more tightly disciplined by them. The way our research performance is measured and judged comes to be productive of our ways of being and our academic selves, and we wish to register some concerns about the consequences of this. We draw upon our own and colleagues' experiences of trying to make sense of and navigate the RAE. These allow us to explore the curtailment of professional and personal freedoms and the reshaping of expectations and obligations that are productive in their effects: reconstructing academic work, and those who do it, in ways that serve the prevailing model of institutional competition. Our concern in each case is that the 'mentalities' sustained by the RAE will outlive our memory of the arbitrariness of their production and our criticality about them, leaving the values and hierarchies reified even harder to contest. We will therefore have ended up valuing what was measured in spite of ourselves.

What is the RAE?

The Research Assessment Exercise is a process by which the research of UK universities has been evaluated in order to determine future funding, or rather, 'to *inform* the selective distribution of public funds for research by the four UK higher education funding bodies' (RAE 2006: 1, itals added). It therefore provides the UK's Higher Education Funding Council for England (HEFCE) with information for the selective allocation of research funds to universities as part of their block grant. The next RAE (2007/8) will be the 6th in the series conducted nationally since 1986. This process of assessing research has been highly controversial and yet is currently informing models being developed for use in Australia and elsewhere (McNay 2006). The RAE is merely the particular instantiation of more general pressures associated with the rise of the audit culture and new managerialism over the last 20 years in the UK and beyond. Yet it has changed fundamentally – at both individual and institutional levels – what is produced and valued in academia.

The most obvious way in which the RAE wields power is in the grading of research outputs (e.g. chapters, books, articles, reports) and the hierarchical ranking of Higher Education Institutes (HEIs) on the basis of a summation of these. A revised 'marking system' for producing these gradings – seeking to measure the quality of each output, and assign it a value on a scale – has been devised and made public before each RAE. Such grading schemes attempt to discriminate between knowledge outputs according to objectively applied criteria and have generally sought to make explicit how value is assigned and by whom through publication of the criteria and of the panels of judges.

Despite such attempts at transparency, the rules of 'the game' can be hard to fathom. Differing accounts of 'the rules' emerge from differing interpretations, from the various strategies HEI managers adopt, and because of actual revisions between successive RAEs, which provide some basis in fact to our sense of shifting 'goalposts'. For example, some of us were academically socialised (in the social sciences) into prizing book authorship and aspired to win book contracts after our initial publications of chapters or articles, only to find when we eventually did that the message about what is valued has changed, and, in line with scientific rather than arts disciplines, the journal article is the prized form of publication. The broad adoption of a value-system rooted in the sciences is the most general example of the hierarchies of knowledge forms, favouring empirical research and, within that, quantitative methods. Between the 2001 and 2008 RAEs, an explicit shift instituted across disciplines was the emphasis on quality of research output, not quantity. This grew out of a widespread recognition (including by the Government, see McNay 2006) that the RAE process had skewed academic production by pressuring academics to write multiple outputs on the same findings.

In the 2006 Budget speech, and between first and second drafts of this chapter, the Government announced its intention not to conduct further Research Assessment Exercises after 2007/08, and even considered abandoning that one (Sastry and Bekhradnia 2006) (see HEPI website for details). This news did not salve our concerns about the existing and ongoing consequences of the process to date. In exploring how both knowledge production and practices of the academic self have changed under RAE conditions, a model of power is employed that exposes both the productive and repressive functioning of institutional power (Foucault 1981; Henriques *et al.* 2002). Our disquiet about the RAE come from our perception that 1) we do not share some of the values it embodies, which run counter to our own understandings of what constitutes valuable, socially responsible research; 2) the political consequences of these values are undesirable; and 3) the process is not as value-neutral as is implied by the rhetoric of measurement. Here we will focus primarily on the consequences for knowledge production and aspects of academic subjectivity and touch briefly on the values and objectivity arguments. We now turn to the vexed issue of how indeed to measure research value/output, which means engaging with the RAE's technical detail.

Measuring what we value

For the 2008 RAE the aim of the evaluators is not simply to award each unit of assessment (UoA) (usually a Department) a single grade as in the past, but to produce 'Overall quality profiles' that reflect the percentage of their research activity that is rated in each of five grades. These grades are: 'world-leading in terms of originality, significance and rigour' (4*); 'internationally excellent' in terms of originality, significance and rigour (3*); 'recognised internationally...' (2*); 'recognised nationally...' (1*) and 'falls below the standard of nationally recognised work' ('Unclassified') (RAE 01/2005: 24, Table 2, cited in Johnston 2005: 117). This grading is applied three times for each UoA in order to grade 'three overarching elements: research outputs, research environment and esteem indicators' (RAE 01/2005: 10, #38, d, ii, cited in Johnston 2005: 116). The weighted sum of these gives the quality profile, where different subject panels can decide what weighting to give research outputs relative to the other two elements for their disciplines (e.g. Johnston 2005). Sub-panels – comprised of academics who 'are currently or have recently been active in high quality research' – will decide which indicators will be used for each element (RAE 01/2005: 5, #18, cited from Johnston 2005: 115). Because of this complexity, the exercise is a massive task for universities and assessors. In addition, the commitment this time to read almost all published outputs (in response to earlier criticisms) means that the 'burden of RAE 2008 will be much greater than ever before' (Johnston 2005: 116).

But what does 'international' mean as an indicator of quality? The widespread concern has been that research on locally relevant matters and practitioner-led disciplines maybe wholly characterised by 'low status' research since large sections of the discipline's work may engage only a UK audience, yet may still make a significant contribution

(Lewis 2002, cited in McNay 2006). One of us takes pride in a short publication in a practitioner journal because a Health Visitor responded saying how useful she found it to show to new mothers, yet the article is low status by RAE terms because of its style, length and location in a non-academic publication. Despite later reassurance in 2005 that 'World-leading', 'internationally' and 'nationally' in this context refer to quality standards not to the nature or geographical scope of particular subjects (RAE 01/2005: 24, #3, cited from Johnston 2005: 117), this concern remains. Johnston, for one, remains critical – and like McNay and Lewis he is an ex-panel member. He says:

> These are very fine distinctions, to say the least: how do you distinguish something that is 'internationally excellent' from something that is 'recognised internationally' on the same criteria – 'originality, significance and rigor' – always assuming that you can define an absolute standard associated with 'internationally'? (Johnston 2005: 117)

The meaning of *international* in terms of relevance, place of publication or as some purported indicator of standard has been a matter of debate and confusion. It adds a level of variation between panels (in addition to their choice of weightings) because some have elaborated this whilst others have not. In the past, the Sociology panel recognised that 'work that has not received international attention can be of international quality' (HEFCE 1999: 175, cited in McNay 2006) and in the last 2001 RAE, even those involved in making assessments were sometimes unclear about what counted as 'international excellence'. For instance, Lewis reported (of her experience on the Social Policy & Administration and Social Work panel) that:

> One of the interesting quirks of the RAE is that it was concerned to measure the quality of research, but what was meant by 'quality' was never defined. Somehow we were all meant to be able to identify it – and grade it – when we saw it. (2002: 5, cited by McNay 2006)

This is akin to what McNay (2005 personal communication) and other education theorists call 'the elephant mode of marking' where assessors use their confidence that 'they will know one when they see one' to excuse limited criteria. In addition, as Johnston (2005) asks, how are assessors to know how many submissions should be in each grade band (in fact, how many world-leading articles were published in each discipline since the last RAE)? As lecturers we are expected to know which type of grading system we apply: criterion-referenced or norm-referenced (e.g. Rowntree 1987). In the former it doesn't matter how many are assigned each rank, just that they meet the criteria, but in the latter, exactly where they fall relative to the whole group is the key defining feature of their grade. Given that the exercise is to allocate a limited amount of money, the gradings are surely relative to the whole set of work done and so a normal distribution of 'quality' might be assumed. The brief criteria provided might be more meaningful if assessors were told to assume this distribution of grades.

A normal distribution however assumes the whole population is represented, whereas not all the research conducted is submitted for assessment as we shall see. Other ways in which institutions 'play the RAE game' affect the pattern too. The mean ratings have improved markedly over time, particularly between the 1996 and 2001 RAEs, leading Sharp (2004: 202), for instance, to conclude that 'the size and stability of the differences are sufficient to cast some doubt on the consistency of assessment standards across time and subjects'. However, the meaning of rising grades is ambiguous: are individuals and/or institutions producing better research, getting better at 'playing the game', or is there 'grade inflation' like some claim affects our degree marking? In addition, the goalposts have shrunk so that only a narrowing band of departments/UoAs at the top receive any money, rather than the higher ranked UoAs receiving progressively more money. Having a *measure* therefore doesn't appear to guarantee that we know what it *means*.

Furthermore, these wrangles over assigning value distract us from the inequity of ranking against each other institutions with dissimilar comparators (Turner 2005) or applying the same pressure for research outputs to staff who are primarily teachers as to those who are primarily researchers. It is commonly recognised that being a lecturer at a new (post-1992) university tends to carry a much larger teaching load than in an 'old' university, yet the RAE makes no allowance for this. In addition, departments engaged in professional training feel unfairly treated since their teaching, tightly regulated by external bodies, cannot be squeezed to make more room for research.

RAE08's emphasis on quality of research output goes some way to addressing this, but the attempt to give 'quality' an objective status and quantifiable character seems optimistic. Stating criteria lends the appearance of objectivity when actually the application of these criteria is harder than their neat definitions suggest. How far can claims to rational objectivity be upheld when subjective judgements clearly form a key element in the assessment process? How can a process designed to discriminate between different standards of output 'treat [all outputs] equally', as one institution tried to reassure staff? We shall discuss what counts as knowledge and which forms of research are valued later, but first we will discuss an area in which it appears the RAE has a rather conservative impact – in the disciplinarity of individual's work and ultimately in departments' recruitment practices – and we will highlight some of the political consequences of this.

Disciplinary difficulties

As before, the RAE08 covers research across the disciplines which are divided into 70 sub/disciplines. Disciplines are clumped into 'Main Panels' A to O, so that for example, main panel K includes the units of assessment called Education, Psychology and Sports-Related Studies, and main panel J covers Law, Politics and International Studies, Social Work and Social Policy Administration, Sociology, Anthropology and Development Studies.

Despite today's widespread encouragement of inter-, multi-, and trans-disciplinary studies and even broad recognition of the arbitrariness of disciplinary boundaries and distinctions, the assessment exercise reifies distinct disciplines in that each 'unit of assessment' (or department as it usually is) must choose which to be entered under. Whilst statements from the sub-panels try to reassure practitioners of interdisciplinary work by appointing experts from a wide range of specialisms within a discipline, this does not avoid the problem of having to choose one sub-panel. Some departments will fit comfortably into one or other category, but many others may house academics whose disciplinary allegiance is varied. For instance, a School of Education may well include researchers whose work is informed by, intervenes in or might for some other reason sensibly be situated in Psychology, Sociology, Cultural Studies, History, Geography or Social Policy. The task for the main panels is to ensure a degree of 'equity and consistency in working practices across a group of cognate disciplines' (RAE 01/2005: 9, #37, c, www.RAE.ac.uk) and so in the second tier of the assessment process psychological and educational research will be assessed to 'common criteria' (RAE 01/2005: 9, #38, a) because they are co-located in main panel K above. Sociology and Education are, however, in separate main panels. This points to the importance of the overarching criteria across all the panels.

Whilst it would seem inappropriate to insist that all panels operate identically, do the ratings really mean the same when McNay's (2003) comparative analysis of panels shows that the 2001 Anthropology panel gave 5 or 5* ratings to 70% of units whereas Economics only gave this grade to 32%, and when disciplines sampled very differing amounts of the research output: 'a minimum of 10%' in Business and Management Studies, 'at least 25%' in Sociology, and for History 'an absolute minimum of 50%' (cited in McNay 2006). McNay (2006) concludes that panels with clearer, perhaps more demanding criteria, awarded a higher proportion of top scores. Some commentators believe that whereas differences between panels in the last RAE were only apparent afterwards, prior knowledge of their refinements and weightings would have altered the gaming behaviour of players (see McNay 2003 and Lucas 2005). Instead, switching between disciplines happens to good effect between RAEs as potential units of assessment get better at 'playing the game'. McNay (2006) describes how, between 1996 and 2001, the number of submissions in Education fell from 103 to 83, and for Sociology from 61 to 48 as disciplinary allegiances shifted strategically for anticipated better funding outcomes. For example, the American Studies panel received only 13 submissions despite 40 current UK programmes and so concluded that staff's research outputs had been disaggregated back to 'parent' disciplines rather than being submitted for this interdisciplinary subject. Therefore 'what is clear is that the structure of the subject panels and their perceived behaviour influences the way institutional managers conceive of subject boundaries' and, over time, institutional managers have learnt to play the RAE 'game' in more strategic and effective ways (McNay 2006: 153).

Yet, even playing the RAE game still involves the prioritising of particular types of publication. Interdisciplinary academic areas may be seen as too dilute, and similarly, journals that are explicitly interdisciplinary can be regarded as too wide-ranging and not discipline specific enough, even though they may be the natural home for publications from collaborative, interdisciplinary research (which we were encouraged to do relatively recently). Here our objection is to the political consequences for feminist research of the RAE's powerful reinforcement of the values it enshrines. In particular, our concern is for feminist research work that is informed by several disciplines and 'owned' by none. This position may have intellectual and political advantages, but is not recognised or valued in a discipline-based scheme. Submissions to the Women's Studies sub-panel were lower than might be expected in 2001, which can be read as a conservative or mainstreaming impulse to be counted within larger units of assessment. McNay (2006) reports that over a quarter of submissions to the Sociology panel were women's or gender studies and were therefore referred to the Women's Studies sub-panel. This sub-panel only received four other submissions via other panels, none from arts and humanities, which suggests it did not examine work reflecting the real range or worth of research in the area.

Similarly, feminist journals may be assigned low status where they do not fit disciplinary categories and hence are assumed to have low impact factors. Journals such as Feminist Review, Feminist Theory, Feminist Studies, and Women's Studies International Forum do not fit disciplinary boxes, and by virtue of their wider spread across the citations indexes may rank lower on any particular index. It will be interesting to see how feminist journals which do have disciplinary identities, e.g. Feminist Economics, fare by comparison to those which stand to lose most as a consequence of the valuing of disciplinary location.

Whilst drawing together different disciplinary expertise when submitting a funding bid is believed to strengthen it, when it comes to publishing its outputs, tensions may develop over where to publish interdisciplinary findings, particularly when specifically interdisciplinary forums are deemed too low status to count for the RAE or are viewed as diluting the disciplinary integrity of an individual's submission. Disciplines differ in how multi-authored papers are received and in how author order is read. Where author order is intended to indicate effort involved yet coincides with alphabetical order, it may be assumed simply to reflect alphabetisation. Author naming can become a contentious issue or, conversely, a strategic (and sometimes cooperative) ploy in which team members still 'needing' a publication can be named first. Clearly pressures against team-working have wider implications beyond the RAE for the sharing of expertise, the dissemination of research findings and contributing to research that *makes a difference*. At times then the requirements of the RAE – and resulting practices – can be experienced as running counter to what Stanley has called research which produces 'useful knowledge' and 'unalienated knowledge' (Stanley 1990).

Knowledge production: what counts, where and who says?

So how do we work out what types of outputs count and where to publish in order to be rated well in the RAE? One of us was told by a senior colleague that he wouldn't submit to a journal he didn't know the editor of. This type of personal contact, along with knowledge of journal hierarchies and citation indices are a form of 'insider information' that might be more available to individuals who are networking with senior academics and panel members, a practice that not all find comfortable or possible, as Gillies and Alldred examine in Chapter 6. This question shows a status-conscious, strategic approach that can distort the relationship between research and publishing (see e.g. McNay 1997). Research findings should surely be published in the journal most likely to reach the audience intended, which is not necessarily the one ranked most highly in RAE terms. Professional and practitioner journals tend not to be highly ranked, even though they may be peer reviewed and inform practice. Our earlier example of the publication eliciting a letter from a practitioner raises questions about how the value of a piece of work is to be measured. There is the potential for conflict with funders where they may want research findings disseminated in practitioner and/or service-user publications that will not be highly ranked by RAE assessors but will meet the intended audiences. Lewis is critical of the hierarchy assumed:

> A piece of local, empirical work which is useful to people in the locality and is written up in an accessible way could be classified as sub-national because it is not couched in academic/discipline based formats, but from other perspectives, could be of international excellence in terms of quality (Lewis 2002: 5, cited in McNay 2006)

The definition of research employed is 'original investigation undertaken in order to gain knowledge and understanding' (RAE 01/2005: Annex B, cited in Johnston 2005: 116). The RAE08 aims to focus on 'quality' and not be distracted by quantity by only allowing four publications per academic, and by reducing the need for a coherent theme across a UoA, which is thought to have led to a selective representation last time, involving the omission of departments' 'odd ball' researchers who did not fit into the themes that could otherwise be narrated.

Evidence of what types of knowledge are valued – gathered from the circulation of journal rankings and citation data – appears to runs contrary to the spirit of institutions' guidelines based on guidance from the RAE that 'equity' is the first principle of the RAE and that 'all types of research and all forms of research output shall be assessed on a fair and equal basis' (Institutional memo, 08/07/05). The Orwellian resonance grows when comparing guidance from different institutions. For example, guidelines from the Sociology panel states that 'edited books, research reports, reports to statutory, official and private-sector bodies' are suitable forms of output, yet Tina's contribution to the earlier Women's Workshop book (3 co-authored chapters and co-editorship) is not considered high status enough for inclusion. Feedback from mock RAEs provide contradictory messages about how the Education panel will receive practice-related, as opposed to theoretical work.

The valuing of academic over practitioner-oriented publications illustrates one of our qualms about the political implications of the RAE process generally. In what Lewis (*ibid.*) describes as a passive approach to informing policy or practice whereby academics simply publish their findings in existing status-conscious places and expect 'users' to find them, we see responsibility for changing the world relegated to an optional extra that some academics may do if politically motivated. It represents academic findings as apolitical, that only when *applied* (by others) do they have political effects. This decouples knowledge production from politics and absolves academics of responsibility for the uses to which their work is put.

A clear hierarchy among different methods and approaches to research is embedded in the assessment exercise. Improving the quality of research, in RAE2001

> was often seen as conforming to a specific definition of quality, so that economists saw work in econometrics and other quantitative approaches being valued above other methodologies (Harley and Lee 1997), and psychologists noted that lab-based psychology gained higher grades than other modes of working (Marks 1995). Their behaviour, in choosing what to research and how, changed accordingly. (McNay 2006: 149)

This inevitably has consequences for what research work is conducted in future, engendering a conservative impact on research methodologies employed. In the case of education, McNay (*ibid.* 149) argues:

> The feedback from the 2001 Education panel called for more large-scale, quantitative, longitudinal studies. That presented several problems: of delivering within a short time-scale before the next assessment, of relevance to the work of many staff who work closely with professionals at the teaching-learning interface, and of attracting funding to a significant number of such projects. No doubt some are trying even now to develop such work, to be 'fit for

purpose' in the RAE, if of limited utility in improving the quality of practice, or informing teaching, which I see as major objectives of much work in social science.

Studies such as by Fisher and Marsh (2003: 74) describe the impact the RAE process has on disciplines, such as Social Policy and Administration and Social Work 'that need to adapt to the rubric essentially derived from a different tradition and research base'. The RAE influences the way in which knowledge is organised and bounded (McNay 2006). For an exercise that presents itself as merely 'measuring' what is there, the RAE has powerful effects.

The distorting effects of the RAE are recognised at the highest levels including by the Parliamentary Select Committee and the Economic and Social Research Council (ESRC). The latter explicitly notes the distinction between RAE requirements and the research councils in areas such as 'interdisciplinarity, applied research and research related to professional practice and engagement with users' (ESRC 2004: 26, cited in McNay 2006: 147). Yet McNay highlights the irony of citing the ESRC's concern given that its own funding is more responsive to Government agendas (instead of those generated 'bottom-up' from the research community) than the other research councils.

Whilst the RAE necessitates that academics think about what type of research to do and where to try to publish research findings, it is at the institutional level that we will each be initially judged. The question of *who* is returned under the RAE and *where* is usually in the hands of those occupying more powerful positions within our institution. Our own disciplinary identities and allegiances or political commitment to making particular interventions may be irrelevant to bureaucratic decisions about which RAE panel our work is submitted to. Through regular reviews and mock RAEs our individual efforts are subject to internal and external scrutiny and our potential value in relation to the RAE assessed. It is hard to believe that individuals will not be made visible or vulnerable in this process.

Quantitative, ideally large-scale, findings are valorised, with theoretical, reflexive work at the far end of the continuum of research approaches and the conventional distinction between academic and applied work is shored up. It appears that, in spite of the huge amount of critical work on epistemology, methodology and reflexivity by feminist and other scholars, the legacy of objectivism and positivism continues to influence what is most valued – and ironically perpetuated by – the RAE. The RAE presides over a lamentable narrowing of forms of knowledge production and a shift towards the most normative scientific models of research. Even the prizing of journal articles over books or other outputs in the RAE regime reflects and validates scientific models of research, seeing outputs as discreet packages of new knowledge that get us further up the mountain towards 'Truth' (Rorty 1980).

The same presumptions about the value of forms of knowledge production are embedded in the evidence-based movement in education which seeks research findings that inform practice and support (but do not critique) policy implementation. Qualitative research is devalued and quantitative research privileged in 'systematic reviews' of 'the evidence' and this has implications for what (and whose) perspectives are taken into account in the development of policy, for instance, rarely including the views of those who are the targets of the policy (Graham and McDermott 2005; Dixon Woods *et al.* 2004). It has political consequences for the relationship between research and policy, and for the way research questions get framed. It influences the type of projects that get funding, the types of new journals starting up or surviving the market and the type of funding available through the funding bodies' choice of funding streams and thematic priorities. The 'evidence base' that is deemed relevant to inform practice seems to have got narrower over the past decade by the elevation of quantitative methods and relegation of qualitative methods in policy discourse. Large-scale or longitudinal studies are beyond the reach of many of us and funding bodies will err on the side of caution in awarding grants of the size required for these only to those who are seen as pre-eminent in their field and based in prestigious research universities. This leaves the skills of those of us trained in qualitative approaches undervalued and our experience and commitment to, for instance, feminist or critical approaches further marginalised. Academics with an established record of attracting research funding are more likely to attract funding in future making it difficult to establish a foothold in grant-winning. The introduction of a metrics-based system (see Sastry and Bekhradnia 2006) will worsen this: money will be awarded precisely on the basis of money previously won from research councils and other funders (Bekhradnia 2006), making the system itself inherently conservative.

The systematic review illustrates the controlling and reductive aspects of audit culture in the extreme, in its 'rage for clarity, transparency and certainty of outcomes', as Maggie MacLure writes:

> Exasperated by the inability of education research to deliver the kind of seemingly hard evidence offered by health and medicine,

systematic review favours quantitative methods and embodies a scarcely-concealed positivism that places qualitative research far down the 'credibility hierarchy' (Hammersley 2001, p. 545). (MacLure 2005: 394)

However MacLure argues persuasively that it fails ultimately in its goal of improving quality because it reviews only those studies that address the pre-defined question and meet the strict criteria for 'quality' research. The 'tiny dead bodies of knowledge disinterred by systematic review', as she puts it 'hold little power to generate new understandings' and by trying to regulate reading, writing and interpretation, 'suppress[...] aspects of quality in research and scholarship that are at least as important as clarity, countability and accountability – such as interstitial connectivity, critique, interest, expertise, independence, tacit knowledge, chance encounters with new ideas, and dialogic interactions between researcher, "literature" and "data"'. (2005: p. 394)

Performing academic subjects

What then are the consequences of measuring research performances for academics ourselves? As we become increasingly self-conscious of performance indicators and – individually audited and more visible through them – our research performance becomes inextricably caught up with our academic decisions, actions and selves, but many authors point to the ways in which academics feel it compromises some of the shared principles underpinning academic identities (Henkel 2000) and violates traditional academic values (Harley 2002; Lucas 2005). The overall impact of RAE-induced pressures has been to create a more individualistic orientation and more competitive ethos. In compliance with the new regime we have to become more instrumental in our decisions about what work to take on and as a result, activities that are not valued in RAE terms, lose out. For instance, many of the smaller and perhaps more 'everyday' pieces of work that academics do such as reviewing and refereeing the work of others for journals and for funding bodies are either invisible or don't count highly in the RAE. Evidence of an increasing instrumentalism is seen by journal editors in finding people to agree to referee articles. For instance, a recent article submitted to a feminist journal now needs a 9th and 10th referee to be approached, because all so far have said they are too busy. Similarly the editors of a proposal for a journal special issue pulled out realising they'd be 'better off' publishing their collection as a book. This is even happening for a journal that approaches *feminist* academics, colleagues who therefore have a political interest in the journal, not only an academic one. It represents an insidious undermining of the idea that academic work might be to promote social justice.

We are expected in the next RAE to comment on how much work went into a joint-authored publication, but how much work goes into a joint publication 'normally'? Against what should we compare our contribution vis-à-vis our co-author's? What about ideas generated in dialogue? This institutionalises the individualising notion of the originating subject. A performative model of the subject is assumed where it suits – such that increasing pressure on individual academics is expected to productively enhance our investments in particular types of knowledge claims and production practices – and, it is intended, to increase our overall productivity. But it is the Cartesian subject who is assumed when the originating subject is required to produce glamorous 'new' knowledge. We suspect that increasingly strategic decisions are made in order to prioritise individual outputs over more collegiate modes of working. Our concern is that the instrumentality, individualism and competitiveness the RAE produces in us will not be easily shaken off afterwards. It will leave us changed subjects. In this sense it will have been productive irrespective of whether it made us work any harder.

Disciplined selves

Among those writing on new managerialism and performative regimes in higher education (HE) are analyses of the consequences for individuals of the resulting organisational cultures. Valerie Hey (2004) explores the 'perverse pleasures' of our over-commitment to intellectual labour in 'greedy institutions' and McWilliam (2004) explores how individuals shoulder the burden of risk minimisation in the post-welfare universities (of the UK, Australia and New Zealand) and her analysis of the self-auditing academic subject is relevant here. More specifically, Henkel (2000) and Lucas (2004, 2005) each explore the RAE's impact on individuals and their academic identities.

Hey (2004: 33) describes being 'perplexed by the clash between corridor... critique of the impact of audit and managerialism and our manic productivity'. Our commitments have been powerfully reworked so that we have become instrumental in our own exploitation, over-complying or over-zealous, suggesting that there is 'more to our punitive work rate than can be explained as compliance with the escalating demands of higher education restructuring (Marginson 1997; Morley 2002).' (*ibid.* 34). The Foucauldian (Foucault 1977) understanding of how individuals come to do the work of institutions in 'policing' or disciplining themselves fits: power works *through* us to stimulate in us the desire to succeed in these terms which we may previously have been critical of (Foucault 1981). What role do we play ourselves in 'buying into the particular economy of new times performativity and [what] rationales [do] we offer about our commitments and performances' (Hey 2004: 35) when we know what academic culture desires and come to want that too. 'Even our language is instructive' Hey points out: 'we learn the texts of our discipline, we do disciplined enquiry, we must be rigorous, and we offer our work as submissions' (*ibid*). There is something deeply ascetic, self-denying and yet egotistical in this peculiar practice that indeed reveals something of the origins of the English university in Medieval monastic vocational devotion. We even allow ourselves only short-lived pleasures 'success is always postponed in the race for the next prize' (*ibid*.: 40).

In *Ethics in Qualitative Research* (Mauthner *et al.* 2002) we wrote about the old-fashioned motive to 'make a difference' and feminists' use of academic work for social change, but does this get 'eaten up by the desiring machine of professional identity projects fuelled by ambition and personal and positional gains?' (Hey 2004: 41). Hey suggests that

> If we are honest about what we 'get out' of the current settlement, even so far as recognising the perversity of our pleasures, we might be in a better position to stop martyring ourselves – as punishment for those inadmissible 'guilty pleasures' (in intellectual work, in competitive endeavours, in status, in winning, etc) and put our skills and capacities to 'better public and civic use' (2004: 41)

The individualising, competitive, perhaps even masochistic space of academia can be deeply compromising for feminists (Burman 1996; Morley 1999), yet we help each other comply, compete *and* resist. Now the language of 'collaboration' has been colonised by the new managerialism that saturates universities and we are expected to do it for instrumental reasons (ideally with someone at a higher ranking institution), but some inspiring collaborations buck the RAE audit process. Collaborative productions that publish under a group name, such as the Hall Carpenter Archives (e.g. 1989) or even invent for themselves a name, such as the collective that published under the name Beryl Curt (e.g. 1994) resist the individual attribution and fantasy of the originating subject standard practice shores up.

Valuing what we can measure

A popular critique among educationalists of today's over-testing of pupils in UK schools is that we cannot measure that which we value, and instead we come to value that which can be measured. This is one of the most troubling effects of the RAE. In addition to the way it enables us to discipline ourselves, the academic terrain itself will bear the imprint of the RAE into the future. Whatever system replaces it, when we hear ourselves referring to '5*' departments in the future, we will know that its logic has won out. The power of the RAE lies in this inevitable process of reification. No matter how qualified, tentative or complex the outcome measures are, as soon as a number or rank is assigned, the qualifiers and caveats fall away. All 'Ah buts' and explanations of strategic play-offs will fail to register, in much the same way we sometimes feel students' perception of our detailed formative feedback is utterly dominated by the summative feedback (the grade). They sometimes seem not to hear our explanations of (and implications of) their mark, they just want to know what they '*got*.'

We have described some of the values underpinning the hierarchies of research outputs and research methods embedded in the RAE, and our disquiet surrounds their conservative or de-politicising effects. We may not share these values, but it is the fact that they are *assumed* that is problematic. In the valuing of certain types of knowledge over others, is the assumed supremacy of quantitative methods that rest on the naïve objectivity that feminists engaged with in the 1980s and 1990s. What is alarming is not that there exist those who do not share our epistemological perspectives, but that their views are encoded in a practice which does not admit its partiality, thus actively undermining the recognition that different views exist. Positions stated explicitly can be argued with. Instead it is implicit that bigger is better in terms of study size, that numbers are more robust than 'mere' views, that the 'academic' research firmly within disciplinary boundaries is of higher status than applied or interdisciplinary research, that 'international' is a marker of quality, and that there can be some agreement about the merits of a piece of research on a linear 5-point scale. The individualistic fantasy that academics are originators of new knowledge is reinforced too.

Some of the RAE logics are powerful and worth making explicit. It clearly rests on, and embeds the understanding that competition benefits productivity, at both individual and institutional levels. Indeed if grade inflation were to be taken at face value, competition has been effective in raising grades and the application of market rationalities to education appear vindicated. However, in parallel with GSCE or degree results, the meaning of improved grades is unclear and for the RAE some contribution of better gaming and strategic appointments and manoeuvring are hardly in doubt. Competition has concentrated funding in fewer centres (AUT 2003), but is this necessarily a good thing? It is certainly likely to reduce the range of approaches and topics in a discipline. Indeed, it has 'reduced the originality and quality of much academic research' according to the Commission on the Social Sciences (2003: 5, cited in McNay 2006).

One of the consequences of the measurement of research productivity may have been the rise in status of research, with the resultant individual esteem boosts to 'research active' academics (see Harley 2002; Henkel 2000; Lucas 2005), but the drop in status for teaching and apparently resulting student (dis)satisfaction cannot be ignored and indeed some research-successful universities are now urgently trying to improve the student experience. Pushing research and teaching into competition with each other may prove unproductive for universities. It may ultimately widen the gap between the post and pre-1992 universities which could never compete 'on a level playing field' anyway and see the decoupling of research from teaching to reinstate the division between teaching-led and research-led universities.

One of the most fundamental and least questioned assumptions is that greater funding should follow highest ratings. It seems important to make explicit this logic in order to dislodge its position as the obvious or only rational division of research money: an alternative logic would suggest that enhanced funding followed those departments most struggling to raise their research profile. Indeed this would be an educational, rather than an economic rationale. What is notable is the ease with which one particular logic regarding the allocation of money 'on the basis of the ranking system' comes to occupy the position of common sense. One of the conservative consequences of this is the difficulty getting onto the RAE-ranked ladder which allows existing and entrenched power bases to be retained and strengthened, potentially stifling change or the emergence of new areas of study or groups of researchers.

'How did we ever agree to a linear system of stars?' said one colleague. That such crude feedback will be the eventual result of such laborious efforts by both submitters and adjudicators is bemusing. How we 'agreed' to it, if this isn't to flatter ourselves regarding our power, was through clever use of the process of peer reviewing (Lucas 2004). Its adoption of peer evaluation as the central evaluative mechanism is the key feature that buys credibility for the assessments. It is seen as democratising the process, so that our investment in peer review manufactures our consent (see also Wisker 1996). In addition, the process of consultation and revision of the RAE itself helps to buys our faith in an improving mechanism, which, in fact, mirrors science's belief in its own gradual progress towards Truth.

We mistakenly assume (against our intellectual commitments) the objectivity of a process so bureaucratised. The technical language of criteria and the complexity of subdivisions of evaluations all serve to convince us that this is a rational process. However, as the European Studies panel noted, the 'more precise' rating scales reduce panels' discretion (McNay 2006) and loses some of the potential benefit from peer evaluations. Moreover, behind its proclaimed logic and transparency, the different interpretations of submission guidelines we find between (and even within) particular HEIs, imply that such guidelines are more subject to interpretation than their presentation admits. What it sold us as an objective way of ranking research outputs turns out to rest on highly subjective judgments every step of the way (Johnston 2005).

The heart of the matter is that evaluating human knowledge practices and production presents a problem far messier than is implied by the types of technical solution considered. Even the crudely simplified rating on 5 (or even 7) points, eventually collapses into two categories – either side of the (regionally variable) threshold for receiving any funding. It perfectly illustrates Bauman's (1992) analysis of the rational, bureaucratic 'solutions' that modernity looks to. Psychoanalytic reflections on the RAE might highlight the search for a process that promises to manage and contain our anxiety which is fuelled by the increasingly competitive environment. The irony is that we invest in the RAE because we value our research (as well as the funding) and the identity perks offered, but that the result of this (over?) investment is a system that fails to reflect what we value, and worse, undermines our political values and potentially our commitment to research of social value.

References

AUT (Association of University Teachers) (2003) *The Risk to Research in Higher Education in England*, London: AUT.

Bauman, Z. (1992) *Modernity & Holocaust*, New York: Cornell University Press.

Bekhradnia, B. (2006) New research funding plans are even worse than before, *GuardianEducation* 20/06/06, p. 10.

Burman, E. (1996) Introduction: Contexts, contests and interventions, in E. Burman, P. Alldred, C. Bewley, B. Goldberg, C. Heenan, D. Marks, J. Marshall, K. Taylor, R. Ullah, S. Warner, *Challenging Women: Psychology's Exclusions, Feminist Possibilities*, Buckingham: Open University Press.

Commission on the Social Sciences (2003) Great expectations: the social sciences in Britain, accessible on the ALSISS website: www.the-academy.org.uk

Curt, B. (1994) *Textuality and Tectonics: Troubling Social and Psychological Science*, Buckingham: Open University Press.

Dixon Woods, M., Agarwal, S., Young, B., Jones, D. and Sutton, A. (2004) *Synthesising Qualitative and Quantitative Evidence*, London: Health Development Agency.

ESRC (Economic and Social Research Council) (2004) Memorandum from the Economic and Social Research Council (2004) in evidence to the House of Commons Parliamentary Select Committee on Science and Technology, *The Work of the Economic and Social Research Council*, HC 13, London: The Stationery Office.

Fisher, M. and Marsh, P. (2003) Social work research and the 2001 Research Assessment Exercise: an initial overview, *Social Work Education*, 22 (1) 71–80.

Foucault, M. (1977) *Discipline and Punish*, London: Allen Lane.

Foucault, M. (1981) *The History of Sexuality Volume 1: An Introduction*, Harmondsworth: Penguin.

Graham, H. and McDermott, E. (2005) Qualitative research and the evidence base of policy: insights from studies of teenage mothers in the UK, *Journal of Social Policy*, 35 (1) 21–37.

Johnston, R. (2005) Commentary: on preparing for more subjective judgements: RAE 2008, *Perspectives*, 9 (4) 115–120.

Hall Carpenter Archives (1989) *Inventing Ourselves: Lesbian Life Stories*, London: Routledge.

Hammersley, M. (2001) On 'systematic' reviews of research literature: a narrative response to Evans and Benefield, *British Educational Research Journal*, 27 (5) 543–554.

Harley, S. (2002) The impact of research selectivity on academic work and identity in UK universities, *Studies in Higher Education*, 27 (2) 187–205.

Henkel, M. (2000) *Academic Identities and Policy Change in Higher Education*, London: Jessica Kingsley Publications.

Henriques, J., Hollway, W., Urwin, C., Venn, C. and Walkerdine, V. (2002) *Changing the Subject: Psychology, Social Regulation and Subjectivity*, London: Routledge (second edition).

HEPI (Higher Education Policy Institute) www.HEPI.ac.uk

Hey, V. (2004) Perverse pleasures – identity work and the paradoxes of greedy institutions, *Journal of International Women's Studies*, 5 (3) 33–43.

HEFCE (Higher Education Funding Council for England) (1999) Research Assessment Exercise 2001: Assessment panels' criteria and working methods, RAE 5/99, Bristol, HEFCE.
Lewis, J. (2002) Assessing the Research Assessment Exercise: an expensive (mad) lottery?, Presentation to the AUA Annual Conference, April.
Lucas, L. (2004) Reclaiming academic research work from regulation and relegation, in M. Walker and J. Nixon (eds) *Reclaiming Universities From a Runaway World*, Open University Press (and Society for Research into H.E.).
Lucas, L. (2005) *The Research Game in Academic Life*, Maidenhead: SRHE/Open University Press.
MacLure, M. (2005) 'Clarity bordering on stupidity': where's the quality in systematic review? *Journal of Education Policy*, 20 (4) 393–416.
Marginson, S. (1997) Markets in education, Sydney: Allen & Unwin.
Mauthner, M., Birch, M., Jessop, J. and Miller, T. (2002) *Ethics in Qualitative Research*, London: Sage.
McNay, I. (2003) Assessing the assessment: an analysis of the UK Research Assessment Exercise, and its outcomes, with special reference to research in Education, *Science and Public Policy*, 30 (1) 47–54.
McNay, I. (2006) Research assessment; researcher autonomy, in C. Kayrooz, G. Akerlind and M. Tight (eds), *Autonomy in Social Science Research. The View from the United Kingdom and Australia*, Elsevier.
McNay, I. (1997) *The Impact of the 1992 Research Assessment Exercise on Individual and Institutional Behaviour in English Higher Education*, Chelmsford: Anglia Polytechnic University.
McWilliam, E. (2004) Changing the academic subject, *Studies in Higher Education*, 29 (2) 151–163.
Morley, L. (ed.) (1999) *Organising Feminisms: The Micropolitics of the Academy*, London: Macmillan.
Morley, L. (2002) *Quality and Power in Higher Education*, Buckingham: Open University Press.
RAE (Research Assessment Exercise) 2006 www.RAE.ac.uk, accessed 6.1.06
RAE 03/2005 rae2008: Research Assessment Exercise. Guidance on Submissions. July. Available at http://www.rae.ac.uk/pubs/2005/03/rae0305.pdf.
RAE 01/2005 rea2008: Research Assessment Exercise. Guidance to Panels. January. Available at http://www.rae.ac.uk/pubs/2005/01/.
Rorty, R. (1980) *Philosophy and the Mirror of Nature*, Oxford: Blackwell.
Rowntree, D. (1987) *Assessing Students: How Shall We Know Them?* London: Kogan Page.
Sastry, T. and Bekhradnia, B. (2006) *Using Metrics to Allocate Research Funding*, HEPI website downloaded June 7th.
Sharp, S. (2004) The Research Assessment Exercises 1992–2001: patterns across time and subjects, *Studies in Higher Education*, 29 (20) 201–218.
Stanley, L. (ed) (1990) *Feminist Praxis: Research Theory and Epistemology in Feminist Sociology*, London: Routledge.
Turner, D. (2005) Benchmarking in universities: league tables revisited, *Oxford Review of Education*, 31 (3) 353–371.
Wisker, G. (1996) *Empowering Women in Higher Education*, London: Kogan Page.

9
Feminism, the Relational Micro-Politics of Power and Research Management in Higher Education in Britain

Natasha Mauthner and Rosalind Edwards

Introduction

One of the distinctive contributions of feminist scholarship to the social sciences has been to open up the black box of theoretical and empirical knowledge construction processes. By placing reflexivity at the centre of their research practices, feminists have discussed a range of aspects of power relations in the knowledge production process. For example, in addition to looking at what counts as knowledge generally (Collins 1990; Harding 1991; Rose 1994), they have considered how the construction of knowledge is influenced by power relations during fieldwork, particularly inequalities in terms of power and privilege between researchers and respondents (Edwards 1990; Finch 1984; Ribbens 1989; Ribbens and Edwards 1998; Wolf 1996); power relations during data analysis and interpretive stages (Glucksmann 1994; Mauthner and Doucet 1998, 2003); and power issues in writing about and representing the 'Other' (Standing 1998; Wilkinson and Kitzinger 1996; Wolf 1996).

Despite these lively feminist discussions on power vis-à-vis our research respondents 'in the field', rarely have we turned this critical reflexive gaze onto our practices and relationships with collaborators 'in the office'. There has been relatively little feminist analysis of issues of power and ethics within research teams. The few examples where the principles of feminist self-reflexive research have been applied to academic collaborations include discussions of female contract researchers' relationships with women in research teams (Reay 1999, 2000; see also Mauthner and Bell this volume), doctoral student-supervisor relationships (Heinrich 1995; Hewson 1999; McIntyre and Lykes 1998; see also Almack and Churchill, and Lucey and Rogers, this volume), and power between women and feminists in academia more generally (Edwards 2000; Fox Keller and Moglen 1987; Onyx 1999). For the most part, however, power dynamics within feminist collaborations remain a largely invisible aspect of the research process, discussed and negotiated in private, confided about to colleagues and friends, or simply buried along with the painful emotions these issues arouse.

The particular perspective we investigate in this chapter is that of feminist research managers within the British higher education system. We have not worked together as colleagues on research projects, but over the past decade or so, we have both been involved in research management following time as contract researchers. For this reason, we came together to write this chapter, our first collaborative venture. After getting her PhD, Natasha worked as a contract researcher before moving on to core funded research management posts. She has since gone on to a lecturing post involving teaching, research and administrative responsibilities. Ros also worked as a contract researcher after her PhD and then was promoted into core-funded research management posts. She currently manages an externally funded programme of work comprising a number of interlinked projects, in addition to working on other individual research projects.

As will be evident throughout our discussion in this chapter, research management involves a wide range of tasks and responsibilities. Both of us attempt to approach these management activities from a feminist perspective, taking a collaborative approach and operating with an ethic of care that acknowledges interdependencies. We are, however, working within the context of 'new managerialism' in higher education that creates more hierarchical power relations and provides challenges and tensions for such a feminist approach. Furthermore, while we may attempt to be collaborative and eschew hierarchies, research management involves the institutional power to 'hire and fire' researchers, and research managers usually have greater job security and are paid more than those they manage. It is the very fact that we are in a position of power that enables us to attempt feminist research management in the face of new managerialism.

We discuss our understandings of feminist research management and new managerialism further below, along with our conception of power. This takes us from a review of the organisational forces underlying the practice of power in research management into a more nuanced consideration of the relational 'micro-politics' of research management in terms of power resources embedded in divisions of labour, divisions of responsibilities and divisions of rights. We want to show the ambivalent and contested nature of power, beyond simpler notions of collaboration versus hierarchy, in our daily research management experiences. This ambivalence and contestation – within a context where power relations are always present, whatever form our research management practice takes – leads us to argue that a feminist approach to such practice necessarily involves open reflexivity.

Feminist research management

Generally, there is an important distinction to be made between 'women in academic management' and 'feminists in academic management' (Adler *et al.* 1993). Not all women managers regard themselves as feminists or manage in feminist ways (Edwards 2000). While feminist management can proceed from a number of feminist perspectives (from liberal to radical), in general it is characterised by a commitment to social equity and social change, and a guiding awareness of gender issues and intersections with other social divisions. It involves an explicit attempt to challenge the unequal distribution and exercise of power, hierarchical structures and hegemonic institutional practices (Hughes 2000; Strachan 1999). It advocates consultative, egalitarian and collaborative ways of working and of knowledge production (Mountz *et al.* 2003; Ramazanoglu 1990; Tanton and Hughes 1999). Also central, at least to our particular approach to feminist management, is an ethic of care and a desire to create a more caring working environment, which recognises our mutual interdependence, and the personal benefits and rewards of collaboration and interdependence over competition and individualism (Hughes 2000).

In relation to research management 'in the office' specifically, feminist management involves attempts to break down power differentials between team members and institute a non-hierarchical way of working with one another that recognises interdependency and acknowledges that being 'equal' members of a team can mean being the same and/or being different depending on the circumstances. We have attempted to implement this model through varying combinations of the following: sharing involvement in the research tasks (e.g. data collection, analysis, writing-up, dissemination and publication); sharing information, resources and rewards; giving all team members equal intellectual property rights over the data, the research and publications; discussing and agreeing dissemination strategies; team members taking responsibility for different publications but, in principle, giving team members co-authorship; sharing decision-making, power and authority; drawing up agreements for all team members at the outset of a project allowing these issues to be discussed, negotiated and agreed upon; and discussing issues of power and equity as they arise during the course of a collaboration.[1] We are selective about the research projects, or parts of them, in which we implement feminist research management practices, depending on the nature of the project, the type of funding, and the people we are working with. For example, a feminist approach may not be appropriate in some types of research consultancy. Thus there can be a distinction between being a feminist and acting as one.

This chapter is concerned, nonetheless, with attempting explicit feminist research practice. The institutional and organisational contexts in which we attempt to be feminist research managers, however, are infused with the culture and conditions of 'new managerialism' that cut across our ideals and practises.

New managerialism in higher education

New managerialism in higher education (Deem and Brehony 2005), as well as more broadly in public sector services (Clarke and Newman 1994), is an organisational and cultural process that promotes hierarchical power relations and particular values and interests. While new managerialism certainly has not invented hierarchical power relations, which have always infused higher education systems and practices, it has given power a particular shape. New managerialism is an approach that arises out of state higher education policies and funding regimes (Deem 2004), and which promotes the exercise of management itself as primary and is dedicated to measurement and overt external accountability. It is characterised by 'best practices' such as the monitoring of employee and self performance, planning strategies, and working to meet financial targets, performance indicators and quality audits. New managerialism serves to legitimate managerial interests and actions that are not necessarily the same as the best interests of employees.

The policy and funding context of research within the higher education system is replete with new managerialist language and values of targets and accountability and related appraisal and auditing mechanisms (rather than creative knowledge work). Higher education institutions are positioning themselves competitively in knowledge economies and 'external' research markets (Brannen and Edwards

1996, 1998). Notably, the Research Assessment Exercise assesses the research quality of 'units of assessment' submitted by each university – evaluating and selectively grading the quality of research outputs, external research funding, research 'culture' and so on, and then unequally distributing resources to universities on the basis of this grading (see also Alldred and Miller this volume). This process draws research managers and academic peers into the new managerialist culture. Academics need to be 'research-active' in particular ways for their university's grading, and research managers are charged with an interventionist approach that ensures their staff produce what counts as 'high quality' publications and acquire prestige grant income, while the RAE audit is subject to peer review, ensuring that the exercise is legitimated by academic control (Shattock 1999). Furthermore, grants for research programmes and individual projects increasingly are monitored and audited by research funders in an ongoing fashion, with those managing the programmes and projects ensuring that: performance indicators are met, research timetable strategies are in place and implemented, risk analyses produced, requirements for research products and presentation are met, research utility is achieved in terms of research-end users, and so on.

The features and practices of new managerialism construct a subject position for research managers to fill, and produce the instrumental reflexivity and surveillance through which people in these posts come to know and enact themselves as managers in relation to others (Pritchard and Deem 1999). When research managers are also attempting to know and enact themselves as managers of others from another sort of managerial subject position, such as that informed by feminism, there can be real tensions, with feminist managers likely to be pulled in different directions (Edwards 2000). Analyses of the situation at this level may provide us with an explanation of tensions and their sources in practising feminist research management in the contemporary higher education context. They tell us little, however, about the ambivalences and complexities involved in the 'micropolitics' of how power is relayed and contested in the everyday practices and transactions of research management.

Relational micro-politics and power resources

Joan Beckwith has discussed power structures and discourses from a feminist post-structural perspective. She argues that power is 'a complex tapestry of individuals, discourses and structures' (1999: 391).

This brings together the power embedded in social structures and institutions, resulting in structural inequality, oppression and power, and the workings of power, embedded in language, difference, and deconstruction. Similarly Louise Morley (1999) has drawn attention to the 'micro-politics' of the academy. As discussed elsewhere in this book, she uses the term to refer to the ways in which power is relayed in the everyday practises associated with working in higher education: 'a subtext of organisational life in which conflicts, tensions, resentments, competing interests and power imbalances influence everyday transactions in institutions' (p. 4). Thus, power is not possessed; rather it is exercised. But it is not exercised in a merely straightforward way. It is subtle, complex, disconcerting and – above all for our discussion of feminist research management – relational.

Feminist research management, as we have noted above, involves attempting to juggle competing discourses of power and subject positionings around hierarchy and audit, and collaboration and interdependency. The ethical dilemmas, emotional upsets and intellectual strains we face as feminist research managers arise from often unspoken power struggles within research teams that relate to these competing discourses. But power is especially relational in that it is invested in an individual's position or status *as related to* another individual's position or status, *as part of* an institutional system, and *as played out* in personal relationships between the people in those various positions within that system.

In terms of understanding where we derive power from within the relational micro-politics of research management, the notion of 'power resources' is key, in that power derives from access to and control over resources (Bradley 1999; Logan and Huntley 2002). These power resources can derive from characteristics such as age, gender, class, race and personality (what Heinrich 1995 terms 'personal power'). Power can also be drawn from shifting and changing resources such as: positionalities (e.g. professional rank; job status; etc);[2] institutional affiliation; social networks and social capital (see also Gillies and Alldred this volume); research and life experiences; knowledge and intellectual capital; time-of-arrival-on-the-project; manner of entry into the project; and proximity to/distance from the field both physically but also in terms of level and degree of involvement in fieldwork (Mountz *et al.* 2003). Thus, the balance of power is not static but continually shifts as research relationships, situations and access to power resources change. No single relationship can be characterised by a set power dynamic. For example, when a contract researcher secures a core-funded administrative or teaching position she can access greater power resources and this may shift the balance of power within a research team in which she is involved. If a collaborator is also your head of department she exercises structural power over you, which she loses when she is no longer head of department (Deem et al. 2001).[3] The relational nature of power means that the balance of power can change as our power resources change. Moreover, power does not necessarily flow from status, seniority, and rank. In certain situations, a more junior colleague can exercise power over a more senior one. One example of this that we note further below is where researchers working on projects have power resources by virtue of their detailed knowledge of the project and the data, or through access to influential social networks.

Before we begin our detailed discussion of the everyday challenges, tensions and complexities involved in the relational micro-politics of research management, however, we need briefly to discuss the ethics of doing so.

Ethical dilemmas

One of the ethical dilemmas we faced in writing this chapter was how to discuss difficult situations, experiences and feelings without betraying our colleagues, breaking confidences or threatening our research collaborations. The fact that Mary Ellen Logan and Helen Huntley (2002) used pseudonyms to write about power struggles within their research team testifies to the level of sensitivity surrounding these issues. We experimented, in our first drafts of this chapter, with using specific examples drawn from our own experiences. Writing personalised accounts rekindled painful emotions, however, and made it more difficult to write in such a way that avoids both blaming the other party and feeling we have to justify ourselves (although we would not claim to have avoided this completely). Consequently, in order to protect our colleagues, and ourselves, we decided not to include in our public account any specific examples drawn from our own experiences. Instead, we analysed these incidents in private, distilled the critical issues in relation to power, feminism and research management, and used these key points in order to construct an account of the day-to-day tensions and dilemmas we face in our attempts to be feminist research managers.

A further dilemma we faced is the extent to which writing about the tensions of being a feminist research manager risks undermining and criticising our very achievements. As one of us has previously written in a review of the literature on feminists in higher education (Edwards 2000: 328), 'Perhaps it is not wise for women to be open about their own managerial mistakes and dilemmas, potentially undermining themselves, in a situation where others may be quick enough to do so'. (See also Beckwith 1999: 390) This potential to undermine does, of course, depend on the audience. Among our own close networks (and in relation to other authors in this edited collection), open reflexivity can be regarded as positive and a demonstration of strength. But we will not know the perceptions of a wider audience.

In what follows then, rather than a personalised account, we self-reflexively and critically analyse our experiences to demonstrate the contradictions between feminism and management whereby internal and external forces thwart our attempts to implement feminist principles within our research management practices. For the sake of order, we discuss these experiences in relation to three 'divisions' that have implications for the relational micro-politics of feminist research management: the divisions of labour that permeate research teams, and the divisions of responsibility and of rights that flow from these divisions of labour.

Divisions of labour

The British model of research management is one in which, as research managers progress, they are expected to run several research projects or oversee a whole programme comprising a number of interlinked projects at the same time. For some, this also occurs alongside additional teaching and administrative responsibilities. The accumulation of research grants can be critical to ensuring job security as well as career progression. The management of multiple research projects, however, enforces an 'academic division of labour' (Stanley 1990: 7), within and across individual projects and within and across the research teams undertaking them, which can run counter to both our scholarly instincts and feminist principles.

Often contract researchers are employed to spend most if not all of their time working on a single project. They have some administrative responsibility in terms of the day-to-day running of the project, and they may also have some informal management responsibility for more junior researchers and/or support staff associated with the project. The majority of their time, however, is devoted to the everyday elements of the research process. Generally, the researcher will organise and conduct most of the fieldwork, thereby acquiring a close and detailed understanding of the data. Depending on the researchers's skills, abilities and confidence, they will also be involved in carrying out literature reviews, analysing the data, and writing publications, presentations and other dissemination activities.

As research managers, we have responsibility for administering and managing several research projects or a research programme, and the staff working on them. We have overall responsibility for administrative and managerial work including (and not limited to): liaising with funding bodies; producing interim, annual and final reports; drawing up various strategies and monitoring their implementation, such as for 'knowledge transfer' communication and dissemination; preparing and attending advisory group meetings; managing project budgets and timetables; managing research and support staff, co-grant holders and non-academic partners; securing resources for project staff; linking research projects and programmes and staff into the university's departmental and faculty processes and activities; and networking with the wider academic community and with other sectors (e.g. policy; voluntary; media). The time taken up by these administrative and managerial responsibilities demands that we lessen our involvement in the actual research process, particularly time-consuming tasks such as data collection and analysis. Intense intellectual input on our part tends to be concentrated in the early stages of the research process – especially the writing of grant applications – as well as in the latter stages when we write up publications and engage in other forms of dissemination. During the course of a research project, our intellectual contributions tend to be more strategic and distant from the field, in terms of offering direction, guidance, advice and support; though, depending on the researcher and our time commitments, we may also take primary or some responsibility for analysing the data.

Contract researchers have written about how they experience this division of labour, and how it can leave them feeling that their intellectual labour is conflated with or appropriated by grant holders (Reay 1999, 2000). There are few accounts, however, of grant holders' and research managers' – particularly feminists' – perspectives on these issues (exceptions include Porter 1994; Wakeford 1985). From our own experiences, the research management model enforces upon us a way of working and a division of labour that, as scholars and feminists, we find problematic because it runs counter to our scholarly and feminist ideals. As scholars, the passion, enthusiasm and intellectual satisfaction we derive from our work comes from immersion in a set of theoretical ideas, an intricate knowledge of our data, and generating new theoretical and empirical contributions to a particular field of knowledge. Yet as we progress in our careers as research managers, we have less and less time to devote to this intellectual work and deeply grounded knowledge. The new managerialism of the knowledge economy takes priority over creative and collegial intellectual endeavour.

This situation can create feelings of envy towards contract researchers who have, as we see it, the luxury of devoting most if not all of their time to research and to a single project. It can leave us feeling distanced and marginalised from the knowledge construction and production process, and concerned that the quality and integrity of the research may be compromised. Depending on our collaborators, we can feel frustrated that colleagues are not carrying out the research in the same way or to the same standards that we would like, envious that they are 'hands on' researchers and we are not, and/or guilty that we are not 'pulling our weight' in visible and direct ways (see further below). In delegating tasks and activities, letting go of our intellectual goals, standards, ownership and control can be a struggle. This is particularly so in cases where we are emotionally and intellectually attached to and vested in the project. While collaborative research has the potential to be more intellectually stimulating, more productive, and more fun than solo research, this all depends on our relationships with team members.

Quite apart from our own ontological insecurities about our alienation from the everyday process of the research, the micro-politics of such structural status divisions run counter to our feminist ideals of grant holders and contract researchers taking equal (whether the same or different) shares in all aspects of the research process. Such divisions impose power and status differentials on team members that compromise our feminist attempts to equalise power.

Paradoxically, although the administrative and managerial responsibility that we have as research managers is invested with institutionalised status and power (see below), it may not be recognised or valued as 'work' by contract researchers, and in some cases by co-grant holders, line managers and university institutions. For example, research-related administrative and managerial work may or may not be taken into account when allocating teaching loads and departmental administrative tasks, and this type of work is not recognised and rewarded in the RAE. Written accounts and our own experiences suggest that contract researchers can regard the only 'real' work on a project as the work they are involved in – fieldwork, data analysis, and writing publications – and that intellectual 'ownership' of the research can only be achieved through this type of investment of time. In this sense, 'equal' comes to mean 'the same as' rather than 'equal but different'. Our administrative and managerial responsibilities carry with them considerable amounts of 'labour', particularly in cases where contract researchers or co-grant holders, for whatever reasons, fail to 'deliver' their contribution to the project or programme on time, or to the required quality, or in the format required. There is a great deal of variation among contract researchers in terms of their skills, experience, expertise and working patterns, and thus what tasks they feel confident to undertake. Some researchers may lack the confidence to analyse the data and request that we take responsibility for this aspect of the project. Others may feel daunted at the prospect of conducting a literature review. Researchers also vary in their desire and ability to take the lead in writing up publications. This variation in skills, abilities and confidence means that, as grant holders and research managers, the responsibility falls on us to undertake these uncompleted tasks. When researchers take sickness or other types of leave, or depart from a project part-way through, it is our responsibility to ensure delivery of the project to the funding agencies, either by conducting the research work ourselves or by appointing another researcher and taking them through an institutional and project 'induction programme'. This managerial labour and responsibility tends to be invisible.

Furthermore, the discussion of divisions of labour between contract researchers and grant holders can obscure the more or less explicit divisions of labour that exist between co-grant holders. In some cases, a junior grant holder can experience feelings towards a senior grant holder that are similar to those experienced by contract researchers towards grant holders. For example, more junior grant holders may be more involved in the research than the overall research manager because they have more time or prioritise this aspect of their work. In turn, because the research manager's administrative and managerial responsibilities may leave her little time or desire to engage in a period of sustained and time-consuming intellectual work, this can leave junior grant holders or contract researchers feeling resentful and angry, and create tensions and disappointments within the team.

The process of conducting collaborative research can be messy and unpredictable and the responsibility for picking up the pieces of a project when this process fails to run smoothly falls on us. Moreover, the emotional labour involved in managing researchers, team relationships and associated inter-personal dynamics is an added task and responsibility. These aspects of academic *work*, undertaken by research managers, can be overlooked or rendered invisible partly, we suggest, because – despite the pervasive structural and discursive facets of new managerialism – both ourselves and our colleagues have yet to fully recognise and incorporate the role and implications of being a 'research manager' (see also Deem *et al.* 2001). The clashes and tensions between the new managerialist subject position and other subject positionings, such as creative intellectual and feminist researcher manager, are not only played out for us in our struggles over our identity as feminist academics, but also in our colleagues' conceptions of 'what counts'. On the one hand, we may applaud this challenge to the dominance of the new managerial ideology. On the other, we have to deal with the consequences.

Divisions of responsibilities

In our discussion above it is evident that divisions of responsibility are associated with divisions of labour in the research process, and that these have concomitant power resources. Here we take our musings on these responsibilities further to draw out the relational micro-politics involved more explicitly. The division of labour introduces a power imbalance that is difficult to reconcile with our feminist aspirations to equalise power and dismantle the hierarchies involved in research management generally, and in research teams specifically. The distinct research tasks and responsibilities that contract researchers and grant holders undertake are invested with differential value, recognition, status and power. Research grants earn grant holders status, visibility and acknowledgement within university institutions. In contrast, the researchers employed on the grants tend to experience poorer pay and conditions of service, economic insecurity, less status, and access fewer privileges and material resources (e.g. decent office space and computing equipment). Furthermore, they tend not to be formally recognised as part of the institutional and academic community, are often geographically marginalised by being located in separate buildings, and can be excluded from staff meetings, committees and the politics of the organisation (e.g. Platt 1976; Porter 1984; Woodward and Chisholm 1981; Allen-Collinson 2003). Administrative and managerial responsibility for projects and programmes places managers in a position of structural power over contract researchers, and can situate a principal grant holder in a position of 'informal' power over other grant holders. Whether we choose to use our status and position as a power resource or not, this role can be forced upon us, or at least assumed, by contract researchers, co-grant holders, the university system, funding bodies and academic social networks.

Funding bodies, for example, tend to have a hierarchical or 'breadwinner' model in dealing with research team members (also see Porter 1994). While all team members can be named on research grant application forms, most funding bodies require that just one principal applicant must be nominated, even where applications are multi-institutional and from peers. If the application is successful, all further correspondence between the funder and the research team is solely with the identified principal applicant. This also has financial implications for universities' research income, where the grant holders are located in more than one institution. The 'lead' institution, in which the 'breadwinner' grant holder is located, administers the grant. The co-grant holders and their institutions have to 'claim' their allocated budget resources from the lead institution, and these claims have to be 'approved' by the principal grant holder. Research managers similarly oversee and approve contract researchers' claims for reimbursement of expenses and so on.

These procedures, presumably put in place because of their efficiency for the funding organisation, impose a hierarchical and individualistic research management model that creates distinctions and unequal power relations between collaborators. They structurally compromise our attempts to implement egalitarian and collective research management practices. They accord power and responsibility to just one member of a research team, and their institution, in a context where we have tried to break down power hierarchies. Even if we may not exercise it, the power resource conferred upon us as research managers and as principal grant holders can be threatening to other team members (both co-grant holders and contract researchers).

In some cases, however, and despite our feminist principles and ideals, we find ourselves having to use our structural power in order to fulfil our administrative and managerial responsibilities. As we have said, responsibility and accountability for the completion and delivery of the research project lie with the research manager as grant holder. The feminist research management ideal of equity and equality obfuscates our obligations, responsibility and accountability to funding bodies, just as it conceals contract researchers' obligations, responsibility and accountability to us as their line managers. Contract researchers, and secondary co-grant holders, can seemingly 'opt out' of collaborative efforts because they do not feel the managerial responsibility carried by the research manager. Moreover, there are also cases where we feel our feminist approach has left us open to 'abuse'. The egalitarian and caring environment we try to create can be mistaken for a lenient and indulgent approach whereby colleagues can consistently fail to deliver, yet expect continued sympathy and understanding. In such cases, we can either take all responsibilities and tasks on ourselves and feel hard done by, or abandon attempts at sharing and use our institutional power in order to get colleagues to fulfil their 'contractual' obligations to the project or programme. This is one reason why feminist research managers may ricochet between different management styles – collaborative one moment and directive the next (also see Edwards 2000). In turn, such inconsistencies can lead to tensions not only with contract researchers but also with co-grant holders who may sit in a different place along the feminist idealism-pragmatism scale. Our feminist research management practices can therefore set up false expectations amongst team members; expectations that are bitterly shattered when we find ourselves having to revert to hierarchical and authoritarian management practices.

The resistance to structural power inequalities demanded by a commitment to feminist research management means that power can come to be exerted, asserted and maintained in more subtle and personal ways. A feminist rhetoric of collaboration, interdependency and egalitarianism can thereby conceal more insidious exertions of power resources. This personal power can be used by research managers to remind research team members of who really is the boss in ways that we are not always aware; but it can also be used by team members to challenge research managers' structural power even where this power is not exerted over others. For example, the micro-politics of body and verbal language can be used as ways of communicating power (Morley 1999). Using the term 'I' (rather than 'we') in the context of a team meeting, conference paper, or advisory group or funder meeting, can create and communicate distance from other team members, by signalling individual ownership of intellectual ideas. Such explicit or unconscious linguistic strategies can be used as a way of positioning oneself in competition, rather than in collaboration, with research team members. Similarly, the ways in which team meetings are managed can signal authority, control and power. Issues such as who chairs the meeting, whose office the meeting is held in, late arrival at a meeting, or taking phone calls during a meeting, can all be used as symbols of power, authority and priority.

One of the recurring themes within feminist and non-feminist discussions of academic collaborations is the power of the research manager versus the powerlessness of the contract researcher. There is an assumption that power positions and accompanying resources map straightforwardly onto rank positions: that the view from below is that of the contract researcher and the view from above is that of research manager or grant holder. Our experiences, however, suggest that research managers can experience themselves as powerless, and contract researchers can exert power over them and other team members. Being a research manager involves navigating and negotiating multiple relationships in which we exercise more or less power – relationships with contract researchers, co-grant holders, the institution, funding bodies and other social networks. Each of these relationships is the focus of power and associated struggles. As research managers, we can feel exploited by a more senior grant holder who is not pulling their weight, or who gets credit and recognition for work that we have done. Moreover, contract researchers have greater power resources than they perhaps realise. They can exert structural power over, for example, secretarial and support staff. Although, of course, this is similarly a complex set of power relations and power flows, with administrative and support staff having their own power resources. As we noted earlier, they may have intellectual power over research managers by virtue of, for example, their detailed knowledge of and access to the data; power and knowledge which can leave us feeling intellectually threatened and insecure. As research managers, we feel we are constructed by our researchers as all-powerful. What may not be apparent to them are the power struggles and inequities that, as managers, we are confronted with, and indeed often the lack of power we experience in our positions.

Divisions of rights

Earlier on, we reflected on contrasting views on how intellectual ownership is 'earned' and the relative importance of different types of academic work in this process. Here, we explore the related question of whether claims to research areas and ownership of intellectual ideas lie with individual researchers or with the research team as a collective. As feminists, our premise is that collaboratively-produced knowledge constitutes collective intellectual 'capital'; intellectual property rights over collective work belong to the research team rather than to individual researchers; and all intellectual property rights issues should be discussed and negotiated with team members.

Concomitantly, we do not feel that research managers who have contributed very little, for example other than being inserted on a grant application as a symbolic 'big name', should be included as an author on publications towards which they have contributed nothing. Yet in our research practises, we work with collaborators – contract researchers and co-grant holders – who do not necessarily share these feminist ideals, or even when they do, they may vary in the extent to which they put them into practice. We ourselves similarly may vary because we are fed-up or pressured, or especially disenchanted with someone's input. Some colleagues accept authorship on all papers initiated and written by other team members, but produce and submit single-authored publications. Some will apply for research grants that directly draw upon existing collaborative research projects but do not include other team members. In some cases, these colleagues have consulted and negotiated with other team members; in other cases there has been no prior discussion.

In addition to our own and others' 'failings' as feminists, our feminist approach can leave us open and vulnerable to non-feminist opportunists who put themselves, their interests and their careers first, as well as to ideologically committed feminists who may use structural or other forms of power (e.g. rank, age, experience, social networks) to justify non-feminist practices. These infringements on collective property rights embody individualistic and competitive positions that cut across the collegial, interdependent and collaborative structures we attempt to put in place and practise as feminist research managers. In some cases, these may be deliberate acts borne out of ambition and careerism. In other instances, they may be more benign and the result of carelessness and thoughtlessness; for example, by colluding with, rather than challenging, colleagues' interpretations and representations of collectively-produced knowledge as individual scholarship. Again, we ourselves may have been ambitious or thoughtless either because of the subjective position created for us by new managerialism or because of our own aspirations and careerism. Whether deliberate or not, these micro-political acts can leave whoever is on the receiving end feeling angry, betrayed and violated; as well as naïve not to have exercised power resources and placed such trust in others in the first place.

The strength of emotions generated by these situations stems from the profound disappointment we can feel when other women, and particularly feminists, behave in such 'unsisterly' ways. We feel let down by unfulfilled expectations of 'sisterhood', and particularly disappointed when colleagues fail to act upon their feminist principles and commitments. As Sally Munt eloquently writes:

> As a woman my cruellest struggles in academia have been with other women – haplessly, with other feminists. I want to emphasise that these transactions are not the most overtly vicious, and that they can be unintentional. The damage is not always in external consequences, but in the broken expectations of fellowship [sic], the unexpected and deeply internalised disappointment that seeps from a perceived betrayal. (1999: 424)

Yet as Beckwith (1999) points out, we need to be wary of blaming and disparaging women. We need to examine and question the unrealistically high expectations that we have of other women and feminists, and particularly our expectations about how women should *do* power, because they are based 'on problematic constructions of femininity, unsustainable assumptions of sisterhood, and failure to take account of the impact of gender relations' (Beckwith 1999: 392). As we have stressed, non-feminist practices must be understood in part within the context of the hierarchical and new managerialist academic systems we operate in, which require constant auditing, encourage competition and reward individualism. However, the tensions also stem from recognising that we each have individual and independent professional and intellectual identities, aspirations and ambitions, and that we should not restrict one another from achieving these; whilst at the same time creating and valuing relationships of mutual interdependence, where using joint work as a launch pad for solo work can pose a threat to the bond and cause a fear of abandonment (see Fox Keller and Moglen 1987).

There may well be tensions here between the desire for individual recognition and collaborative working. Nonetheless, actually experiencing such tensions depends on a range of factors such as: the collaborators; whether they share our disciplinary, departmental, and institutional affiliation; how long we have known them; the nature of the collaborative research relationship and collaborators' research practices; whether the collaborators are friends as well as colleagues; the nature of the project, and how emotionally and intellectually attached we are to it; where this particular project fits into our portfolio of work. Depending on such issues, there may or may not be tensions. For example, in our experiences, the most intellectually rewarding and productive collaborations are ones in which the knowledge has been constructed and produced in such an organic and symbiotic way that we find it difficult, if not impossible, to distinguish individual ownership and origins of ideas. Within the context of such collaborations, there can be times when we do not experience the desire for individual recognition in the first place. Similarly, we may feel our responsibilities and attachments to junior colleagues strongly, and – in circumstances where we feel safe in our own reputations – are happy (or perhaps munificent) to let them take the limelight. Generally, if our desire or need for individual recognition is accommodated through solo research and writing projects, there may be less of a need to pursue recognition within joint work.

Whatever the scenarios, positive or negative or both, as feminists we need to take responsibility for and be reflexive about the ways in which we treat and are treated by colleagues.

Conclusion

In this chapter, we have discussed our aims as feminist research managers, challenging the traditionally hierarchical nature of research relationships and teams. We have, however, also highlighted how, as research managers operating within the contemporary higher education context of new managerialism and traditional hierarchical structures, the micro-political implications of relations within and beyond the academy (e.g. the RAE, funding bodies, social networks) uphold and reinforce the very power structures and differentials we seek to break down. As Morgan Tanton and Christina Hughes have observed:

> The terms management and feminism are in one sense an anathema. Feminism is about collectivity, social equity and social change. It represents an anti-hierarchical political position. Management on the other hand usually represents control, authority relations and conservatism. (1999: 245).

As one of us has noted elsewhere (Edwards 2000), whilst forms of feminism can provide alternative models of management for women, attempts to operate in collaborative and cooperative ways, and a guiding awareness of gender issues and intersections with other social divisions, can lead to paradoxes and tensions within a new managerial and market driven higher education system:

> Feminist academics who have progressed through the patriarchal academic hierarchy – however few of them there may be – have

to combine the exercise of academic power with their feminism, something ... that is fraught with tensions. (p. 325).

As we have tried to demonstrate in this chapter, despite their best endeavours feminist research managers run the risk of simply replicating and perpetuating the hierarchical power structures and conventional micropolitical relations they struggle to overcome (Cancian 1992; Ferguson 1984; Porter 1994). However much we may try to avoid it and reflect upon situations, the new managerialism invites a subject positioning for feminist research managers that creates real tensions and frustrations for attempts to inhabit an alternative subject positioning.

This chapter, however, should not be read as a confessional account of our own and others' failings, or as a warning against the possibility of resisting the onslaught of new managerialism as part of research management. Rather, we would argue that feminist research managers, along with others who wish to undertake this position and exercise power resources in non-hierarchical and collaborative ways need not only to be personally reflective, but importantly, they need to be openly reflexive and publicly voice the issues involved in working within structures that cut across and constrain them.

As part of that endeavour, here we have attempted to name, acknowledge and work with the power resources and differentials that characterise management of research teams and collaborations. We are not so naïve as to believe that naming power equalises or eradicates it; but it does allow power to be discussed and negotiated. Although less evident in our account above, we also want to remember the potential of empowerment alongside stressing the importance of naming and negotiating the structures and discourses that bring constraining, co-opting and hierarchical power resources and practices in their wake. While, as with other subjugated practices, feminist research management may be obfuscated, collaboration and reflexivity represent characteristic forms of feminist resistance to hierarchical domination.

Another issue that we have attempted to vocalise and make evident is the emotionality of the relational micro-politics of feminist research management. The emotions resulting from our own and others' infringements or misuse of power resources, particularly feelings of anger, resentment and betrayal, are rarely recognised or discussed within research teams. We believe it is important to be open about and develop a practice of dealing with the emotions generated by the research process and within research relationships (see Ramazanoglu 1990). Some of the solutions, ironically, may have to draw on new managerialist type of practices – using them towards empowerment rather than managerial surveillance and auditing, however. Just as we have consent forms and ethical guidelines for how to do research with our informants (Edwards and Mauthner 2002), we may need protocols and ethical guidelines for working with colleagues. This may involve drawing up a set of written guidelines for all team members to agree on concerning the conditions of collaboration, order of authorship, and other issues. This sort of acknowledgment of power resources and differentials, and of the potential for conflict of interests, allows ways forward to deal with them.

Reflexivity has become a hallmark of feminist research (Mauthner and Doucet 2003). Yet as we noted in the introduction, research managers remain silent and unreflexive, at least in public, about research collaborations and relationships. Just as feminists have emphasised the importance of articulating the links between empirical and theoretical knowledge production and knowledge construction processes, so too we need to highlight the links between the new managerial knowledge economy and the relational micro-politics of research team dynamics in the practice of feminist research management.

Postscript

The editors of this book have pointed out that this chapter could be read as a glossing over of our own investments in research management. We respond to this by offering some reflections on where we are at in our research management careers, and the different places we have each come to as a result of the tensions of feminist research management described above. After seven years in research management, Natasha decided to leave it and move into a lectureship, in large part motivated by her dissatisfaction with the dominant research management model. The intellectual, scholarly, emotional and ethical strains, compromises and costs became too great and began to outweigh any political or career rewards of research management. Natasha's investment was in and for *feminist* management, rather than management per se. She left research management when she felt that it did not allow her to meet this commitment. Meanwhile, Ros's investment is bound up with intellectual academic status as well as feminist management practice. She struggles on with research management and the person she has become in exercising these responsibilities, because she feels that at least some of the receipts from her investment are worthwhile.

Notes

1. Although these principles are features of feminist practice within research teams (e.g. Ramazanoglu 1990; Mountz et al. 2003) they can also characterise other non-feminist attempts to create non-hierarchical team relationships (see Woods et al. 2000; Platt 1976).
2. Power vested in academics by the educational system in the form of their professional rank and status within the university has been termed 'structural' (Hewson 1999) or 'legitimate power' (Heinrich 1995).
3. Head of Department posts can be permanent or run for fixed periods of time, with the latter more common in pre-1992 universities.

References

Adler S., Laney, J. and Packer, M. (1993) *Managing Women: Feminism and Power in Educational Management*, Buckingham: Open University Press.

Allen-Collinson, J. (2003) Working at a marginal 'career': the case of UK social science contract researchers, *The Sociological Review*, 51 (3) 405–422.

Beckwith, J.B. (1999) Power between women, *Feminism and Psychology*, 9 (4) 389–397.

Bradley, H. (1999) *Gender and Power in the Workplace: Analyzing the Impact of Economic Change*, London: St Martin's Press.

Brannen, J. and Edwards, R. (1996) Introduction: from parents to children – the generation of a research programme, in J. Brannen and R. Edwards (eds), *Perspectives on Parenting and Childhood: Looking Back and Moving Forward*, London: South Bank University/Institute of Education/Economic and Social Research Council.

Brannen, J. and Edwards, R. (1998) Editorial, *International Journal of Social Research Methodology: Theory and Practice*, 1 (1) 1–6.

Cancian, F.M. (1992) Feminist science: methodologies that challenge inequality, *Gender & Society*, 6 (4) 623–642.

Clarke, J. and Newman, J. (1994) The manageralisation of public services, in J. Clarke, A. Cochran and E. McLaughlin (eds), *Managing Social Policy*, London: Sage.

Collins, P.H. (1990) *Black Feminist Thought: Knowledge, Consciousness and the Politics of Empowerment*, London: HarperCollins.

Deem, R. (2004) The knowledge worker, the manager-academic and the contemporary UK university: new and old forms of public management, *Financial Accountability and Management*, 20 (2) 107–128.

Deem, R. and Brehony, K. (2005) Management of ideology: the case of 'new managerialism' in higher education, *Oxford Review of Education*, 31 (2) 217–235.

Deem, R., Fulton, O., Reed, M. and Watson, S. (2001) 'Managing UK universities – manager-academics and new managerialism', *Online Journal of Academic Leadership*: www.academicleadership.org, June.

Edwards, R. (1990) Connecting method and epistemology: a White woman interviewing Black women, *Women's Studies International Forum*, 13, 447–490.

Edwards, R. (2000) Numbers are not enough: on women in higher education and being a feminist academic, in M. Tight (ed.), *Academic Work and Life:*

What It Is To Be An Academic, and How This Is Changing, Vol. I of International Perspectives of Higher Education Research Series, London: JAI.
Edwards, R. and Mauthner, M. (2002) Ethics and feminist research: theory and practice, in M. Mauthner, M. Birch, J. Jessop and T. Miller (eds), *Ethics in Qualitative Research*, London: Sage.
Ferguson, K. (1984) *The Feminist Case Against Bureaucracy*, Philadelphia, PA: Temple University Press.
Finch, J. (1984) 'It's great to have someone to talk to': the ethics and politics of interviewing women, in C. Bell and H. Roberts (eds), *Social Researching: Politics, Problems, Practice*, London: Routledge and Kegan Paul.
Fox Keller, E. and Moglen, H. (1987) Competition and feminism: conflicts for academic women, *Signs*, 12(3) 493–510.
Glucksmann, M. (1994) The work of knowledge and the knowledge of women's work, in *Researching Women's Lives from a Feminist Perspective*, edited by M. Maynard and J. Purvis, London: Taylor and Francis.
Harding, S. (1991) *Whose Science? Whose Knowledge?*, Milton Keynes: Open University Press.
Heinrich, K.T. (1995) Doctoral advisement relationships between women: on friendship and betrayal, *The Journal of Higher Education*, 66 (4) 447–469.
Hewson, D. (1999) Empowerment in supervision, *Feminism and Psychology*, 9 (4) 406–409.
Hughes, C. (2000) Is it possible to be a feminist manager in the 'real world' of further education? *Journal of Further and Higher Education*, 24 (2) 251–260.
Logan, M.E. and Huntley, H. (2002) Gender and power in the research process, *Women's Studies International Forum*, 24 (6) 623–635.
Mauthner, N.S. and Doucet, A. (1998) Reflections on a voice centred relational method of data analysis: analysing maternal and domestic voices, in *Feminist Dilemmas in Qualitative Research: Private Lives and Public Texts*, edited by J. Ribbens and R. Edwards, London: Sage Publications.
Mauthner, N.S. and Doucet, A. (2003) Reflexive accounts and accounts of reflexivity in qualitative data analysis, *Sociology* 37, 413–431.
McIntyre, A. and Lykes, M.B. (1998) Who's the boss? Confronting whiteness and power differences within a feminist mentoring relationship in participatory action research, *Feminism and Psychology*, 8 (4) 427–444.
Morley, L. (1999) *Organising Feminisms: The Micropolitics of the Academy*, Basingstoke: Macmillan.
Mountz, A., Miyares, I.M., Wright, R. and Bailey, A.J. (2003) Methodologically becoming: power, knowledge and team research, *Gender, Place and Culture*, 10 (1) 29–46.
Munt, S.R. (1999) Power, pedagogy and partiality, *Feminism and Psychology*, 9(4) 422–425.
Onyx, J. (1999) Power between women in organizations, *Feminism and Psychology*, 9 (4) 417–421.
Platt, J. (1976) *Realities of Social Research: An Empirical Study of British Sociologists*, Brighton: Sussex University Press.
Porter, M. (1984) The modification of method in researching postgraduate education, in R.G. Burgess (ed.), *The Research Process in Educational Settings*, London and New York: The Falmer Press.

Porter, M. (1994) 'Second-hand ethnography': Some problems in analysing a feminist project, in A. Bryman and R.G. Burgess (eds), *Analyzing Qualitative Data*, London and New York: Routledge.

Pritchard, C. and Deem, R. (1999) Wo-managing further education: gender and the construction of the manager in the corporate colleges of England, *Gender and Education*, 11 (3) 323–342.

Ramazanoglu, C. (1990) *Methods of Working as a Research Team*, WRAP Paper 3, London: The Tufnell Press.

Reay, D. (1999) Fantasies of feminisms: egalitarian fictions and elitist realities, *Feminism and Psychology* 9 (4) 426–430.

Reay, D. (2000) 'Dim dross': marginalised women both inside and outside the academy, *Women's Studies International Forum*, 23 (1) 13–21.

Ribbens, J. (1989) Interviewing: an 'unnatural situation?', *Women's Studies International Forum*, 12 (6) 579–592.

Ribbens, J. and Edwards, R. (1998) *Feminist Dilemmas in Qualitative Research: Private Lives and Public Texts*, London: Sage Publications.

Rose, H. (1994) *Love, Power and Knowledge: Towards a Feminist Transformation of the Sciences*, Cambridge: Polity Press.

Shattock, M. (1999) Governance and management in universities: the way we live now, *Journal of Education Policy*, 14 (3) 271–282.

Standing, K. (1998) Writing the voices of the less powerful: research on lone mothers, in J. Ribbens and R. Edwards (eds), *Feminist Dilemmas in Qualitative Research: Public Knowledge and Private Lives*, London: Sage.

Stanley, L. (1990) *Feminist Praxis: Research, Theory and Epistemology in Feminist Sociology*, London: Routledge.

Strachan, J. (1999) Feminist educational leadership: locating the concepts in practice, *Gender and Education*, 11 (3) 309–322.

Tanton, M. and Hughes, C. (1999) Editorial, *Gender and Education*, 11 (3) 245–249.

Wakeford, J. (1985) A director's dilemmas. In R.G. Burgess (ed.), *Field Methods in The Study of Education*, London and Philadelphia: The Falmer Press.

Wilkinson, S. and Kitzinger, C. (eds) (1996) *Representing the Other*, London: Sage.

Wolf, D. (1996) (ed.) *Feminist Dilemmas in Fieldwork*, Boulder Colorado: Westview Press.

Woods, P., Boyle, M., Jeffrey, B. and Troman, G. (2000) A research team in ethnography, *Qualitative Studies in Education*, 13 (1) 85–98.

Woodward, D. and Chisholm, L. (1981) The expert view? The sociological analysis of graduates' occupational and domestic roles, in H. Roberts (ed.), *Doing Feminist Research*, London: Routledge and Kegan Paul.

Index

Academic careers, 1, 2, 7, 13, 19, 20, 21, 36, 38, 41, 43, 53, 66, 71, 79, 106, 111, 113
Academic practitioner mix, 71, 78, 83
Academic subjectivities, 16, 28, 34
Academic standards, 82
Administrative/managerial responsibility, 175–180
Agency, 18, 44, 50, 90, 98, 102
Almack, K., vii, 12
Aldrige, J., 130
Alldred, P., vii, 13
Ambivalence, 36, 49, 62, 66, 113, 119, 135, 170, 172
Anxiety, 11, 20, 22, 47, 127, 138, 165
Asian, 53
Assessment, 78, 82
Authenticity, 39, 53, 55–56, 59, 62, 66
Autobiography, 124–130, 142–143
Autonomy, 18, 19, 27, 46
Authority, 29, 32, 33, 48, 49, 59, 60, 62, 97, 100, 112, 122, 123, 124, 125–127, 128, 129, 131, 135, 137, 181

Beckwith, Joan, 172, 184
Bell, L., vii, 12
Black, 62, 64, 66
Black, P., 39, 44, 47–48
Birch, M., viii, x, 6
Bourdieu, P., 1, 2, 5, 38, 39, 43, 47, 49, 51, 84, 110
Bowler, M., 20

Childhood experiences, 20, 24
Churchill, H., viii, 12
Codes of practice, 20, 71
Collective ethos, 97, 98, 102, 103
Competition, 4, 14, 53, 66, 148, 164, 181, 184

Class, 18, 36, 38, 39, 53–59, 63, 66, 71, 109, 110
Class relations, 38, 50
Working class, 1, 21, 27, 37, 40, 43, 45, 46, 48, 57, 105, 106, 113, 114, 115
Middle class, 18, 44, 107, 110, 111, 114, 116
Collaboration, 168–170, 173–174, 178, 181, 184–186
Collaborative writing, 8, 88
Competition, 164
Contract researchers, 12, 53, 54, 63, 111, 168–169, 174, 176–179, 180–183
Craib, I., 28, 29–30, 33, 134
Creativity, 96, 97, 100, 101, 132
Cross-cultural research, 61–62, 64–65, 67
Culture, 53–55, 57–62, 64, 67, 106, 111, 113, 115
Cultural arbitrary, 110, 113

Delamont, S., 22–23
Disabling niches, 54, 56, 63, 66
Disappointment, 29–30, 31, 32, 33, 34, 178
Discrimination, 4, 59, 63, 107, 109, 115
Disillusionment, 29–30, 34
Distribution of resources, 2, 18
Division of (research) labour, 170, 175–179
responsibilities, 170, 179–182
rights – see also intellectual property rights, 170, 182–185
Duncan, Simon, 137

Editorial power, 10
Edwards, R., ii, viii, ix, x, 14
Emotions, 21, 22, 23, 89, 128, 169, 174, 183, 186
Emotional labour, 178

Emotional resources, 18
Empowerment, 18, 21, 42, 51, 58, 62, 81, 84, 86, 186, 187
Enabling niches, 54, 56, 60, 61, 63, 66
Epistemology, 96, 100, 158, 135
Equal opportunities, 107, 108
Equality as sameness/difference, 170, 177, 178, 180
Ethic of care, 169, 170
Ethical dilemmas, 7, 174–175
Ethnic identity, 53–54, 56, 58–60, 62, 65
Ethnicity, 8–9, 12, 53–67
Evidence
 evidence based practice, 122, 134, 159
 representation and mis-representation of, 132–133, 137–141
Expertise, 56, 59–61, 63, 77, 94, 95, 99, 123, 125, 127, 129, 135–136, 137, 155

Fathers, 24–25, 30, 31, 32, 33
Feminism, 21, 38, 40, 55, 58, 59, 61, 71, 74, 75, 79, 81, 83, 84, 85, 88, 99, 103, 116, 135, 172, 174, 175, 185–186
Feminist managers, 14, 169, 170–171, 173–175, 180, 181, 183, 185–187
Foucault, M., 2, 19, 33, 62
Freud, S., 24
Funding bodies, 148, 159, 160, 171, 172, 176, 178, 180, 182

Gillies, V., ii, x, ix, 13
Gender, 12, 18, 21, 33, 38, 43, 53–55, 57, 59, 62, 66, 71, 85, 91, 92, 93, 98, 101, 115, 170, 184, 185
Getting published, 8
Grading, 149, 150, 152, 172
Grant holders, 178–181, 183

Habitus, 38–39, 43–44, 45, 48, 49, 51, 110
Hammersley, M., 127, 134, 137, 141
Harrington and Harrison, 138–141
Hey, Valerie, 113, 161, 162
HEFCE, 148

Hierarchy, 20, 26, 112, 118, 156, 157, 173
Hoggett, P., 18, 26
Hughes, Christina, 185
Huntley, Helen, 174
Hyperrationality, 19

Idealisation, 28–29, 30, 33
Identity, 70, 75, 78, 79, 82, 83, 84, 85
Identity politics, 53, 63, 65
Independence, 23, 57, 105
Inequality, 50, 107, 109
Insider, 57, 59–60
Institutional power relations, 13, 14, 17, 19, 26, 139, 161, 181, 193
Institutional denial, 3
Intellectual labour, 176
Intellectual property rights/ownership, 170, 178, 182
Internal world, 20
Interpersonal dynamics, 3, 6–8, 9–11, 22, 89
Intimacy, 20, 21
Intrapersonal dynamics, 3
Intersubjectivity, 20
Investment, 20, 22, 108, 110, 132, 161, 165, 178, 187

Klein, M., 24
Knowledge economy, 171, 177

Lacey, J., 27
Literature review, 13, 122–144, 176, 178
Logan, Mary Ellen, 174
Loss, 13, 98
Lucey, H., ii, x, ix, 11, 21, 28, 35
Lutzke et al, 140

McNay, Ian, 151, 154, 155, 157, 158
Mand, K., ix, 9, 12
Mauthner, M., ii, ix, 1, 6, 13, 15
Mauthner, N., x, 14
Miller, T., viii, x, 6, 14, 15
Micro-politics, 89, 93, 169, 172–174, 177, 181, 183, 186
Morley, L., 4, 21, 38–40, 43, 48, 50, 70, 84, 85, 91, 92, 93, 101, 112, 173
Munt, Sally, 184

Networking, 13, 105–119, 124, 126, 176
Niche market, 53, 55, 63
New managerialism, 20, 92, 148, 161, 162, 169, 171–172, 177, 179, 183–187

Objectivity, 150, 152, 153, 155, 130, 135
Oedipal relations, 24
Old boy networks, 106

Past, the, 20
Peer review, 111, 165
Pels, D., 142
Performativity, 84, 88, 90, 91, 92
Performance indicators, 84, 93, 148, 160, 171, 172
Personal/political, 3
Phd research, 12, 36–51
  non-traditional student experiences, 39–42, 43, 44–45, 49
  access to doctoral research, 36–37, 42–43
  getting started with PhD studies, 45–47
  motivations, 41–42
  working class experiences, 37, 38–39, 40, 42–44, 46, 47–48
  and childcare, 45, 48, 49
  and empowerment, 42, 44, 50–51
PhD supervision relationship, 16–34
  support and guidance, 20
  Parental, 23, 24
  Seduction, 31
  Pleasure, 31
  Conflict, 19, 29, 31
Political dilemmas, 7
Positive discrimination, 63
Postcolonial feminism, 55, 58–59, 61
Poststructuralism, 3, 18–19, 89
Power
  Creative, 3, 18,
  Destructive potential, 3, 18
  Discourses, 90, 172, 173, 186
  Dynamics, 3, 5, 9, 10, 12, 13, 14, 37, 38, 55, 66, 90, 117, 143
  Effects, 3
  Ever present, 3
  Fluid, 3, 12
  Institutional, 17
  In research teams, 13
  Levels of, 17
  Network, 19
  Personal possession, 17
  Practices, 3
  Relational, 3, 38, 55, 58, 60, 61, 66
  Sites, 3, 17, 78, 89–90, 103
  Structures, 5, 50, 131, 172, 185, 186
Practitioners, 89, 70, 71, 80
Productivity, 13, 92, 96, 147, 161, 164
Production of knowledge, 2, 5, 12, 13, 19, 26, 51, 58, 66, 112
Professional competencies, 71, 81, 83
Professional education, 71, 76, 78, 82, 84
Professional qualifications, 71, 73, 74, 80, 81, 82
Projective identification, 28
Psychoanalysis, 16, 21, 24
Psychosocial, 11, 22, 34
Public/private, 3, 116
Public sector, 71, 74, 80

Quality assurance, 84

Race, 53–55, 62–63, 65
Race Relations (Amendment) Act 2000, 62
Rassool, Naz, 127
Rationality, 3, 22, 105
Reality, 24, 29
Reay, Diane, 39, 40, 44, 46, 48, 117, 119
Reflexivity, 13, 36–49, 90, 101, 102, 125, 135, 142–143, 158, 168, 172, 175, 186, 187
Reinherz et al, 139
Research Assessment Exercise, 8, 13, 14, 56, 67, 136, 147–165, 172, 177, 185
Research management
  authoritarian/hierarchical, 169–171, 180, 181, 184–186
  collective/egalitarian, 180, 181, 183

Research outputs, 149, 150, 152, 154, 163, 165, 172
Research quality, 149–153, 172
Research, routine tasks, 92, 96
Research team/s, 88–103, 168, 170, 173–175, 177–183, 185, 187
Resistance, 29–30, 33, 42, 44, 49, 51, 90, 98, 102, 181, 186
Reynolds, Tracey, 115
Ribbens-McCarthy, J., ii, viii, x, 1, 6, 13, 15
Rogers, C., x, 2, 11
Rose, N., 19

Scott, J., 17, 33
Secrecy, 11
Self, the, 20, 28
Self-help books, 16
Silverman, D., 20
Skeggs, B., 38–41, 43–44
Social capital, 13, 70, 106, 108, 109, 111
Stanley, Jo, 118
Status quo, 5
Structuralism, 19
Symbolic violence, 47, 110

Tanton, Morgan, 185
Teaching, 37, 74, 76, 77, 78, 80, 81, 91, 110, 152, 164
Teamwork, 13, 88, 90, 96–100
Transference, 24–26, 34
True self, 19
Truth, 19

Unconscious, 3, 20, 21, 24, 27
  Anxiety, 20, 22, 24, 29, 34
  Desire, 20, 31
  fantasy, 20, 24, 27, 29
  envy, 27–28
Units of Assessment, 153–155, 172

Values, 5, 43, 62, 71, 81, 105, 112, 147, 148, 150, 154, 163, 171
Van Eerdewegh et al, 140

Weller, S., xi, 9, 12
Wisker, G., 49
White, 8, 54, 57, 105, 110, 111
Women's Workshop, 1, 3, 2, 5–7, 36, 50, 75, 106, 107, 112, 113, 118, 119, 126, 157
Writing, 70, 71, 78, 79, 82, 83, 84